AND THEY
CALL IT
HELP

Other Books by the Author

Kiss Daddy Goodnight
The Home Front: Notes from the Family War Zone
Solomon Says: A Speakout on Foster Care
A Child's Guide to Freud

For Children

*How to Turn Lemons into Money: A Child's Guide
to Economics*
*How to Turn Up into Down into Up: A Child's Guide to
Inflation, Depression, and Economic Recovery*
*How to Turn War into Peace: A Child's Guide to
Conflict Resolution*
The Thump, Blam, Bump Mystery
Arthur Gets What He Spills

AND THEY CALL IT HELP

The Psychiatric Policing
of America's Children

LOUISE ARMSTRONG

Addison-Wesley Publishing Company

*Reading, Massachusetts · Menlo Park, California · New York
Don Mills, Ontario · Wokingham, England · Amsterdam · Bonn · Sydney · Singapore
Tokyo · Madrid · San Juan · Paris · Seoul · Milan · Mexico City · Taipei*

All acknowledgments for permission to reprint previously published material can be found on page 306.

Many of the designations used by manufacturers and sellers to distinguish their products are claimed as trademarks. Where those designations appear in this book and Addison-Wesley was aware of a trademark claim, the designations have been printed in initial capital letters (e.g., Wite-Out).

Note to the reader: Except for professionals, names have been changed for confidentiality. Names of psychiatric and treatment institutions have also been changed except where clearly indicated or where the names appear in a purely reportorial context (data, quotes from news or official sources, etc.).

Library of Congress Cataloging-in-Publication Data

Armstrong, Louise.
    And they call it help : the psychiatric policing of America's children / Louise Armstrong.
      p.   cm.
    Includes index.
    ISBN 0-201-57794-1
    1. Child psychotherapy—Residential treatment—Political aspects—United States. 2. Child psychotherapy—Residential treatment—United States—Moral and ethical aspects. 3. Adolescent psychotherapy—Residential treatment—Political aspects—United States. 4. Adolescent psychotherapy—Residential treatment—United States—Moral and ethical aspects. 5. Social control. I. Title.
RJ504.5.A77   1993
362.2′1′083—dc20   92-34929
                                                CIP

Jacket design by Designed to Print
Text design by Dede Cummings/I.P.A.
Set in 11-point Caledonia by Pagesetters, Inc.

1 2 3 4 5 6 7 8 9-MA-9796959493
First printing, March 1993

For Tom, Alexi, Noah.
And in support of child advocates,
psychiatric survivors, and common sense.

Contents

Acknowledgments

To BEGIN: I am much indebted to all those kids and families who chose to speak with me. And to Ira Schwartz, Gerry Coles, Bill Johnson; Leonore Behar; to child advocates Richard Danford, Jeannie Matulis, Barbara Lurie, Amy Rossi, and Chris Zawisza, who went out of their way to help me make vital connections; to those whose work informs this book (Thomas Szasz, Paula Caplan, Erving Goffman, R. C. Lewontin, et al., Jeffrey Moussaieff Masson, Florence Rush, Peter Breggin, Denis Donovan, Bob Friedman, Jack Levine, Gary Melton, attorneys at the San Francisco Youth Law Center and the Center for Youth Law, Diana Autin and Joan Harrington at Advocates for Children in New York . . . far more people than I can name); to Amy Elman, who deserves an Olympic medal for swift, smart research; to the many, many others who gave generously of their time, their information, and their support. And, of course, to my most perspicacious editor, Nancy Miller.

Special thanks are reserved for those now adults who have been abused in the psychiatric system and who, calling themselves psychiatric survivors, have joined together as the National Association of Psychiatric Survivors and done groundbreaking work toward change.

Finally, an acknowledgment that is rueful. An entire group (or class, if you will) of kids is not represented here. I speak of gay kids, who, according to all advocates I spoke with, get the worst of what psych technology has to offer—not because they are "sick," but because they defy the ideology of the social norm. While serendipity was not with me in getting their story, these kids deserve a forum. I hope they will get one.

Out of Control:

An Introduction

"Is this gonna be in a book for real?" Joey asks.

Joey is ten—a sturdy, serious child. His gaze is direct from behind thick-lensed glasses. Temporarily in his grandmother Lucy's care, he sits beside me in her office, regarding me with a mixture of curiosity and apprehension. Lucy has arranged for me to meet Joey. She has told him why I am here: to try to understand what it was like for a ten-year-old boy to spend forty-two days on the locked ward of the adolescent unit of a private psychiatric hospital.

Yeah, Joey, I say, it'll be in a book. "But not with your real name, so you don't have to worry about that."

"I just don't want people to know I've been there," Joey says softly. The quiet shame in his voice puts blood in the veins of the word *stigma*.

"Would you mind, Joey, telling me what it was like for you to be in Psychiatric?"

Joey pauses. He looks at his hands, then back at me, then at his hands. . . . Then, looking back at me—with astonishing composure for a ten-year-old kid—he rises to the occasion. "Okay," he says firmly. "So. It's a hospital. It's not exactly a hospital for crazy people, but—it's for kids with emotional problems. Drug dependency, suicide. And there's five units. There's a teen unit, chemical dependency, a women's program . . ." The women's program, Lucy has told me, is where Joey's mom was (and now is again) after she signed

1

herself and Joey and Joey's fourteen-year-old brother into Psychiatric. "And there's an adult unit." There is also a children's unit but, as Joey explains, it was shut down for lack of a sufficient under-twelve population. So—"I was on the adolescent unit. Basically, there was a lot of kids there who'd been raped. Who had drug dependencies. Who'd been abused. Who'd been in gangs. Things like that. And they had a Time Out Room, which is when you're out of control."

"What does 'out of control' mean, Joey?"

"Well, see, there's two kinds of out of control," Joey explains patiently. "If you're, like, just mad—then they'll send you to the Time Out Room. Angry, things like that. And you go there, and there's like a bed and some mattresses—no blankets or anything. It's just like a cold room—where you go and stay until you calm down. Then," he adds, "they could escort you if you won't go."

"Escort?"

"That would mean, like—they'll carry you there, or drag you there." Joey notices my frown at the word "drag." "Like what they call dragging is one person lifts your feet and somebody gets your arms." Oh, right, *dragging*.

"There's also another thing—if you're like 'going off.' Going off? That would be, like, going berserk. Then they'll—uh—put you in restraints. And that's like—they put a rope around this wrist, and this wrist, and one around your waist, and like, same thing with your ankles. So you can't, like, move around or anything. Or hurt yourself. Or hurt other people."

It is certainly impressive. In less than two months, this ten-year-old kid has mastered another language: the language of—depending on your viewpoint—his treaters, his guards, his helpers, his captors. He has mastered the rules, the byways and folkways of life in an entirely different universe.

What is searing and poignant to me, as I listen to Joey, is the desperation that has informed that learning: Joey had to know his own total powerlessness in the face of the articulated threat of forcible restraint. He had witnessed the threat made good on, and so he had to have experienced viscerally the image of a swarm of Gullivers dragging, roping a single Lilliputian (Joey), one already inside their fortress and legally in their power—to restrain, to isolate, to medicate, to declare sick or well, to retain or release. Since his mother and his brother have also been paying guests at Psychiatric, he has to believe this place, these people, are benign in their intentions. Joey does not like it when, during our conversation, I seem to question the rights, the motives, or the means of those who have had him in thrall. He will say to me that it is all to "help." He will say that the drugs, the restraints, the seclusion are all necessary for those kids who (unlike him: he has learned the rules; he is good) are so "sick" they are "out of control."

≈

This book is the story of my journey into the world of children and adolescents in institutional settings that are designated "psychiatric" or "therapeutic." In many ways it is the continuation of prior journeys—into the world of child sexual abuse, into the world of child welfare and foster care. All of these worlds are contiguous: many kids in psychiatric hospitals or residential treatment centers, or therapeutic "schools," have been abused. In the dozen years since its "discovery" the main focus of the issue of child sexual abuse has come to be on the children's subsequent emotional disturbance/pathology. Kids who disclose abuse are routinely evaluated in those terms, and labeled, and at risk of a full range of "treatments," including institutional placement. Kids in foster care are routinely labeled in language that derives from the psychiatric and are placed accordingly—as emotionally disturbed, seriously emotionally disturbed, behaviorally disturbed, conduct disordered. In the state of Connecticut, "at least a third of foster-care children wind up in some kind of institution like residential treatment centers, psychiatric hospitals and group homes."[1]

This much I already knew.

However, during the late 1980s the media went ablaze with stories of the epidemic of white middle-class kids being placed in secure, private, for-profit psychiatric facilities by fearful or misguided, or duped, or sometimes vengeful, parents:

"CAGED KIDS: Behave or Mom and Dad Will Put You in the Nuthouse."

"TREATING TEENS IN TROUBLE: Can the Psychiatric Ward Fill In for the Family?"

"COMMITTED YOUTH: Why Are So Many Teens Being Locked Up in Private Mental Hospitals?"

"DON'T PUT ME AWAY, MOM, PLEASE!"

"GROWING UP BEHIND LOCKED DOORS."

In 1986, 36,000 American teenagers spent time on locked wards in private psychiatric hospitals—an increase of 400 percent over the previous decade.[2] A 1985 study commissioned by the University of Michigan Center for the Study of Youth Policy showed that over 270,000 kids under eighteen were hospitalized in that year for psychiatric reasons—more than double the number in 1971.[3]*

Typically, the media stories would lead with (for example) a homecoming princess placed in the hospital because she argued with her parents. A boy locked away because he was failing chemistry, which his parents took for a sign of depression. A kid who had run away from violently confrontational or abusive parents and was then perceived as "a danger to himself."

The stories depicted the kids as normal, behaviorally average, for our culture. (It was this that was the source of the moral outrage.) And they depicted the parents as feeling unable, or sometimes unwilling, to cope with adolescent problems. (And then also duly recited as contributory the litany of ills said to beset contemporary American life: the increase in single-parent families, in dual-career families; the temptations of drugs; the hedonism of popular culture.) Just to be balanced (and to raise the confusion level), there would

---

* As is not unusual with heralded epidemics, this concern over skyrocketing admissions was new largely in the amount of publicity generated. In 1970, concern was sounded that "Admission to inpatient status of children and adolescents has increased sharply in recent years. It has been estimated that resident patient populations are expected to decrease for the population 25 years and over, but increase by sizable amounts in the age groups under 15 years. . . . There were more than 5,000 children and adolescents under age 15 in state and county mental hospitals in 1963, and it is estimated this will increase to over 13,000 by 1973" (Henry H. Weiss, Ph.D., and Evan F. Pizer, M.D., "Hospitalizing the Young: Is It for Their Own Good?" *Mental Hygiene* 54, No. 4, [October 1970], p. 198).

generally be included quotes from several psychiatric professionals or representatives of psychiatric associations warning us that the problem was not the wrongful incarceration/treatment of kids, but the epidemic of emotional illness among our young that was *not* resulting in incarceration/treatment.

One of the higher-profile professionals quoted in rebuttal was Dr. John Meeks, a member of the board of directors of the National Association of Private Psychiatric Hospitals and medical director of the Psychiatric Institute of Montgomery County, Rockville, Maryland, who found it "hard to believe that there's any major problem" with overhospitalization.[4]

Part of the outcry concerned the major advertising and marketing campaigns launched by the competing hospital chains—Charter Medical Corporation, Community Psychiatric Centers (CPC), Hospital Corporation of America, Psychiatric Institutes of America, National Medical Enterprises—which blatantly played to both schools and parents, presenting psychiatric institutionalization as a reasonable response to—variously—failing grades, moroseness, moodiness, rebelliousness. . . . The ads flagrantly played to parents' fears of drugs, juvenile justice involvement, teen suicide:

A picture of a smiling boy of around eight, proudly displaying a math test, with the headline MADE POSSIBLE BY CHARTER HOSPITAL OF SAN DIEGO. Subhead: "Finally Achieving . . ."

An ad by Charter Pacific Hospital, headlined, ARE YOU WORRIED ABOUT YOUR CHILD?

"Do you know a child or adolescent who

"1. Has a long-standing or recent decrease in school performance?
"2. Has experienced a change in one of the following: appetite, sleep patterns, concentration or energy levels?
"3. Has difficulty taking directions from authority figures?
"4. Is hyperactive or demonstrates impulsive behavior?
"5. Is very emotional, frequently crying or having temper tantrums?
"6. Has recently been traumatized?
"7. Has had a recent onset of aggressive behavior?"

The message? "Call us for help."

IS YOUR TEENAGER FAILING LIFE?

IS YOUR TEENAGER RUNNING AWAY WITHOUT LEAVING HOME?

IS YOUR TEEN SUFFERING?

About these, Dr. Meeks offered the opinion that advertising was not an effective way to increase a hospital's census "since physicians generally do not refer patients on the basis of advertisements."[5]

In light of the fact that, according to Joey's hospital records, *the secondary referral for Joey's hospitalization was recorded as "TV,"* this struck me as somewhat disingenuous. Although it is necessary for a hospital-affiliated physician to sign off on the admission, later news stories would show that, in fact, in some hospitals the signing off occurred without the physician/psychiatrist ever having seen the kid. More important, these kids were not all being "physician-referred." Rather, they were being parent-volunteered.

In Meeks's view, however, the advertising was nothing if not a good thing because it might make it "easier for parents to accept the need for hospital treatment of their child." Advertising, Meeks asserted, "has done more to destigmatize psychiatry than all the fancy educational programs."[6]

Most of the mainstream media reports identified the root cause of the new explosion of kids-as-psychiatric-hospital-fodder as being the willingness of third-party insurers to cover the costs of inpatient treatment—alongside their reluctance to provide coverage for out-patient treatment. Insurers, interviewed, expressed their own concern that, were they to cover outpatient treatment, hordes of America's parents would throng through the gates seeking psychiatry's (unquestioned) benefits. While evidence emerged everywhere that the boom in psychiatric hospitalization was reimbursement-driven, this did not seem to me the issue of focal importance. For one thing, in the face of an outrage that seemed overwhelmingly moral and ethical, it struck me as oddly deflating to look for the solution in the zone of free-market capitalism: in adjuring one industry to control another. Secondly, that focus did not address what appeared to be a cultural predisposition to buy what the psychiatric hospitals were selling. Thirdly, my hunch was that a singular focus on reforming insurance would, in the end, have the potential for doing great damage to precisely the limited population that actually was in need: kids who truly required hospital attention—some of whom required chronic care.

A secondary cause of the explosion of juvenile inpatients was said to be the inadvertent side effect of an attempt to solve a different juvenile outrage, the placement of "incorrigible" juveniles, those guilty of status offenses (offenses that would not be seen as such if committed by an adult: truancy, running away . . .), in adult jails or juvenile detention centers. The Juvenile Justice and Delinquency Prevention Act of 1974 was intended to discourage states from locking kids up. This "transinstitutionalization" of kids—diversion from juvenile justice lockups to psychiatric lockups—certainly seemed plausible. But as an explanation it raised a question: The greatest number of kids in the for-profit psychiatric hospitals were parent-, not court-, placed: the funding source was private insurance, not Medicare or the state and federal government. The question, then, was: If court-involved kids were being diverted to psychiatric detention, but were not to be found in the private, for-profit hospitals, *where in fact were they going?* (And why, in the press reports, was this piece of the story absent?)

The best surmise was that less affluent kids were being sent to less costly entities, which fell under the heading of residential treatment centers, or to state hospitals.

In 1989, the National Mental Health Association published a report titled *Invisible Children Project,* which included a final report and recommendation.[7] Its survey, which received far less linage in the press than kids placed in private, for-profit institutions, reported *only on kids placed by public agencies.* Among their findings were that in the calendar year 1986 "States placed at least four thousand children for the period surveyed in out-of-state residential treatment and psychiatric facilities at an estimated cost of $215 million."[8] Of these placements, 91 percent were initiated by state agencies other than the mental health authority, with child welfare leading (46 percent), followed by education (28 percent) and juvenile justice (only 17 percent).[9] So of the kids placed in residential facilities designated as being for "treatment," the greatest number were placed there by the child welfare/foster care system—a system whose doings were almost entirely shielded by the word *confidentiality*;* a system that had arrogated to itself fully as much authority as institutional psychiatry to categorize and label kids. And a system whose first and last resort was all too often expediency. Regardless of who or what triggered these placements, the average length of stay was reported as 15.4 months. Ten years was the longest reported stay.

Additionally, 22,472 children were placed in state psychiatric hospitals nationwide in 1986. The average stay there was 4.2 months, at an average daily cost of $299.16[10] (approximately $2,100 per week, or $9,000 per month—a bargain compared to Joey's hospital bills, which ran over $8,000 a week).

While only sixteen states responded as to how many children they had placed in residential treatment centers within their own state, over 14,228 such placements were reported by those sixteen states.[11] (Which means that the total number *could* be three times that many overall.) What lay behind the fact that just sixteen states responded? From my own previous investigations I could only surmise that quite probably the remaining states simply didn't know. (There are not cracks in the states' existing foster care placement systems; there are gaping crevasses.)

And so, adding these numbers—which themselves do not give anywhere near the full picture—to the number of children placed

---

* As I discovered in researching *Solomon Says: A Speakout on Foster Care* (New York: Pocket Books, 1989), "confidentiality" is a shibboleth—the screen from behind which Oz presides. It is based on no legal theory and is unsupported by research. "Measuring the instrumental argument for privilege and nondisclosure laws would seem to call for empirical research, but such research has rarely been attempted. *Rather the laws of privilege and nondisclosure have evolved, or stumbled along, as legislatures and courts have made fairly crude guesses about social behavior, and have responded to an uncertain mixture of unsupported instrumental assertions and the politics of professionalism* [emphasis mine]" (Michael Wald and Robert Weisberg, "Confidentiality Laws and State Efforts to Protect Abused or Neglected Children: The Need for Statutory Reform," *Family Law Quarterly* 18, no. 2 [Summer 1984], p. 185).

in private psychiatric hospitals, the image that began to emerge was far graver. If, as Ira M. Schwarz and Jeffrey Butts's Michigan study showed, about two-thirds of the children placed in private, for-profit psychiatric hospitals were so placed for relatively minor personality disorders and nonaddictive drug use—for behavioral (or misbehavioral) infractions, for challenging authority, for family conflict, for school failure[12]—everything I knew led me to believe that the state-as-parent would have even less patience with these "disorders" than individual mothers or fathers. The state's version of an "adjustment disorder" could well be the child's failure to welcome placement in foster care, or the child's increasing irritability as he was yanked from home to home to group home without warning or, often enough, reason.

What we appeared to be looking at was the increasingly routine use of "treatment" as punishment: the psychiatric policing of children.

≈

"Cruise for Fall," announces the Charter Hospital flyer, before going on, "Ladies and gentlemen, grab your suitcases. Here it is. 'Cruise for Fall.' An all-expenses-paid cruise for two to the Caribbean for 8 days and 7 nights.

"This is a new and exciting incentive program designed to encourage you, the Charter Hospital staff, to take an active role in Marketing our hospital to the community.

"Each time you perform one of the marketing activities described on the back of this flyer, you will be awarded an appropriate number of entry forms. Simply fill out each entry form and forward them to the Personnel Department . . ."

Well, now. And what, on the back of the flyer, are these activities "you" (ladies and gentlemen) might perform?

"1. Admission. (Employee-generated admission must be documented on intake form. At the time of admission, employee is automatically eligible for 5 entry forms.)"

Five points? For just *one* kid? Wow.

"2. Intake resulting directly from employee marketing effort. (Must have employee's name documented as a referral source on intake form. Employee's name need not be the only referral source identified.)"

Other points come from: Successful return of an AWOL patient. Bringing a new or approved referral source or community member to the hospital for lunch/tour. Marketing visit to a new or approved referral source. And even—successful completion of intake form by a nurse.

This was bounty hunting. It also made the news, hyping the issue. Clearly there was something particularly repellent about the kind of incentive programs commonly used to boost sales of Amway products or Mary Kay cosmetics being used to secure a child-census for psychiatric wards.

As stories peppered the popular journals and the airwaves, the American Academy of Child and Adolescent Psychiatry attempted to clarify its own position[13] and distance itself from the publicized hanky-panky. It issued its own set of guidelines for inpatient admission of juveniles and specified as unacceptable: participating in programs that paid reimbursement to doctors for admission; participation in programs that did not require admission decisions to be made by a qualified psychiatrist; and participation in programs that used misleading, guilt-provoking, or unduly alarming advertising. (In other words, in the case of the first and the third, participation in grossly unethical practices.)

Perhaps in the spirit of "the best defense is a strong offense," the Institute of Medicine of the National Academy of Sciences issued a report in 1989 claiming that 12 percent of America's population under the age of eighteen (7.5 million children and teenagers) "have a diagnosable personality disorder." Only 2.5 million, we were ruefully told, were receiving treatment. Meanwhile, the National Institute of Mental Health was urging a fourfold increase in funds for research on children's disorders.[14]

As I would come to find common, underlying this claim— allowing it—was the blur of language, the hodgepodge mixing of everything in the psychiatric stew. It is a long way from a *diagnosable* disturbance to the kind of hellish childhood that produces chronic emotional anguish and perhaps behavior that disturbs society—and a long way from there then to severe psychiatric illness on the order of autism or schizophrenia.* And it is so far from all of those as to be a separate but corollary conversation to get into basic classist and racist reality:

"If you are an adolescent and black and you are seriously emotionally disturbed, the chances are that you will end up in the justice system, rather than in a treatment setting. If you are a Native American child and you are seriously emotionally disturbed, you will likely go without treatment or be removed legally and geographically from your family and tribe. If you are a child who is Hispanic and seriously emotionally disturbed, the assessment is not going to be in your own language. If you are an Asian child and seriously emotionally disturbed, you will probably never come to the attention of the health care system."[15]

While these facts feed the expansionism of establishment psychiatry, they are not its focus. "Our Nation is needlessly wasting its most precious national resource—our children and adolescents," stated Lewis L. Judd, then director of the National Institute of Mental Health, in an NIMH press release announcing the availability of a research plan for childhood mental disorders. "A shocking 12 percent of our youth suffer from mental disorders—often for life. We must do something about this situation now, and we can."

Ah. But within the body of the research plan itself,[16] even 12 percent does not seem on target: "How many children and adolescents in the U. S. have mental disorders?" the authors ask. "This fundamental question does not yet have a definitive answer. Recent studies suggest that between 17 and 22 percent (or 11 to 14 million children) suffer from some type of diagnosable mental disorder. But even the most conservative estimate is that 12 percent of the 63 million young people in this country under the age of 18 suffer from clinical maladjustment. Of these 7.5 million youngsters, nearly half are presumed to be severely handicapped by their mental disorder.

---

* This discrete and definitionally limited population is not the focus of this journey. Indeed, the thesis will emerge that these children could be more attentively served were they, in fact, psychiatry's primary focus.

And even in less severe cases, a child or adolescent may have difficulty coping with the demands of school, family, and community life."

It seems reasonable to suggest that the reason the "fundamental question" of how many children and adolescents in the United States have mental disorders "does not yet have a definitive answer" may well be the fact that the fundamental question is itself absent definitive definition. "Some type of . . . mental disorder"? "Clinical maladjustment"? "*Presumed to be* severely handicapped"? "*May* have difficulty coping with the demands of school, family, and community life"? (What difficulty? Which demands? Which schools? Which families? Which communities? And—*who doesn't* at some time?) This pitch on behalf of "science" contained language that seemed to me as misleading, guilt-provoking, and unduly alarming as the advertising put forth by clearly marked for-profit institutions, clearly designated entrepreneurial. In fact, it would seem to contain the seeds from which corrupt marketing practices grow.

All of this, it appeared to me, could be taken as "scientific" only in the sense that the official poverty line is scientific: Lower the income level that defines poverty, and you get fewer poor people; raise it, and you have an epidemic.

Conduct disorders, adjustment disorders, identity disorders, oppositional defiance disorders . . . it would seem we were, on the one hand, talking about the use of psychiatry as a police technology, a form of social control. To the extent that this is true, it is entirely consistent with the history of child psychiatry in this country. In the nineteenth century, expertise was taken to lie with physicians, pediatricians. The primary concern was with delinquency, the focus on moral character. Direct intervention focused on the reform of delinquency, the alteration of conduct. "From 1850 to 1880, observations which focused on the psychological dimensions of child welfare came largely from those who had been entrusted with the responsibility of providing care for neglected, dependent, and delinquent children."[17]

Charles Loring Brace, founder of the New York Children's Aid Society, directed his attentions to "saving" vagrants, criminals; to rehabilitating those who deviated from the ideal of social respectability, behavioral conformity, and economic self-sufficiency. The children targeted were a public eyesore, nuisance, or perceived threat.

By the early twentieth century, theories of heredity and congenital factors—of the biological basis of social misfortune—held sway: that crime, insanity, degeneracy, and pauperism were inherited.[18] When William Healy founded the Chicago Juvenile Psychopathic Institute in 1909, it was in the service of the Chicago Juvenile Court. Child welfare workers joined physicians as the authorities in service to the judiciary.

The first inpatient psychiatric centers in the 1920s—at Bellevue Hospital, the Franklin School in Philadelphia, children's institutes at Allentown and Kings Park State Hospitals—were established to deal with the behavior disorders resulting from the widespread encephalitis epidemic of 1919. They specifically admitted children who were behaviorally aggressive, not mentally deficient, brain damaged, or psychotic. The first adolescent psychiatric unit, at Bellevue, set up in 1937, dealt with teenage boys referred by the court as offenders—for truancy, stealing, running away. . . .[19]

But if we are talking about psychiatry as a policing mechanism, we are also, in recent years, talking about it as ideological imperialism. If psychiatry is discrete from psychology and psychotherapy in its medical base, in its institutional and pharmaceutical bias, its expansionism only serves to legitimize the expansionism by the entirety of what the French call the psy sector (inclusive of anything to do with psychiatry or psychology),[20] the colonizing of an ever-growing list of thoughts, behaviors, ideas, feelings—"problems in living," they have been called—as requiring the psy technology; falling within the psy purview to spot, to evaluate, to prescribe solutions for. Adults, adult women in particular, are subscribing to this expansionism for themselves without question. A trip to one Maine bookstore revealed before me an entire aisle, five shelves high, of books on healing (from your own abuse, from your parents' abuse of themselves); on having the courage (to heal, to create); on being an adult child (of alcoholics) or codependent; on hugging the child within. Could it be that the people who were so busy hugging the child within were the very same people who, as parents, were busy throwing the child without out?

Women have long been both the greatest seekers of psy services and the group most heavily victimized by them. As mothers, they have been grotesquely scapegoated and villainized by psy experts. A study by Paula Caplan and Ian Hall-McCorquodale found that in 125 articles in psy journals, seventy-two different kinds of psychopathology were attributed to mothers, including loneliness, marijuana use, minimal brain damage, self-induced television epilepsy, school phobia, delusions, bad dreams, chronic vomiting, frigidity, intellectual ineducability, truancy, and—incest.[21]

Since 1952, the bible of coined pathologies has been the *Diagnostic and Statistical Manual of Mental Disorders* (DSM). It codifies the language reserved to professionals; it offers them the menu from which only they can choose the appropriate category within which to place the combined qualities and behaviors of the object before them. While any psy professional's judgment might be countered by another's reading of the same object, the object herself, simply by virtue of being the object, cannot contradict the category in which she is placed.

This Book of Judgment will command lengthy exploration later. For now, it is important only to know that the original DSM "listed 60 types and subtypes of mental illness. Sixteen years later, DSM-II more than doubled the number of disorders. The number of disorders grew to more than 200 with DSM-III in 1980. The current guide, DSM-III-R (1987), includes tobacco dependence, developmental disorders and sexual dysfunctions, school learning problems, and adolescent rebellion disorders. DSM-IV (in preparation) will add more disorders. Clearly, the more of the ordinary human problems in living that are labeled 'mental illnesses,' the more people will be found to suffer from at least one of them—and, a cynic might add, the more conditions that therapists can treat and for which they can collect health insurance payments."[22]

At issue for me, setting out, was less the obvious entrepreneurial greed than the increasing dominion of the psy sector over all of human *being*—now including preadulthood. And the fact of our *acquiescence* in that dominion in substitution for all social and political thought.

In short, what bothered me most was not *what* was being sold— or that, in a capitalist, free-market society, it *was* being sold—but that we were buying it to such an all-encompassing degree. As Lois Weithorn, author of the seminal law paper on the private psychiatric hospitalization of children, writes, "It is unlikely that the medical characterization of troublesome behavior of children and adolescents would lead to increasing juvenile psychiatric admissions, even in the presence of the legal and economic factors . . . if that characterization were inconsistent with current social attitudes. The medical construction need not be the only culturally acceptable formulation, but it must be at least minimally congruent with predominant values. For example, no matter how legally accessible, convenient, and monetarily well-subsidized policymakers made it to control troublesome juveniles with public torture, this remedy simply would not be accepted in our current sociocultural milieu. It is alien to what the prevailing populace believes, or what it thinks it should believe. In the United States in the 1980s, we prefer to think of ourselves as providing solicitous care and treatment to troublesome children and other dependent persons who may manifest problems."[23]

That these judgments about "illness" (or pathology, or syndromes, or disorders) are made in service to the culture, in service to the social order, in accordance with fashionable norms, is evident in their historical fluidity. (Whatever happened to melancholia? Neurasthenia? That homosexuality has been excised as an official disease state is certainly good news. But it remains sobering that twenty years ago, how many thousands were branded and "treated" for that then-incontrovertible "fact" of illness?)

And what is to be made of this: that within the psy world, there is no agreement as to what we are talking about, much less *whom* we are talking about? (Kids who are behaviorally problematic? Kids who are emotionally troubled? Kids who are unsuccessful in the world of childhood as socially defined?) Are we talking about delinquency? Misery? Social deprivation?

Or are we talking about disease?

In the course of my journey I would tour the bewildering laby-
rinths of language on which the psy sector rests; the confusion of
concepts bubbling within it. From neurobiology, with its conviction
that psychological, emotional, and behavioral distortions (disorders?) reflect an underlying biological or neurological or chemical
flaw, to the location of flaw in parental failure (to set limits, etc.),
with sometimes both at once; from pharmaceutical medication to
behavioral modification (with, often, both at once); from genuine
caring about individual suffering to canny and outright efforts at kid
control; from good intentions to forthrightly greedy ones. . . .

Always, I found it essential to return these abstractions to their
rightful owners for identification: to return to those individuals who
were the objects on which the abstractions were supposedly based;
to whom they theoretically pertained. It is commonplace for critics
who wish to dismiss evidence challenging prevailing ideology to
invoke that word which has become epithet: anecdotal. I can only
assure the reader that none of the people, none of the kids, encountered in these pages is unique, extreme, unrepresentative. Of the
hundreds I spoke with, those found here selected themselves out on
the basis of their ability to articulate what had happened to them,
what they thought, how they felt. Only the most cynical critic, I
think, will want to characterize what they tell of as "a short, entertaining account of some happening, usually personal or biographical," which is how my *Webster's* defines the anecdote.

But perhaps, given that the psy world plays fast and loose
with language and meaning, the overriding reason to *listen* to
individuals—to place the *practice* alongside the theory—is to avoid
speaking in tongues.

Though mental health professionals are habituated to refer with
the depersonalizing label *case histories* to people who have voluntarily or involuntarily found themselves among their clientele, this
impulse to diminish is not, to my mind, one of the more admirable
features of the psy professions. It asserts a superior expertise on
life—on other people's lives: It assumes it. Period.

Whatever the competing theories, the competing subspecialties,
the competing social institutions within the psy sector, the fact of
competition did not in the end seem to me to lessen the overall

power of institutional psychiatry and the ever-shrinking distinction in American life between health and pathology.

Media stories of the 1980s almost uniformly led off with indignation that kids doing normal kid things, things that were within the range of the average or expectable within our society, or doing reasonable things in unreasonable circumstances, were being shut away for one month, two months, six months in private psychiatric hospitals, often dosed with psychotropic medications, placed in restraints, locked in seclusion. . . . By the end of the stories, however, the need for insurance coverage for *outpatient* treatment was deemed paramount. Virtually none seemed to recall the *normalcy* that had been premised eight paragraphs earlier. None then questioned why these normal kids, in conflict perhaps with their parents, or with the ever-more-stringent codes of social conformity that have come to prevail, needed psychiatric "treatment" at all—inpatient *or* outpatient.

This absence of skepticism about the inherent benevolence of "treatment"—the assumption that, the aberrant hospital scandal aside, such "help" could not do harm—seemed to me to be what gave institutional psychiatry its authoritative power, a power that then was readily extended into other major social institutions: the schools, the courts, industry. . . . A power that brooked no query. As Kentucky youth advocate David Richert was to say to me, "I can tell you about what it was like to negotiate with psychiatrists about accountability—as we were drafting some of what we thought was model legislation. It was unbelievable. We've negotiated with judges and prosecutors and almost everybody, including the mentally ill. I have never met a more defensive, more patronizing group of people in my whole life than these people.

"There's an assumption they work on, which is (*a*) only *we* operate as working in the best interests of the child; [and therefore] (*b*) anybody who has any view different from ours is necessarily *not* operating in the best interests of children. . . .

"Frankly, in our state, they bullied one of the most powerful men in the state. Not because he was afraid of them. He was afraid that if they testified, the legislators would say, 'Oh, they're *psychiatrists*. They must know what they're talking about.' In other words, it wasn't that they were a powerful lobby. It was the assumption even legislators have that psychiatrists basically know what's best for children."

What's "best" for children? That would surely include adequate shelter, food, paid care within a home environment, decent educational opportunity. . . . Surely what's best for children is *not* hunger and poverty. Yet there is no evidence that psychiatry has ever concerned itself with such matters. "Best" can only mean best in the sense of: It would be best for this child to be medicated, to be hospitalized, to receive treatment.

A metaphor for this confusion between the optimal and the pathological—the blurring of social reality and individual shortcoming; the undifferentiated admixture of social content, professional expansionism, utopian intentions, and victim blaming—occurred early on. I was transcribing an interview with a former administrative executive of a private, for-profit psychiatric hospital for children and adolescents. Although he is no longer with that facility, and is extremely rancorous at the unethical administrative practices that led him to resign, he is very positive about the need for what he terms "value therapy" for kids. So he is outraged, not by the facility's mission, but by its administrative sloppiness.

He expresses ambivalence about talking with me. He believes in inpatient treatment, in hospitalization. He does not want to contribute to "sensationalism." Still, he knows that there are treatment facilities "that are garbage pits that need to have the lid blown off them." But—kids, he says, do need to be hospitalized; kids do need treatment. . . .

What I am trying to pin him down on is *who* it is he believes needs this "treatment." Is he talking about kids who are definably, visibly, "mentally ill"? Is he talking about kids who are reacting as you might expect—quite as you or I might have reacted—to an atrocious life framework? Is he, then, talking about kids who are not so much disturbed as disturbing? Are these kids who have gone hogwild? Run amok? Are they flinging themselves about the universe because they cannot stop themselves (much as they might want to) and are, in some real sense, out of their own control? Or are they kids who are out of *our* (or their parents', or the schools') control?

To illustrate the benign, the "appropriate" use of hospitalization, this former psychiatric hospital executive tells this story:

"I'll never forget a young black boy. He was fifteen. We had him at the hospital for about nine months.

"If there was a kid that needed to be brought in from the airport, I'd get up in the middle of the night and I'd pick the youngster up, try and get them relaxed and transitioned, and bring them for admission to the hospital.

"That fifteen-year-old got off the airplane drunker than hell, served by the airline. This kid had, at fifteen, two girlfriends, four children, a Mercedes-Benz, and some very nice clothes. This kid—ought to be a CEO in an organization. Obviously a very good brain, but he's not using it well."

I remark that it might not be the most realistic dream for a black kid in a ghetto, becoming a CEO. He continues.

"Anyhow. This kid did all the things—darting around at me to see how fast I could run, to see if there were any guards at the airport. And going to the facility, he asked all the usual questions: Is the campus fenced in with barbed wire? How close is the nearest police station?

"I answered very truthfully and explained that my role was not one of explaining consequences, but there wasn't any barbed wire. Rather, a beautiful golf course on one side, a lake on the other side, and a highway at one end. And it would only take a few minutes to get out of that place."

And, I think, only a few minutes more before this black kid on the highway in this very white midwestern community would be apprehended and questioned. I say nothing.

"I followed that kid for the next five months—belligerent; he had a lot of time out; he didn't come to his issues at all for the longest period of time." Skreek! It is chalk on the blackboard: "Come to his issues." Fraught with apparent significance, absent of literal content. I keep silent. He continues.

"He was mean. He was a tough kid. He threatened others. He beat up on others. He got a lot of one-to-one therapy. And slowly but surely this kid started to open up, started to work with it.

"I watched him transfer to another building, a residential

building. And he started getting involved in the school process. Next couple of weeks, he was riding a bicycle. He could have taken off and gone anyplace. But by that time he was doing pretty well. I sat down and talked with him a couple of times, obviously being very careful to observe all the rules. And one time we sat there and he started to sob. My role at that point was simply to listen: not to disrupt, but to listen. Because I know they come back and get their own personal strength back." (Skreek!) "What he was dealing with that particular day was he had never had a chance to be a kid. By fifteen he had two women, four kids, a Mercedes-Benz, drug sales—and he had to start that at around age nine, hoofing drugs for somebody else.

"He never had a chance to be a kid. He never had a chance to expose feeling hurt. By the time he was fifteen he was having to take care of other people's hurt, including little kids'.

"Was he chemically dependent? Slightly so. Mostly alcohol. He didn't really get involved in using drugs."

Yes, I am thinking, but is that a mental . . .

"Is that a mental health issue?" he asks as though reading my mind.

"You have guessed my question," I say. "Are you going to take every kid, one by one by one by one, out of an abusive environment and put them through a wonderful campus life—assuming that is what you are describing this psychiatric institution to be—where they can ride a bike they never could have had before without stealing it? Yes! *Is it a mental health issue?!* By the way," I add, realizing my voice has achieved a certain—um—intensity, "that's a question. Obviously it's a very *passionate* question."

"It sure is," he says. "Yeah." Unexpectedly, since he has been so ardently arguing the case for good therapeutic intervention, arguing the need for incarceration, arguing the crisis, epidemic even, of seriously emotionally disturbed (or disturbing, or wrong-value) kids, he now says quietly, "That's a problem I'm having myself." He ruminates. "Take the classic case, catatonic schizophrenia—okay? A DSM-III situation. It has some real good visible signs: the person who is sitting in a chair with very little movement, or rocking back and forth. Tight muscles. Constrictions in the face and various bodily appendages. Fingers drawn in tight, gnarled. Really visible.

Psychiatric need? Yeah. Okay—somebody can stay catatonic a hell of a long time. There is no treatment. What do you want to do with them in the meantime? That's what we call hard psych."

No treatment? *That's* what they call hard psych? (Because it's so hard they don't know what to do?)

"When you get involved in soft psych—I have a real problem with the soft psych and who should get involved in it. . . ."

At this point I am getting that sense of logical vertigo that will become my companion throughout this journey. But here is where we get to the metaphor I mentioned earlier:

As I was printing out the transcript of our conversation (and brooding about the young black drug dealer, now back in his ghetto but—if the treatment succeeded—perhaps with his adaptations, his survival machine, no longer in tip-top working order), right at this point, right as he was saying, "I think we're trying to shape our destiny and our tomorrow, but while we're arguing about it there are a lot of kids out there who are . . ." Right at this point (I didn't notice it at first: the chatter-chatter of the printer didn't change): "still manifesting the 4e32"j5 -o 1x" gk2,"5z comes down, I think, in part for 5vj"vo 5vj".x"c" k2vob ix" 2-0"iv m"y-o".xki -5 4598xv2vb-8k229 k88"41k32"z . . ."

Two more whole pages of this went by before I noticed. Am I trying to tell you I believe this stuff was driving the machine crazy too? Come on. Do you think, in light of what we are talking about here, I'd be nuts enough to admit to that?

≈

By comparison, little Joey is a model of clarity and insight, an oasis of specificity, of speaking to the point. Let's go back to his guided tour of Psychiatric Hospital, as the real beginning of this journey.

"Each person who's there," Joey is saying, "gets a special therapist doctor. Like when I was there, my doctor was my mom's doctor also. And there was like staff there—just to watch you. And every Wednesday you go on a dinner outing. And on Friday you go bowling."

Bowling. Right. Why not?

"And there's also—like—levels. Okay?"

I have heard of levels, of course. And the things they call "steps" and "points" and "privileges" and "consequences"—the moral economy that underlies most, if not all, juvenile psychiatric institutions; that by which health and improvement, cooperation and conformity are measured; those things that define the proscriptions of your daily activities and your standing in terms of approval/disapproval, good/bad, well/sick. But I want Joey's take on it, so I shake my head.

"Okay. Say—there's three things you can do wrong. You could be on SP or EP—or Strict EP. Strict EP is for Escape Precautions. Which is you try to AWOL from the hospital. Which is run away."

Yes. And which I have also heard called, rather amazingly, *eloping*. "Is that very hard to do?"

"Well, one of the girls—just got a Level 2. She was on the bowling line and she tried to run away from there. But we [*sic*] got her and stuff. And she was put on Strict EP.

"And there is EP, which is if you'd run away from home, but not from the hospital. And SP is Suicide Precautions. And so, like, if you're on any of those, you can't get to Level 2."

Taking a deep breath, Joey sums up. "So." He ticks off on his fingers. "There's Level 1, which is you cannot leave the unit at all. Level 2, you can get a six-hour pass to go home. And you could go to the cafeteria and eat—the food there isn't very appetizing anyway, in fact I didn't eat it because I hated it. And then there's Level 3: You can get an eight-hour pass, and you could bring like radios and stuff to the hospital—when you came home from your pass."

How interesting. If the greatest number of kids in private psychiatric hospitals either have been abused by parents, or are locked in conflict with parents such that the parents have locked them up (in treatment), or such that they have run away from the home, how can it be seen as sensible that the greatest award those in power can confer on you in tribute to your adjustment in the institution is the opportunity to return, for ever-greater periods of time, to the environment that is your problem?

"And when you get to Level 4," Joey says, "that means you get to go home. Or if they think you're ready. I mean, that's not the only way you get to go home. You could be on Level 1 and go home."

Whoa, Joey. "Why?"

"Why?" Joey tries to think why (some of this is beyond the grasp of even a very bright ten-year-old). "The thing is, you can also stay on Level 1 if you're not good, and break all the rules. Because they have something called the Weekly Floor Plan, which is, like, work. Which is about anger and things like that. And if you don't get that finished, you don't get your level raised. You don't get in trouble or anything."

"What is the 'work'? What is it you do about anger?"

"Well—um—it's not always anger. It's different things. Like—if you're abused, you have to do a 'Dear Dad' letter."

" 'Dear Dad' what?"

"They just say, 'Dear Dad.' You fill in the rest. And you do different things. You do, like, paperwork talking about yourself. It's not too much, though. Just like a weekly thing. And they give it to you Friday. And if you don't get it done by Wednesday, then your level doesn't get raised.

"And there's something called 'room check.' Which is every morning—at ten o'clock—you go in and you clean up the room. Hang your stuff up and make the bed. And they come in just briefly, look at your room, look at your bed, see if it seems okay, see if your clothes are folded, things like that.

"And there's a plus, a check, and a minus. Plus is good. Check is okay. And minus is not good. So if you get Monday through Friday all pluses, on Friday you get to watch a movie, and during the movie you get to go to a vending machine for some snacks. They pay for it.

"Also, they have something called 'head check. ' Which is, every half hour in sleeping time, they come in and wiggle you and make sure that you're there and make sure that you're quiet and stuff. And like you also have medicine things.

"At night I was on something. I was in there for 'depression' and 'family problems,' and this was for antidepression. It was like there are a certain number of milligrams a day. It started out with forty-five milligrams, but then I was on a hundred and twenty-five milligrams."

"How did that stuff make you feel?"

"I felt pretty good, except they said it was a little side-effecting. Which was that my heart would sort of beat faster. And it also made me, at night—that's why they gave it to me at night, 'cause it helps you get to sleep. It helps you get tired at night. That's just a side effect. That's why they gave it to me at night. So you won't get tired in the daytime.

"And the kids, if they're there and they don't get better, what happens then is—they have a thing called 'placement.' Which is, after you leave the hospital, you go to another hospital-like place where you can stay longer. My friend is there. She's 'in placement' right now. What it is, it's like the same thing as Psychiatric pretty much, and you could stay there between six months and when you're eighteen. Psychiatric, you can stay, I think, up to ten months."

"Even if your parents run out of money?"

"No. If you don't have enough insurance, then you can't be there. Because it costs, I think, about eight hundred dollars to stay there one day. So."

Pretty good, I think, for a ten-year-old who has been transferred abruptly and without warning or preparation to an entirely strange world. Pretty aware, pretty *reasonable* for a kid who was diagnosed as suffering from "Major Depression."*

As I took leave of Joey and his grandmother, I wondered: How would Joey's report jibe with others'?

---

* A "Major Depressive Episode" is defined in the DSM-III-R as "either depressed mood (or possibly, in children or adolescents, an irritable mood) or loss of interest or pleasure in all, or almost all, activities, and associated symptoms, for a period of at least two weeks. . . . The associated symptoms include appetite disturbance, change in weight, sleep disturbance, psychomotor agitation or retardation, decreased energy, feelings of worthlessness or excessive or inappropriate guilt, difficulty thinking or concentrating, and recurrent thoughts of death, or suicidal ideation or attempts. . . .

"A person with a depressed mood will usually describe feeling depressed, sad, hopeless, discouraged, 'down in the dumps,' or some other colloquial equivalent. In some cases, although the person may deny feeling depressed, the presence of depressed mood can be inferred from others' observing that the person looks sad or depressed." (That's not *all* there is—the person may eat more or eat less, sleep more or sleep less, become more active or less active. . . .)

1

The Fake
Police

THE KEY TURNS in the lock, click. This is the fourth door so far requiring a key. The halls are freshly painted, the floors carpeted, the atmosphere airy: It is like being in some dream-state motel that suddenly, and without your knowing it, has been declared a locked psychiatric facility.

"This," my tour guide, the director of professional relations, is saying, "is the wing for the affective disorders."

At the far end of the hallway a boy, about fifteen, stands with his face to the corner wall, at once a spectacle for others, demonstrating the results of some wrongdoing, and an object one is not supposed to notice or see. Across from him, a thirteen-year-old girl sits glumly on a chair (the chair suggesting some slightly lesser infraction); another prop in this hospital-orchestrated morality play.

In this facility, this is a demonstration of what their admission booklet calls "Progressive Intervention." In the psy version of clear speech, this is defined as "the observation by a patient of others modeling appropriate behavior from a designated space that has been offered to the patient so that the patient can both regain control of his/her emotions and still observe the appropriate behavior of the other patients in the environment." This is the psy way of saying, "We tell the kid to go stand in the corner."

"Down there," my guide says, "is the classroom." A group of ten "affective disorders" mills out from the room. Forming a line, they move toward us, unnaturally silent for kids. Wait. It's important to be clear: What I mean is *unnaturally silenced* for kids.

These are the Hall/Line Rules:

1. Walk in the halls.
2. Line up in line order.
3. The peace sign (no talking) is up in line.
4. Keep your body to yourself.
5. Use good body control.

As the line passes, several kids make eye contact with me. Smile at them? Make the normal approach to them one makes to kids? I have not actually been told that would not be allowed. But it is palpable: Whether or not my talking to them would be a violation, any response on their part would violate imposed order. My *not* talking to them seems to me, however, a far greater violation: It is complicity. In the moment it takes for them to pass by, rendering the dilemma moot, there is a glimmer of understanding. If, even for me, an outsider, an adult, a free agent, to accede to the implicit redefinition of social rules is to confirm and to validate the right and judgment of those in authority here, if even I am angered by this artificial restraint—what is the psychic hurt and rage for the kid held helpless here?

My tour guide is moving right along, chatting amiably, pointing out the sights. We pause in front of chalkboards hung on the wall delineating the controlled transactions that govern this universe. They are recorded in code, next to each kid's name, the privileges and penalties and status changes of the week. The privileges include soft drinks; free time; a radio in your room; extra time, above the three minutes twice a week, on the phone; a courtyard visit; time with a peer . . .

Since my guide is in administration, he is not familiar with what all the codes signify. RE? It stands, he says, for Recognition Experience, but he is not sure what that means. LE stands for Learning Experience, which means that—let's see—"you stand before your peers and detail the nature of your behavior."

There are status distinctions coded on the board as well. CT (coordinator trainee), E (expediter) . . .

"Expediter of what?" I ask.

He reflects a minute. "Probably someone who puts things into place?" he suggests.

There is ET and T and ATT (activity therapy trainee), and SP (senior person) . . .

On the wall over the boards hangs a sign: LIFE IS WHAT'S HAPPEN-ING WHILE YOU'RE MAKING OTHER PLANS. Heavy.

The place is clean. It is modern. Two sets of bunk beds in each room along the living area, each bed tautly clothed. It is boarding-school normal if you fail to observe the pegs on each bed—two at the head end, two down below—for restraints (the tying down Joey has told us about).

Back out toward the lobby, just off the reception area, is a differ-ent room. This one has a heavy metal door, like a bank vault or a meat locker, with three sets of bolts on the outside. The room is maybe six feet square, with cinder block walls. Overhead, a bulb casts an eerie bluish light. In the center of the floor is a drain. The seclusion room.

This is my first tour. This is the first seclusion room I have seen. I stand thinking that if I were a serious inquirer I would walk into that room. I imagine doing so. Imagine asking that they close the door on me so I can see what it feels like. I feel sure they will comply; in my guide's view, we are touring his offices, his plant, his work environ-ment, no more. But the flash of imagining pops like a bubble. I am not that serious. Just looking at that room terrifies me.

"Why," I ask chattily, "is there a drain in the floor?"

Smiling, he explains that kids, you know, will often—well, defe-cate. In retaliation. When they become so, you know, out of con-trol. . . . It is purely my opinion—though in keeping with the spirit of agreeableness in play, I do not express it—that they may have the wrong take here on "loss of control."

It's going to want some getting used to, this universe.

≈

What takes still more getting used to, early on, is the kids themselves, those who speak with me after the fact of having done time in
psych hospitals around the country. The contrast between their
essential rationality, their clarity in reporting on their experience,
and the vivid distortions, the tight-lipped suspiciousness masked in
psy talk, of the hospital reports—all this results, curiously, in a
sense of breathtaking banality.

This is the initial appraisal by a California private psychiatric
hospital of:

PATIENT: Parsons, Delia

IDENTIFYING DATA: This is the first psychiatric hospitalization for this
16-year-old adolescent female who is living with her father at the time
of admission and intermittently attending continuation school.

BRIEF PERTINENT HISTORY: The patient was hospitalized after she had
runaway [*sic*] from home for ten days prior to admission. She had
runaway on two previous occasions, had runaway from a residential
treatment program two months prior to admission, had a history of
truancy and intermittent poor school performance and had a history
of putting herself in dangerous situations such as leaving the house in
the middle of the night and walking on the beach and continuing to
abuse alcohol on an intermittent basis.

She has a long history of difficulty with her parents. She described
her relationship with her father as one of mutual irritation and aggra-
vation. She also states that she was extremely angry with her mother.

Her parents are separated and at the time of admission she was
living with her father but wanted to move out and live with a girl-
friend.

She has a history of what appear to be clear-cut major depressive
symptoms including a severe fatigue, not leaving the home [except,
presumably, to "runaway"], sleep disturbance, and unable to concentrate on her schoolwork. However, she denied these symptoms prior
to admission. She also has a history of probable anorexic symptomatology although the patient minimizes this. . . .

Denies. Minimizes. Aha!

The report goes on to appraise Delia's "mental status" on first finding she is to be locked in a psych hospital:

> On admission revealed the patient to be neat, clean, casually dressed. Her speech was generally coherent. She is alternately tearful and angry. Her overall mood was depressed. There was no evidence of thought disorder, hallucinations or delusions. Her thought process was primarily focused on the injustice of being in the hospital and projecting blame onto her parents. She did not take any responsibility for her own actions. Her memory was grossly intact. She had no insight. She is oriented times three [the psy way of saying she knows who and where she is].

≈

The place I am to meet Delia is at the southern California home of her friend, Tammy, and Tammy's mother, Sandy. I arrive and ring the bell and—ring the bell again. Hmm. I peer through the window to the side of the door and a mime is in progress, a woman energetically vacuuming. Sandy is trying to impose an unfamiliar order for this stranger's visit. As I begin banging on the door, she looks up, clicks off the machine, cheerfully giving the effort up, and lets me in, smiling warmly. The home is modest: the living room aclutter in the way of a house that is accommodating of both young children and teenagers. Apart from her daughter, Tammy, Sandy has two other children, four and five, who at the moment are on visitation with their father. As well as the coloring books and crayons, plastic toys, teen magazines, kids' books, the living room holds a drawing board on which work in progress has been temporarily left off. Sandy is a free-lance illustrator.

Delia has been briefly delayed at her job in a gift shop. Over coffee, Sandy explains how Delia's hospitalization came about, how she came, now, to be living with Sandy.

"Okay. My daughter, Tammy, she and Delia are less than a year apart. They went to school together—I guess for about five years. Basically, Delia's a kid from a divorced family, who has done the back-and-forth thing—one week at Dad's, one week back with Mom—since she was about six years old.

"Delia's—a very intelligent kid. She was into ballet; my daughter was into ballet. They both have an artistic streak in them. I think that that, in and of itself, puts a kid at a disadvantage in society because people expect you to do certain things by certain routines, and follow certain patterns of development—and being that type of person you've already got a mark against you. Because you don't show your intelligence in ways people believe you should.

"Her mother's very paranoid, meaning very suspicious. She always thought that Delia was on drugs, which is interesting because she herself is a pot smoker.

"Around the age of thirteen there was that mother-daughter thing that happens. Which was around the time that Delia and Tammy became friends. So she's been around me and Tammy for about four years. As often as her mother would allow.

"But then her parents started to get this real restrictive thing with her, where they didn't want her to go out, and they didn't—they wanted her to behave and do well in school. And as she started to feel her independence, and do things that a lot of kids do—lying around, wanting to go out when they want to go out, wanting to hang around with the people they want to hang around with—when she started behaving that way after being this model child, I think that really disturbed them, so they tried to tighten the reins on her—normal conflict stuff. I consider that normal teenage rebellion. Not that every teenager's going to rebel, but that's the way it happens when it does. So she went from being this perfect model child with great grades and all, started going off and trying to be her own person. And she and her parents developed quite a power struggle.

"And when one couldn't stand it, they'd send her to live with the other one. Kind of passed her around, depending on who had the most control at the time.

"So by the summer of '89, I asked her parents if she could come and stay with me for a couple of weeks in the summer, because Delia showed an interest in wanting to be at my house. But they wouldn't even let her come and stay with me for a couple of weeks. That was in July. Within a month—August and September—Delia tripped out, ran away to another friend's house. She was involved in what I would call very mild drug use. They smoked pot and they drank—but nothing heavy. Pretty light. And she got a job down there. And I guess the father of the girl she was visiting let her live there. And Delia's parents kind of gave their consent.

"And then one day they changed their minds."

The front door opens, announcing Delia's arrival. Striking, small, fair, Delia offers a ready smile and handshake. For a while, the talk turns to how the day went, and then to where we should go to dinner. This being southern California, this of course involves getting into the car, navigating, parking. . . . It's not until we've ordered dinner that Delia begins her story.

"I was fourteen, and Mom got really worried about me. She thought I was going to ballet too much. I was dancing about three hours a day, except Saturdays when I'd go for nine hours. And I was getting thin, and she thought I was anorexic. At the *least* I was ninety-five pounds."

Since Delia is small boned and no more than five feet one—and since thin is a demand of ballet—I remark that that doesn't seem too terribly thin.

"Well." Delia smiles. "*She* thought I needed therapy. Then her brother died. And she got really weird. So I went and stayed with my dad. And she was saying that I was on drugs, that I was sniffing Wite-Out. She said I did 'ice,' which is a real drug. I hadn't even heard of it at that time. She wouldn't listen that I wasn't on these drugs.

"So I went to live with my dad. And by then she'd given him lists she had gotten my grandparents to start sending, whenever they saw things about symptoms of kids who were on drugs and depressed. Whenever they saw an article like that, my dad would get it. And so if I stayed out late one night, or stayed up all night, he could check it off: 'Doesn't sleep.' Or if I skipped dinner one night: 'Doesn't eat.' Eventually, I would fulfill all of the symptoms. Everybody would. Eventually, he'd have them all down.

"Mom was always very into psychology stuff. Always reading about it. All the books in the house were psychology books.

"And the fact that I didn't like to go to school was a big problem for them. I hated school because I didn't like the people there, really. I didn't feel I was learning anything. I'd much rather have been dancing. Through junior high, I hated school. I would go and get good grades. But I just went for the tests. It was expected. You were supposed to get good grades.

"But when I got to high school, my parents were calling me a drug addict anyway. So eventually I stopped even going for the tests. Because she was gonna be worried *anyway*."

And yet here is a kid who, hospital records show, at sixteen, at the tenth-grade level, tested at a more than twelfth-grade level:

INITIAL ASSESSMENT AND PLACEMENT:

WRAT READING TEST: 12+ grade level. Gray Reading Test: 11.9 grade level. Excellent comprehension and word attack.

WRAT ARITHMETIC TEST: 12+ grade level. Good understanding of most concepts up to and including algebra.

WRAT Spelling Test: 12+ grade level . . .

Delia says, "I can understand how the school thing would be a problem for them. But they took it into a lot more. They took it into that I was really depressed, and I must be on drugs if I'm not going to school. Because I'd always been a good student.

"So I started getting grounded, and I wasn't allowed to go to ballet. And I was getting into trouble at ballet because I was grounded at home. I was getting really frustrated. So after my mom said I couldn't take ballet anymore, when I was sixteen—I ran away."

Ran away. "You mean you left and didn't let them know where you were?"

"No. I *told* my parents where I was. I went to a friend's house. But I wanted to live with Sandy. I'd been talking about living with Sandy and Tammy for about a year. And they wouldn't entertain the idea. I wanted to go talk to a therapist with Sandy and my parents. They said no.

"So part of the reason I went was to force them to listen, that I was serious, that I really wanted to go. But I did let them know where I was.

"And it was like—it was *okay* with them. They came to visit me. They went home. We had a good time.

"I got a job. By then I was living with this other girl from work. Then my parents came down one time to my job. And my father said, 'I want to talk to you outside.' I came out, and my dad said, 'Get in the car.' I said, 'No. Let's just talk out here. What's the problem?' And he said, 'Get in the car.' And put me in the backseat.

"Then my mom came around and she got in the driver's seat. I said, 'What's going on here? If I have to leave, at least let me tell my boss I'm leaving. Where am I going? What are you doing? And why? Why didn't you tell me about this?' "

But is this not strange? In southern California there must be dozens of ways of running away that would be truly dangerous and irresponsible—living on the streets, hanging out at the beach. . . . Delia went to stay with a friend, got a job. And was, reasonably, upset not even to be permitted to decently give notice that she was leaving the job.

"They just started driving," Delia says, "until we got on the freeway. They said we were going to my mom's house. And it wasn't till we got really close to home, and passed home, that they told me we were going to a rehab. They assumed I was on crack. And that I had to be in this rehab."

Here we encounter something I was to encounter often: the interchangeability of substance abuse treatment and psychiatric treatment: the interchangeability of the populations.

What, I ask Delia, was this place like?

"It was houses, a few kids in every house, four houses, two boys', two girls'. About twenty kids altogether. They had school. And we did the cooking and shared work and—there were lots of rules. If you touched somebody, just touched them, then you'd have to do a bunch of chores. There was no touching allowed. It was a rule. If they caught you touching, you'd have an eight-foot ban with that person."

"An 'eight-foot ban'?" (As in my conversation with Joey, I am feeling a bit of a jerk. Although most adults absorb common teen-agerisms willy-nilly from television, the language of *this* world is one only these kids know. It is not *their* language, but the language imposed on them by those who establish the small universes in which they are to be "treated.")

Delia is as patient with me as Joey was: "You always had to remain eight feet from that person. Even if you gave a girl a hug. No touching, no smoking, no saying bad words. Most of the kids were from jail, so if you did that three times, you had to go back to jail. There was me and one other girl who were there because of our parents.

"And—I left. It wasn't locked. The only thing that was hard was— you had to find a way to get home. Because it's way up in the hills. I did it with a friend I'd met there. And I called my dad—he already knew I'd gotten out. And I said, 'I really want to come home. I can't face it all. I'll—I'll go to school.' So I did that, and for a while things were going pretty good. Then the same stuff started happening. My mom was always giving him lists, and he was always asking me, and—my mom, when she'd see me: 'Your eyes! Your eyes are dilated!' And: 'It's *dark*. Turn on the lights. My pupils will get smaller. That's what happens, you know.' I felt like I was always on the spot. And I kept asking to go to Sandy's.

"So last New Year's Eve I left again."

This time Delia went to Sandy and Tammy's house. "And Sandy helped me decide that I was gonna get it straight. We were gonna talk about letting me be at Sandy's no matter what. So I arranged an appointment with this therapist—that they used to make me go see? I figured they'd trust her, and start to talk about what I wanted to do."

With Tammy along for moral support, Delia went to that meeting. "And when I got just outside the building—my dad wasn't there.

"But the Teen Shuttle people were. The fake police."

Delia is correct in her description. California does have what can fairly be characterized as fake police: private enterprises that offer a "service" (to parents and to hospitals): For a fee of some hundreds of dollars, such a service transports juveniles, sometimes forcibly, to treatment programs. There are several such services in California, but the one that "served" in Delia's case was called S & L Teen Shuttle.

"Our twenty-four-hour service covers all parts of Southern California as well as the neighboring states of Arizona and Nevada," says a Teen Shuttle flyer directed to hospital personnel. The flyer goes on to reassure the hospitals on that which is of primary concern to everyone in southern California: that they will be able to get from anywhere to anywhere else. "Centrally located in the San Fernando Valley, Teen Shuttle has easy access to three major freeways. The monitoring of traffic allows us the opportunity to choose our desired route prior to dispatch.

"Upon contact with the child, Teen Shuttle employees identify themselves and explain the situation and their intentions. Calm explanation and discussion is the preferred style of influencing a child to abide by their parent's desire to see them receive treatment. . . ."

And what does *that* look like? Delia says, "One guy was real short, with a beard. Very obnoxious. The other one didn't say much. He was younger. The first guy was about thirty-five. The second one was more like twenty-three. I noticed he was wearing spiked boots. He just kind of stood behind the other guy, I guess in case there was a problem.

"First they said, 'Are you Delia Parsons?' And I said, 'Yeah.' 'Well. Nice to meet you.' And he shook my hand. I was—'Hi.' And then he showed me his badge. 'Well, we're instructed to take you to the da-de-de-de, and you just have to go down there and talk to them for an hour. Your father, he's gonna be down there.' I said, 'I was supposed to meet my dad *here*.' He said, 'Yeah. We realize that. But he has informed us that he wants you to go down there so you can talk to these people. You'll have to talk to them for about an hour.' I said, 'Well, you know, I would rather not go. Is it against the law for me not to go?' And he said, 'Yeah, that would be against the law.' "

In fact, this "service," which I think it could reasonably be argued is an awfully close relative of licensed kidnapping, is entirely legal. (It is only one of the many ironies surrounding the issue of the psychiatric policing of kids that half the world seems to be frantically warning their kids against talking to, much less getting into cars with, strangers. And the other half—at least in California—would seem to be hiring strangers to talk their kids into getting into cars.)

≈

"So," Delia is saying about her encounter with Teen Shuttle, "I said, 'Well, you know, I would rather not go.' Trying to get out of it. So—I went with them. He took my arm and I said, 'I can walk by myself. It's okay. I'm only five one; what am I gonna do?' And he said, 'Oh, you don't know. I've had people shorter than you just fight and run away.'

"All this time Tammy just sat on the steps. She'd been telling me, 'You shouldn't go do this. You shouldn't go! Your father's not gonna be there.'"

Perhaps it is the reasonable tone of Delia's narrative, the triviality of her infractions, the sensible way in which she identified for herself a solution to her situational problem—in contrast with the extreme coercive force that was called into play in response. But the image I am getting is of a war zone, of kids living and trying to survive in an occupied country. The atmosphere has the strangeness of science fiction: of a world where a sinister actuality is masked by a much-propagandized apparent reality: where dreadful things are done to kids—and they call it help. (Perhaps we should call it psy-fi?)

"So they put me in one of those fake police cars—no handles inside," Delia says. "And we went down to the hospital. And over there I said, 'So who am I supposed to talk to? Where's my dad?' They said, 'I don't know who your dad is. He's not here.' He'd met with them a lot earlier. And the woman said, 'I know they told you you were only gonna be here an hour. But you're gonna be here two weeks.'"

Delia was handed forms to fill out. One form told her of her right to speak with the hospital's patients' rights person and request a hearing. She signed that. The patients' rights person came down and spoke with her. Delia requested a hearing.

Then Delia was taken to the second floor. "It was *clean*," she says. "There was a long hallway. About ten rooms altogether. At the end of the hall there was the nurses' station. And there was one room that had a TV and some couches. All—very—clean. Everything was locked. Everything was locked.

"There were windows, but they were really thick and you

couldn't open them except a teeny bit at the top. You could hardly see anything out the windows."

"Did you know what kind of a place this was?"

"No. I didn't know what it was. I didn't know what it was. I knew what its name was. But I didn't know what that meant. And then—I saw my mom out the window. I saw her walking outside, and I thought, Good. She'll explain this to me. But she didn't want to come upstairs. Either that, or they didn't want her to.

"They showed me where my room was. And they said that I had to go play volleyball."

Bowling. Volleyball. These are known in the psy world as RT: recreational therapy.

"They have this cage where you play volleyball. And I didn't want to play volleyball. So I had to sit for twenty minutes and write an essay about that."

≈

According to hospital records:

Examination reveals the patient to be neat, clean, casually dressed, with long hair which she is frequently tossing. Her speech is generally coherent and goal-directed. She is alternately tearful and angry. . . . She is overall depressed in mood. . . . Her thought process is primarily focused on the injustice of her being in the hospital and how it is her parents' fault. . . . When it is pointed out that she is not accomplishing her goals in a functional way, she states that she was just beginning to and that no one was giving her a chance. . . . As evidenced by the above, she has no psychological insight. She consistently minimizes the extent of her problems to this interviewer. . . .

The patient's global deterioration in functioning, total lack of insight, substance abuse, and a history of anorexia, all implicate severe character pathologies. . . . Given her depressed mood and . . . genetic loading, it is likely that she is suffering from early manifestations of a major affective disorder. The family history of alcoholism on her father's side and apparent long-term dysfunction in her mother also suggests a genetic predisposition for substance abuse and character pathology. Therefore, this patient is likely suffering from both a severe personality disorder and a major affective disorder. At this time, this will need to be further evaluated in a structured setting and if appropriate, antidepressant medications will be instituted. . . . Further residential treatment after hospitalization may be indicated.

Delia did get a hearing. The patients' rights person was present, but was not given much of a chance to say anything. Nor was Delia.

She says, "They asked my mom questions, and then they gave me a chance to say something after all the stuff was done. My mom had a prepared three-page thing about everything I'd done in the last three years, and how I was on drugs, and she would notice me not eating. And how depressed I was. So I sat there with my little notepad, and everything I heard that wasn't true, I noted to make a comment on it. But when it got to be my turn all I really had a chance to do was say, 'Well, actually about that fight, this is what really happened. . . .'

"And they just said that I was really defensive; that was a character flaw, so I needed more hospitalization. And I was 'in denial.'"

From the hospital records:

"DEVELOPMENTAL HISTORY: Mother stated that Delia was a planned pregnancy. Father interrupted mother saying that he sort of did not want the pregnancy. Said it was a little quicker than we wanted her. Mother and father were a little annoyed with each other in the way they perceived their marriage and life in terms of Delia. . . . When asked to describe the patient as an infant, mother and father said that she was very healthy. Father said that she was hard to put to sleep. Mother interrupted father saying that she was not hard to put to sleep. Father repeated that she was hard to put to sleep.

"And," Delia adds, "the judge for the hearing was another therapist. From the hospital. Affiliated with the hospital."

"How did you feel at first?" I ask Delia.

"At first? You're shocked. I couldn't believe, at first, that my parents really did that. I thought it was some kind of mistake, and they're gonna show up. And I'd be able to talk to them. That something could be worked out. Because I'd made the *appointment* to talk to them. I figured I was going to—whether it was here or there. So I didn't really believe I was gonna stay. And mostly at first it wasn't scary as much as—I just felt hurt.

"It's confusing. Because when you go in—and you want to cry—if anything, you *don't* want to cry. Because you don't want them to think that you need to be there. So you feel like you have to maintain composure so that you can explain yourself, and explain your position enough so that people will know that you do have a brain, and you do know how to use it.

"See, then again, what you don't realize is that they do want you to cry because that is normal." She shakes her head and smiles. "I don't know *what* they want. What I was trying to do when I got there was to give them what they wanted so I could get out."

The word that hospital records use to indicate this cooperation is "manipulative."

At this point, Sandy, who has been quiet so far, says to Delia, "I think one thing you need to remember is that during that time you knew that I was there, Tammy was there, and we were telling you that we were going to get you out."

Delia nods. "I had friends. I did have people that I could call.

"It didn't get scary until after—two days. I started to get really scared. Because then I started talking to other kids there. And they told me the same story that I thought that I had—not in terms of our lives; our lives were totally different. But the story: 'You're gonna be here an hour. You'll be here three days. You'll be here two weeks.' Some kids were there six months. And they were all told the same thing I was. And they all, also, had friends. And that's when it started to get really scary.

"And then, talking to the psychologist. When I first met her, I was crying and saying, 'What do I do? What do I have to do to fulfill all the requirements at this place so I can graduate?'

"And she said, 'Well, there's nothing you can do, basically.' And she said, 'Be good.' And didn't say about anything after that. She told me there was absolutely nothing I could do but go to a residential home and unless I did that, then I'd go to juvenile hall . . . that's for kids who haven't committed major crimes. Either that or they just don't have anywhere else to go. Not a fun place to be at all. That's when it started to get really scary, when I realized I didn't have any power."

≈

What is the *idea* here? What is the legal theory that permits all of this "voluntary" psychiatric incarceration of children and adolescents—by parents or by the state-as-parent? Where does the blanket permission come from, given the enormous deprivation of liberty involved? And, secondarily, what makes operations like Teen Shuttle legal? (Secondarily because, after all, if we do not question the rationale of the end, arguing the *means*—however mean they may seem—is no more than diversionary.)

≈

To all intents and purposes, the current dilemma began on October 1, 1963, with the birth of the baby who would become known as "J.L." in the landmark Supreme Court case *Parham* v. *J.R. and J.L.* [1] When he was eight hours old, Jackie was adopted by a Georgia couple, Dr. Jackson Larrabee and his wife. Three years later the couple divorced. The adoptive mother was granted legal custody. She remarried and bore a child. Accounts vary as to why what happened next did happen. One account has it that she "no longer had a place in her new marriage for Jackie." Another account has it that the child had to be sacrificed/scapegoated for the marriage to be preserved. Yet another says Mrs. Larrabee "really cared for Jackie and it was a painful, traumatic decision to give him up."

Nonetheless, Jackie was given up—to Central State Hospital in Milledgeville, Georgia, a mental institution. Jackie was six years old at that time. He would remain in Central State for the next five years and five months of his life. Because he was placed in compliance with parental will, his commitment was the kind called "voluntary." Jackie, of course, did not volunteer.

Because this was a psychiatric hospital, after all (albeit a state, not a private, facility), Jackie did require a diagnosis. And so he was labeled "hyperkinetic" and as having an "adjustment reaction to childhood." Neither the social worker nor the lawyer nor the psychiatrist who were to know Jackie during his hospital stay ever recorded seeing the alleged hyperactive behavior. In fact, what they uniformly testified to was a child who was extremely needy, who wanted more than anything else to have a home, to be loved. Others who worked with Jackie described him as attractive, with "light colored hair that seemed to have a mind of its own." A hungry child, hungry for love, acceptance, attention.

It wasn't until 1975 that a young attorney, David Goren, then working for Georgia Indigent Legal Services, was introduced to Jackie by a social worker, and there began what was later to become truly a federal case. Goren started to look into how Jackie got there, what the procedures were, "and what was so incredibly wrong with this kid who desperately wanted to be out of the hospital, but who was there 'voluntarily' according to the law."

On December 5, 1975, the Middle District Court of Georgia convened a three-judge panel to hear Jackie's case, now framed as a class action suit on behalf of Jackie (J.L.) and J.R., a child who had been placed in Central State by the state as guardian, but who had also been there over five years, and forty-four other members of their "class"—children in Georgia mental institutions unnecessarily, and for an average stay of 458 days. Most of the placements were what the law called "voluntary." Which meant, then as now, that the adult in legal charge of the child so volunteered.

There was reason for optimism. Eight years earlier, the Supreme Court decision In re *Gault* 387 U.S. 1 (1967) had established that kids charged with delinquency had rights and protections: the right to notice, the right to counsel, the right to cross-examine witnesses, the rights—excepting that of jury trial—accorded adults charged with criminal behavior.

It could reasonably be argued that children placed "voluntarily" in a mental institution indefinitely sometimes have a visible conflict of interest with those seeking to place them. That there should, at the very least, be some clearly intelligible definitions of the boundaries of "illness" that make a child "suitable for treatment" in a full-fledged mental institution. That there should be, at the least, periodic review.

Hospital documents had begun showing recommendations that Jackie be placed in foster care as early as 1973. Why was he still there—on Ritalin, amphetamine sulphate, and other drugs—developing into what the hospital uncharitably described as "an insecure child who feels he must have your attention with his endless requests" or, as David Goren put it, a kid "who needed love incredibly."

When a loss of liberty of these considerable proportions is at issue—an indeterminate sentence of confinement, a lifelong label—there would seem to be a strong case that the system should outfit a person fully with the protections due any citizen under the Fourteenth Amendment—even if that person is a child member of a family, or a child ward of the state.

When Jackie's case went to the district court, the court emphatically agreed. However, when it went, on appeal by the Department of Human Resources, to the Supreme Court, it effectively said no to all of the above.

In truth, the district court had a certain advantage. Although the testimony of the director of the Office of Child and Adolescent Mental Health Services, Atlanta Division, was part of the written record, it must have been a significant educational experience to actually hear him in person.

Asked when he thought hospitalization was the appropriate treatment for children, he said:

"It can be quite a variety of circumstances that can make it appropriate for a child to be hospitalized. One would be a very acute, severe degree of disturbance. The child's behavior is quite out of control, and he needs to be in a contained environment until some stabilization is achieved through medication, through program therapy and so on that brings about a greater degree of capability on the child's part to function within normal controls."

He continues: "Other situations, due to social circumstances the child's interaction with his parents may be in sort of a vicious pattern where it's getting worse and worse; and the parents are not able to change or interrupt this vicious circle and a disturbance builds. It may be appropriate to hospitalize the child as part of breaking the cycle and achieving a more stable relationship. . . ."

Asked then whether the standard often applied to *involuntary* adult commitment—dangerousness to self or others—was pertinent to children, he said: "More characteristic [of] what we see is a very aggressive, intense, aggressive response, a variety of different behavioral patterns. In effect the statement is a *prognostic one.* It's an effort on the part of the diagnostician to say, 'As far as I can judge, putting all this picture together, the behavior I see and the history I gain, the evidence I see of the parent-child interaction and so on, *this is a condition that I predict will clear up with not too much intervention.' "* [Italics mine.]

If I am correct, what he has just said is that a *guess* that the future will be just fine "with not too much intervention" is grounds for psychiatric incarceration.

He went on. And on.

He was asked: "One of the contentions that's been made in this case is that parents sometimes attempt to scapegoat a particular child as mentally ill and everybody else in the family is healthy. In your experience is that a phenomenon you've seen?"

He replied, "I'll qualify the way you worded it by saying or taking out the words 'parents try to.' Parents certainly do . . . it's probably fairly common in terms of families in general of patients we see in child psychiatry. . . ."

Does the same thing go on in private hospitals?

"There would be a parallelism. . . . The parents may come in saying, 'I can't handle it anymore; do something.' And, they say at the hospital or it might be the psychiatrist who says, 'I think hospitalization is indicated.' The parents would agree and that would decide it."

Okay. But if, as he has testified, adjustment reaction to childhood is really a prognosis, a prediction of what might happen in the future, a label describing behavior that some Significant Other now finds socially unacceptable, doesn't that depend on the person doing the labeling?

"It certainly would have to be true, yes, that the person would agree that the intensity, the level, the extent of his behavior was socially unacceptable. What social unacceptability means, it means that the social group is not accepting; and that's why they brought them there in the first place."

He then goes on to testify that "The problem here in part is the history and tradition of mental hospitals, which have been dumping grounds in the past. As we try to move out of this, there are a lot of people who still treat them as dumping grounds."

"Dumping grounds," then, were the very words used by the witness called on to defend the psychiatric hospitalization of children, of Jackie and others similarly situated.

The district court underscored children's liberty interests. It acknowledged that the child's interests might differ from the parents'. And it allowed as how psychiatrists make mistakes, and thus should not have unfettered power.

Yet the Supreme Court disagreed. Why? Because the justices did not lend weight to the evidence of the use of mental hospitals as "dumping grounds" (despite the testimony of a psychiatrist supporting hospitalization). Because, they said, it is not the hospitalization of the child that is the stigma, but the "symptomatology of a mental or emotional illness." And because of the natural bonds of familial affection that prevail. And because even adolescents have not got sound judgment. Because the protection of adversary proceedings would deter parents from seeking needed treatment for their children, and would just worsen whatever parent-child conflicts existed.

Basically they disagreed because they made the assumption, *despite the evidence*, that what was at issue here were mentally ill children. That the issue was one of "medically indicated treatment." As law professor Gary Melton (University of Nebraska, Lincoln) has argued,[2] "*Parham* marked . . . a pronounced turnabout in the assumptions believed to underlie juvenile mental health law. In engineering this reversal, Chief Justice Burger relied on a panoply of psychological assumptions . . . without supporting evidence."

Among the fourteen whole-cloth, unwarranted assumptions, Melton includes: that there was no evidence of the use of mental hospitals as a dumping ground; that "The state through its voluntary commitment procedures does not 'label' the child." Rather, stigma results primarily from the "symptomatology of a mental or emotional illness"; "The law's concept of the family rests on a presumption that parents possess what a child lacks in maturity, experience, and capacity for judgment required for making life's difficult decisions. Most important, historically it has recognized that natural bonds of affection lead parents to act in the best interests of their children"; and that adversary proceedings "will deter parents from seeking needed treatment for their children."* As Melton contends, "the majority opinion in *Parham* represents a construction of the supposed reality of how hospitalization occurs, derived from idyllic notions of how the family and the mental health professions should be. As such, this opinion reflects both a representation of myths (of wishes for a world that isn't and perhaps never was) as facts and an antiempiricist bias among the Court's conservative members."3

The most dangerous assumption, however, was that these decisions were first and foremost "medical" ones: that they were based on a fixed and reliable determination of definable pathology by a medical professional.4 This assumption infused journalists' stories in the 1980s. The stories were predicated on the assumption that, although it might be shocking that normal misbehavior led to lock wards, nonetheless the children at issue had sufficient mental disturbance to require some form of psy treatment. Once you enter the psy world or once you are brought into it, the hypothesis is you are sick.

In other words, the hypothesis in the psy world is the antithesis of the hypothesis in law.

Parham left states free to determine their own laws, their own level of oversight and scrutiny.

Prior to *Parham*, California already had in place legislation, the Linterman-Petris-Short Act or L-P-S (California Welfare Institutions Code, section 5000, 1969),5 which required a psychiatric

---

* This last is interesting because, as I was to discover, that is the line of challenge by which psychiatry currently tries to quiet unfavorable reports in the media: that stories such as those about wrongful hospitalization will deter parents from seeking the help their children need.

examination prior to any hospitalization and built in procedural protections, hoops that had to be jumped through to hold a patient for more than seventy-two hours. Interestingly, these liberal provisions had been signed into law by then-Governor Ronald Reagan, whose agenda was to cut expenditures, and whose target was the severely disturbed who required extensive and expensive chronic care.

Two years before the U.S. Supreme Court's *Parham* decision, in July of 1977, the California Supreme Court decided In re *Roger S.*, 19 Cal. 3d 921. Here, a fourteen-year-old had been admitted to Napa State Hospital by his mother against his will. The court held that his parent could not waive his due process rights. Although *Roger S.* did not specifically require a court hearing, it did suggest the court might be an appropriate forum, and it did determine that legal counsel should be provided the minor. Although it can reasonably be argued that *Roger S.* should apply to private facilities as well as state facilities (since both perform the same functions and private facilities are licensed by the state), it can also be argued otherwise (since the decision did not directly address the private placement issue). California child advocates then pursued passage of another bill, which would specifically give kids over fourteen placed in private facilities similar rights. The hospitals caught wind of it and submitted their own bill—requiring simply that there be the right to a hearing (without legal representation or friendly witnesses) before a psychiatrist who could be a member of the hospital staff. And that the finding need only be that "further inpatient treatment is reasonably likely to be beneficial to the minor." Or, at least, not actively harmful. This, SB 595 [section 6002, Jan. 1, 1990], passed. (And indeed, although this bill was reactive on the part of the hospitals, ironically, staff discovered that these hearings actually served their interests: that it was only following these ceremonial demonstrations to the child of her powerlessness, and the strength of the forces aligned against her, that she "became involved" in the "treatment.")

Clearly both the legislature and the courts were invested in the same mythology about the "medical" nature of the whole business, and in the oracular wisdom of psychiatry, that had obtained in

Parham. And so when a furor arose as the press began reporting on Teen Shuttle–like operations, advocates considered filing suit. And decided against.

According to Jim Preis, executive director of Mental Health Advocacy Services in Los Angeles, they looked first at the legal theory. Certainly you could sue if the operations acted negligently, but was their work illegal per se?

Remarkably, the answer came up no.

Such operations were considered an "ambulette" service. As such, they were regulated by statute. And the statutes indicated that you could use reasonable force in terms of restraint so long as there was parental consent. Especially (of course) if restraint was "medically indicated."

Considered next, Preis says, was the question of the limits of parental power. Outside of behaviors falling under the child abuse and neglect laws, there were virtually none. Well then, did psychiatric hospitalization equal abuse? Naturally not: It was a medically indicated decision, supported by a professional.

The most basic consideration, however, was that, in a conservative climate—one in which California courts were increasingly prone to take guidance from federal courts—any legal challenge by *your* theory (that kids have some autonomy) would not only likely fall before federal theory (that parents' rights predominate because they act in the best interests of their children), but might lead to the erosion of those gains that had been made.

Bottom line, you would be forced to argue against the psy claim that such "services" were saving the child's life, not kidnapping; to take on the widespread and apparently overriding belief that psychiatry was benign because it was medical; even that the absence of such a service would be denying kids needed medical treatment.

≈

And so we have theory—in law about psychiatry as well as in psychiatry itself—that is aeons away from reality, that is *disproved* by reality—to no effect. Because? Because you are dealing with the doubly disenfranchised: *kids* who are said to be *mentally ill*.

"What were the days like?" I ask Delia.

"It was really structured in that place. They made sure you ate all your food at the appropriate times." In fact, Delia's record is replete with: ate 10 percent of her lunch; ate 40 percent of her dinner—recorded as though she were a laboratory animal. Hospital records show Delia's weight on admission as 135. Either she was not anorexic, or she was awfully *bad* at it. But stranger than this, to me: Even if Delia had the obsession with food that is associated with anorexia, what is to be served by *sharing* that obsession? The fact that she is being effectively graded on how much she eats suggests they believe she is acting deliberately and purposefully—willfully defiant. But if they believed her to be defiant, is that a disease? If one has a disease, is one doing it on purpose? The clear suggestion is that they found her spiteful, and the cure for her "disorder" was to break her will.

"Everything you did was screened," Delia says. "Even the conversations you had with other people. There was always somebody listening and watching. You got points for eating your food. You weren't allowed to have shampoo with alcohol in it because you might kill yourself by drinking it. You couldn't have hair dryers because you might hang yourself.

"And my psychologist—they would try to make something so they could write it down. She would try to make me mad at her, try to make me call her a bitch. So that she could write it down.

"In a family meeting, my little brother was there, and I was very glad to see him. I was rubbing his head, and she said, 'It really bothers me. It's very unhealthy the way you fondle him.' This is something I've done since he was a baby. I don't know why you say it's unhealthy. What are you *implying?*' She said, 'Oh? I'm not implying a *thing. . . .*' And she had this really, really obnoxious look on her face. That was the only time I slipped. And I didn't say it. I just mouthed it (bitch).

"And she said, 'Go ahead. Say it. I saw that on your mouth. Why don't you just say it?' And so I did. And she ended up saying, 'Oh, that's *good!* You did finally release your anger toward me. I've been provoking you, and you just never had the courage to stand up for yourself. I'm glad to see you're getting healthier.' Here I've been trying to restrain myself so I would be able to get out. And it turns out that what you want me to do is say nasty things to you?

"She spent a lot of time trying to make me see that there was no way I could 'rule the show.' And that the only way I could *not* live with my parents was to be emancipated. And I knew I couldn't be emancipated because I didn't have a job. You need to have income for six months. I couldn't live at home. I couldn't be emancipated. There was no way, she said, I could live with Sandy. So the only thing there was, was to be in this hospital, or to go to a residential home. And what she was working on was for me to stay as long as I could—'cause they were getting a thousand dollars every day—and then for me to be in a residential home. That was the consensus where all these professional people were concerned, all the adults.

"I had one counselor—he wasn't a doctor—who was kind of on my side. He used to talk to me sometimes. And I asked him—because my mom was claiming I was anorexic and bulimic. . . . And he said, 'Look, I know you're not anorexic. I believe you.' And I said, 'Well, what extra things can I do to prove that?' So he said, 'We'll make a contract. Every time you eat, make sure somebody writes it down. And then don't go in your room for an hour. If you really, really have to pee, make sure somebody goes with you. And then get weighed. Make sure that somebody weighs you every day.'

"So I did that. I had my weight recorded every day. The first day I was weighed twice—once by the nursing staff and once by the regular doctor. And one of those came out eight pounds heavier than the other. Two different scales." Their scales would seem to be about as reliable as their diagnoses. "After that, I made sure that I was always weighed on the same scale. But what they did was they took the eight-pounds-heavier weight and said that I had lost eight pounds in two weeks. . . . I said, 'If you just look it up, I can swear to you that it's within a pound of what I am now.' And they refused to look it up. So they said I'd lost eight pounds—and that just helped my mom right there, to get those insurance dollars. And then when her insurance ran out, that was it. I went to the next placement. They sent an ambulance."

Our dinners are long finished. As the waitress removes the plates, I notice the restaurant is emptying out. Delia jerks me back to attention, saying quietly, "Kids were put in restraints. I was put in isolation for eight hours—because a kid tried to give me cigarettes."

"Who were the other kids you met there?"

"One girl—her thinking was normal. She was a nice girl, but she was involved in gangs. Her mom was terrible. I could see why she'd rather be with her gang friends than with her mother. Her mother would say, 'I hate you because you're a witch and I can't deal with you.' This girl was fourteen. She wasn't crazy at all. I talked to her, and she was a normal person.

"Two other girls were model students. Miss Model Americas. Ginny, her dad was abusive, and her big brother used to beat her up. Her dad beat her up too. And Trish was there for sneaking out of her window at night, or sneaking in her window after curfew. That's how she got there. One girl, Katya, had tried to kill herself. She was thirteen. And she was in there for nine months."

"Why do you suppose," I ask, "that some kids get targeted? Lots of kids try pot."

"It's their parents. Because—I don't know one kid who's never tried smoking pot. But none of them have been in a mental hospital. It has to do with the parents. Because it's not the police that put these kids in the hospital. It's not the social workers. It's not psychiatrists. It's the parents. The psychiatrists support it. They find the parent who's gullible. My mom's always respected psychiatry so much. She has no novels in her house. She has all books by psychiatrists. And the psychiatrists say, 'Oh, I'll take the kid for you. I can make them all better. You haven't done anything wrong. I'll make them better.' And it takes the stress off people."

"You know," I say, "I just realized I don't have any idea what, in all this, was meant to be 'treatment' for your alleged major depression."

Delia thinks for a minute. "I guess that's what they would call the groups. And how you get points for eating a certain amount at a certain time. They have groups all the time. Recreational therapy. That's when you get in the cage and play volleyball. I had rashes on my face because I just hadn't been outside. It's really unhealthy and you feel it. It's so dead, and it smells so *clean*."

I laugh. I've never heard the word "clean" sound so disgusting.

"Seriously. Just a breeze in the face. The first time I got outside I almost cried because it felt so good. I forgot what it felt like. And that was just two weeks. Not nine months."

I notice the restaurant staff has begun stacking the chairs on the tables. I signal for the check.

"But the worst part of it, the scariest part, I think," Delia says, "is that they can really get you to doubt yourself. They're trained to manipulate. There are psychiatrists out there that can help you. But another brand of psychiatrist is manipulating. They take the things that you say and— Okay, if you say, 'I am not an alcoholic,' they say, 'Have you ever had a drink before?' 'Yes.' 'How old are you?' 'I'm seventeen.' 'So—you're not twenty-one.' 'No.' 'So—you have broken the law. You said you'd never broken the law. And you *must* be an alcoholic. Why would you break the law just to drink when you're not twenty-one?' They keep doing that. 'Why are you crying? You must be depressed.' 'Your mom said this, your dad said this—would they lie? Why would they lie? You must think everybody is out to get you.'

"You grow up thinking this kind of thing can't happen. And just the fact that it does, and so many people are saying, 'Oh, you really need to be here,' and 'You can't be trusted,' can make you doubt yourself. Hearing that all the time.

"And just being in a setting where you're getting patted on the back for things that—I know I shouldn't get credit for that. I'm not doing anything I'm proud of—eating my lunch.

"Being patted on the back for that stuff gets—humiliating. A lot of professionals are telling you that you're crazy—a lot of people, especially kids, after a while are gonna doubt themselves. And if they don't doubt themselves, then they're just gonna give up hope.

"And the fact that they can dull you like that—just dull you and make you give up hope, and tell you, 'There's no such thing as fair.' Things you've relied on. 'It doesn't matter—because *this* is where you are. *We* make the rules here.' And they make you feel like you can't do anything to make a difference. That's the worst part to me."

"All this," I say, "sounds uncannily like enemy captivity."

"The only difference is that they have degrees and they can't hit you," Delia says.

And Sandy adds, "They're allowed to use drugs. They're allowed to put you in restraints. They're allowed to lock you in an empty room. But they're not allowed to hit you."

As my credit card and receipt are returned, I realize I have forgotten something. "The second hospital?" I ask.

"People were crazier at the second hospital. The first person who came up to me was this lady who said I was her sister, and started touching my face. She was in her thirties, and she said, 'You look just like me.' Touching my face. 'What *is* that on your eyes? How did you *do* that?' It was eyeliner. And she said, 'You should teach me. You have to teach me.' And, 'Have you seen my brother? Have you seen *our* brother? Because I haven't seen him in ten years. And you know *what*? You know what's right *here*?' " Cupping her hands: " 'I've got the world in my hands. Can you see it? Do you *see* it?' And she started talking and talking, and she touched her stomach. 'My baby's gone. I had a baby in here, but he's gone. But he's gonna come back. Where's our brother? Are you my sister? Where have you been?'

"That really scared me. There were people like that there. But once I got used to it I wasn't afraid of them. I just felt better because there I could go outside."

"And you got out of there when . . . ?"

"I got hold of a person from Protection and Advocacy to come over and talk to me. I asked her if it would be easier to live with Sandy if I was *in* the hospital or *out* of the hospital. And she said, 'Well—I can't *encourage* you to leave the facility. . . .'

"I said, 'I understand.'

"So I left the hospital. And talked to a lawyer. . . ."

PATIENT: PARSONS, DELIA
DISCHARGE DIAGNOSIS: AXIS ONE:
                               MAJOR DEPRESSIVE DISORDER
                               VERSUS DYSTHYMIC DISORDER
                               SUBSTANCE ABUSE

With this as a matter of record, Delia—who has now got her GED and is talking of going on to college—will have difficulty should she attempt to: become a member of the law bar; become a teacher; join the army; run for political office; get medical insurance. . . . And should she ever, for instance, be raped and press charges, or find herself in a custody battle, the outcome may well be prejudiced based on her "prior psychiatric hospitalization."

"Treatment," as Joey might put it, would seem to be more than a little side-effecting.

2

Dr. Pangloss's
Disciple

"But you *told* me that's when it would be!"

"I know I did."

"So now you're saying it's *not* gonna be Thursday?" Mike is thirteen years old. Fair-haired and freckled, something about the manner in which he presents himself—even distraught as he is now—seems older, more like a mid-teen.

"It's not going to be Thursday, Mike." As Mike starts gesturing in a mute rage of frustration, his law guardian, Ann, puts a hand on his arm. "Mike—I'm working on it. Believe me. . . ."

On the drive out here, through a torrential downpour, Ann has suggested to me that her young client is not going to be happy with what she has to tell him today. She has also implied that there is Something Going On in this place, which may have legal implications beyond the immediate concern for Mike. She has not said much more—partly due to the need to concentrate in virtually no-visibility driving conditions, partly because whatever is brewing has not yet been formally determined.

A fresh torrent of language issues forth from Mike, but tamped into a strained whisper, so others, in other rooms, cannot hear. "Look. You told me four months ago you would get me another place, you told me four months ago I didn't belong here, if I didn't belong here four months ago why do I have to stay here another *day*, much less . . ."

"Here" is, to initial appearance, a typically laid-out southern suburban home. It is, however, described in its brochure as "a home with a therapeutic environment." Like most self-described therapeutic environments, this one has a name that conveys all the authentic goodwill of a stick-on Smiley Face: Res-Q Ranch. It is licensed by the state, the county, and the state social service department as a private psychiatric residential treatment center.

In search of a bathroom, I leave Mike and Ann locked in their exchange and head toward the kitchen. In here, a young boy is seated at the table, chin set on the heels of his hands, a still–partially full plate in front of him. A guy with the build and the bark of a drill sergeant bellows, "Siddup straight or I'll—" and stops as I walk in, glares at me.

"Bathroom?" I ask.

"There." He points, apparently at a heavy door with a small window set in near the top.

I start toward it—it doesn't seem right somehow, this door. . . . "Here?"

The small boy looks over his shoulder at me, grins.

"Across the hall!" barks the drill sergeant. Oh. I get the kid's grin. What I have just been about to try to enter is this facility's seclusion room. (Funny how one just doesn't expect a suburban house to have a seclusion room.) When I emerge from the bathroom, the young boy is still at the table. The drill sergeant is still throwing glower-glances at him. He even spares one for me as I head back to Ann and Mike, still on the living room couch, still locked in fruitless verbal combat.

"You don't *understand*," Mike is saying in an urgent whisper. "I *can't* stay here. It's off the *wall*. They push me around *for no reason*, they locked me up *for no reason*! I don't understand. I don't understand. You *said* I'd be out of here day after tomorrow, now you're saying—"

"I thought we had a placement, Mike. It fell through," Ann says. "You just have to understand that I'm trying. . . ."

Though they are close together on the couch, there is in fact a chasm between them. Mike expects Ann, as the adult empowered to act in his interests, to be able to do what he needs done. But in the world of child welfare this empowerment in fact carries almost no power. Mike is just one of hundreds of kids in this county who, having been removed from their homes, need to be *somewhere*. That is the basic. Somewhere "appropriate"? Somewhere "suitable" for the individual child? Try it.

Two years ago Mike, then eleven, and his thirteen-year-old sister and fourteen-year-old brother were living with their father. Mom had died. Neighbors reported to Protective Services that the father frequently went out at night, leaving the kids alone. Although leaving a thirteen- and fourteen-year-old alone at home in charge of an eleven-year-old may not seem the grossest of misbehavior, particularly in light of scarce alternatives, nonetheless the situation provoked the state to take the kids into custody. For eight or nine months Mike was shunted from foster home to foster home. When no further placement could be located for him, he was placed in Res-Q Ranch, where he has now been for a year and three months.

I have spent many hours on the phone trying to elicit an authoritative distinction between a psychiatric hospital and a psychiatric residential treatment center. There seem to be three claimed differences: staff-to-kid ratio; the number of professional psychiatrists on staff; the amount of money the placement costs. (Res-Q Ranch charges $130 a day.) Two other distinctions are made: Psychiatric hospitals can use drugs; they can have seclusion rooms. Res-Q Ranch, however, is owned by a (nonresident) child psychiatrist and his wife: He can and does prescribe drugs. And, as we have learned, it has a seclusion room.

Enter Lydia. She is the director of Res-Q Ranch, and its head therapist. Conversation interrupted, Ann stands. Mike stares down at his fingernails. Ann explains to Lydia that I was supposed to meet with the owner/psychiatrist. That we have been delayed by the downpour, the road conditions. Lydia says that the psychiatrist has gone home. "Maybe *you* could spend a little time with Louise?" Ann says.

Lydia looks at me. When she says, "Sure," I notice that Ann seems surprised.

Back through the kitchen, past the drill sergeant, the kid still restricted to his chair at the table. (Later, in a brochure called *Welcome to Res-Q Ranch!* I will read: "You may suggest something that you would like for dinner, but you should know that it will not be served at the time or the day you ask for it. You may choose not to eat food items that you do not like, but you must tell us about them when you first arrive." Perhaps the day he arrived this small kid forgot about something he did not like. Perhaps there was some "food item" he did not know about; did not know he did not like.)

Lydia's office (abutting the seclusion room) is what would have been the sun porch of this suburban structure, were it in service as a family home. She waves me to a love seat and takes a chair, smiling sociably. "What would you like to know?"

Smile back. Start small. "How many kids do you have here?"

"We have nine kids—we have a bed capacity for ten. The average length of stay is between a year and two years."

"This is not the first stop on the road for these kids?"

"This is not the first stop. A lot of our kids have been in a lot of other places before this. Foster homes, group homes, lots of different places where they haven't been able to survive appropriately. They'd act aggressively, or they'd run away, or they just had some real problems and couldn't cope in that type of environment. So kids usually go through the less restrictive environments first.

"Some of the kids—we're near the end of the line for them. Other kids—we may be working backwards, where they've come from a hospital setting and are now ready for release to a less restrictive program. We're really one step down from a hospital. It's not a locked facility, but it's a completely supervised facility. The kids can't go anywhere without staff supervision." Supervision: "Siddup straight or I'll—" "Staff means we have four houseparents—two on each shift."

"The big guy in the kitchen?"

"He's a houseparent."

"Are they social work people?"

"The staff we have right now, they're not social work people. They've all—well, not all—the majority have gone to a college-level degree, but not necessarily in the social sciences."

"And the little kid at the kitchen table? How old is he?"

"He's nine. Right now the age range is from nine to fifteen. Now *he's* come from a home environment, a single mother. He's got five other siblings. His mother is unable to care for his needs. He's very aggressive. He acts out against himself and others. He goes to a special school—as do most of our kids, except one."

"Ann's client? Mike?"

"Yes. He's, um, gone from foster home to foster home. And failed in all of them."

Failed in all of them. She has said this evenly, without hesitation. It is what she means to say. But when I challenge her—"You mean the kid has failed? Or the foster home has failed?"—she replies:

"Oh. The foster home! I don't mean the people in the foster homes, but whoever's responsible for the placement, it was not an appropriate placement. The child is difficult to handle, or the placement doesn't know how to handle him or shouldn't be handling it. It's really a matching game. Matching the behaviors to the right placement. I don't believe that it's ever the kid's failure. It's never the kid's problem." How odd. In the flyer that she will shortly hand me, the criteria for admission are (1) behavior disorders, (2) adjustment disorders, (3) depression and suicide, (4) psychotic disorders, (5) pervasive developmental disorders, (6) disorders associated with abuse and neglect, (7) inability to function in the home and in the community, and (8) all other diagnostic categories constituting severely emotionally disturbed (SED). These categories would seem to predicate that failed placements elsewhere, and placement here, *are* the kid's problem.

"But," Lydia is saying, "the nine-year-old still couldn't survive in a regular household. This is actually his second time here. The first time he was here his mother removed him from the facility. She thought she would be able to handle him, and she didn't like the way he was being treated at the facility. About eight months later she desperately tried to get him back in. Now she's very happy with his treatment."

"What is 'treatment'?"

"We have a level system; behavior modification is our basis. The higher on the level system, the more privileges the kids have, but also the more duties they have."

"And the point of the level system?"

"The point of the levels is—uh. These kids really require a lot of structure. A lot of stability. And what the level system helps them to gain is that sense of identification with a certain level, with a certain ability to behave. We try to really encourage them to go up, to gain, and to watch their behavior, to know where they're at. And also to motivate them to change."

"So they can go up and down?"

"Not our kids. The level system used to be like that. Previously. Before I came here, every day you'd be on a different level. Our level system is—it's not up and down every day. And there are privileges: staying up an hour later. Going on different activities. We go on activities four times a week. And they're not minor activities—we go roller skating; we go to museums, to beaches. . . . The level you're on determines what and how many activities you go on."

"Sort of like a behavioral frequent-flyer program," I say (I can't help it). She smiles weakly.

"We also have a consequence policy," she says, "in that for certain behaviors you get consequences."

Consequences. It is a word that pervades the world that deals with children who, having problems, are taken to *be* problems. Establish *consequences*. Enforce *consequences*. To enforce them is known as *consequencing*. Not only is this child pedagogy reminiscent of a more vigorously authoritarian era, but it assumes that the "disorders" are deliberate; that the child is willful and spoiled and that you must constantly show the kid who is boss and, most important, that what you say will happen if the kid does thus and such *will* happen—regardless of behavioral nuance or extenuating circumstance, with the certainty and immutability of natural law. In fact, it can be argued that this policy of dominance is survivable (if you

regard kids as needing to be forcibly conscripted into adulthood)—
but only if you do not allow for the level of bullying that can so
readily spring from the admonition to dispense righteous punishment. Only if the rules are entirely clear and the powers that be
abide scrupulously by them.

"Are these consequences in writing?" I ask. "I mean do you give
kids a list of the rules?"

Lydia goes to the file cabinet and rummages in a folder. She
extracts a flyer and a brochure (*Welcome to Res-Q Ranch!*) and a set
of stapled pages (headed RES-Q RANCH CONSEQUENCE POLICY) and
hands them to me just as her phone rings.

While she is engaged, I read the first paragraph in the *Welcome*
brochure: "Res-Q Ranch is your home while you are away from
your home and family. Here you have an opportunity to work on
your problems. When that happens, you will return home." I am
bemused. Is this a conscious lie? (Mike is not away from his own
home and family because of *his* problem. His *problem*, in his view,
is that he is way from his home and his family. Because his removal
from his home resulted from his *father's* behavior, no matter what
kind of "work" Mike does, changes in *his* behavior will not dictate
or affect his return home.) More chilling than the possibility that
in Mike's case (as in many others) this is an outright lie is the
possibility that the authors of this brochure (and the powers that
be in this place) do not even understand that what they say
is incorrect: that their capacity for thought is that seriously impaired; that their brain cells have been soaking in psy clichés so
long that they are no longer independently capable of interpreting
reality.

I turn to the CONSEQUENCE POLICY.

"A consequence is something that directly follows some behaviors
that you have done," it states.

"At Res-Q Ranch, a consequence is a means of discipline to reduce
undesirable behaviors while providing the opportunity to rethink
the situation during THINKING TIME.

"Most situations that will require a consequence are problems of
conduct behavior which violate social rules, rights of others, or
which are aggressive in nature.

"When you are given THINKING TIME, you will be:

"1) removed from the situation

"2) directly and constantly supervised by staff

"3) sit/stand [*sic*] in a designated area

"4) provided the opportunity to think for a specified length of time about the situation

"5) able to discuss your understanding of the situation and alternate methods of behavior with the staff after your THINKING TIME is over.

"If you refuse to accept the consequence, and continue to seriously disrupt the therapeutic environment, you will be A.C.T. escorted to the designated area. If you begin to harm yourself, others, or the environment, you will be A.C.T. restrained on the spot and then when in more control, you will be A.C.T. escorted to the designated area: If you remain out of control, you may need to be placed in SECLUSION AREA (see Seclusion Room Policies) . . ." These last are not included.

I turn back to the brochure. . . .

"When you are unable to control your behavior of trying to hit others or yourself or destroying things, you are asked by the staff to gain self-control." I try to imagine how the drill sergeant in the kitchen would "ask." "A staff member will remove you from the group. If you continue to lose self-control, you may need help from the staff by physically holding so that you will feel secure and subsequently happy that you really did not hit anyone or destroy things."

Translation: If you don't knuckle under, you will be overpowered and pinned down by this guy with the physical characteristics of a sumo wrestler. But that is nothing if not a good thing because: "You will feel secure and subsequently happy . . ."

"If you continue with loss of self-control, you may have to be placed in a special room. When its doors are locked, it means that you are secluded until you calm down.

"When your behavior becomes very dangerous that means you do not care what happens to you or others and this means you need more protection." Protection. Yes. (But from whom?) "Although the staff may hold you for a period of time, they may not be able to

continue to hold you for too long a period and in that case, the staff
may have orders from the Psychologist or Psychiatrist to have your
feet and hands tied so you don't hurt yourself or others after all the
other ways have been tried first."

I wonder: Would this threatened assault on the child be less awful
if it were not wedded to a brutal assault on the English language?

Lydia returns to her chair.

"I was just reading about consequences," I say. "Thinking time
and so forth."

She nods affably. "Usually, you do thinking time in this nice quiet
little area outside my room, just on the rug in front of my door here,
right in front of the seclusion room." Subtle, that is. "Nice, quiet
little area," she repeats (incredibly). "Where you'll always be monitored by staff." She gives examples of what can lead to "thinking
time": "Stealing: two hours. Refusal to proper hygiene; refusal to do
schoolwork; school suspension; of course running away—"

"Is it hard to run away?"

"It's—we used to make it hard. But we're really trying to put the
responsibility on the kids. If they want to run, they can run any-
time, and they know that. Now the first thing that happens, the
police are called. And the kid will likely be picked up by the police
and will have to face the consequences." More consequences, more
natural law.

"And seclusion?"

"We rarely have to use that seclusion room. The only reason for it
is if the child continues to act up. The only reason we put kids in
seclusion is if they're gonna hurt themselves, hurt someone else, or
they're going to use something violently. Basically, we do it for their
own protection. It's not a punishment."

No. I know that. It's a *treatment*.

"But," I ask, "isn't it scary?"

Much to my surprise, she explodes, brightly, "Oh, yeah! Definitely! Very scary!" This is decidedly more animation than she has
shown thus far. "Seclusion is *not* a fun place for anybody. Ours is nine
by nine. It still gives you that crazy feeling. It's not very pleasant!"

But it's not a punishment. (What do you suppose, in their minds,
a punishment would be?)

"And restraints?"

"We have a wrap mat. It's—sort of like an egg roll wrapper." What a colorful way to think about it. Kind of gives new meaning to the phrase *wonton kid.*

"Is that worse than just the seclusion room?"

"Oh, yeah! *I* wouldn't want—I mean to be physically restrained . . . The seclusion room . . ." She stops, considering. "Except that it's all white. If it were a different color," she muses, "it might be better." She pauses as though mentally reviewing a color chart. "But—it's at least your own little space. And you can pound the walls and you won't get hurt. Throw your body around and you won't get hurt. You can scream and yell."

Gosh. Imagine being free to do all those things in "your own little space."

"But am I right?" I ask. "You only get out when you quiet down? So the more you lash out, the longer you're in?"

"Yeah."

Well, isn't *that* a downer?

No. "See," she adds brightly, *"you* really design how long you're going to be in there."

This woman is definitely Dr. Pangloss's disciple.

≈

As Lydia leaves the room, briefly, summoned by a houseparent, I invite the reader to ponder what this stupid conversation signifies. To realize what grotesquely distorted representations of reality the language of "treatment" can mask. Who, after all, could be against a "structured environment" for kids? And who would argue that a child should not be "restrained" when he is—to use the ubiquitous, all-justifying phrase—a danger to himself or others? Who could be against "thinking time"?

Restless, I get up and wander around the small office, only then noticing the chart on the back of Lydia's office door. It shows that seven of the nine children here are on medication: Mellaril, 300 a day; Mellaril, 400 a day; Mellaril, 125; Mellaril, 110. Lithium, 50; Lithium, 35; Lithium, 60 . . .

I have decided that when Lydia returns I will ask if I may ask the kids themselves what it is like to be in the seclusion room. I am certain she will say she cannot let me, and certain the reason she will give is that it would violate the children's confidentiality. ("Confidentiality" is the rubric under which the child welfare and psychiatric systems disallow children's voices, ensure they cannot be heard.) I am certain that she will cite the legal violation inherent in her breaking that confidentiality.

In the event, I am wrong. Lydia does not say she cannot. The reason she gives why she will not is considerably different. What she says is, "It is absolutely urgent that I get agency permission for everything because—*it's too dangerous.*"

Dangerous? "Why?"

"It's dangerous because—" She laughs. "Um. It's dangerous because—people are scared to take care of this population."

I do not get it. "Why?"

"People are worried if they're gonna get caught—or abuse issues are valid."

Caught? " 'Caught' meaning?"

" 'Caught' meaning accused. People are worried. We've just gone through something like that. There was an allegation of abuse. How it got to this point is there was an investigation of a staff member abusing a child. But then it turned into another investigation about sexual interaction between clients. And then it turned into a whole fiasco about me not intentionally reporting it. To the hot line. Abuse hot line. And in fact it had been reported twice, and the hot line had done nothing about it."

Goddamn. (I begin to get it.) This woman is herself telling me about the cloud over her and this facility; telling me that about which Ann, Mike's advocate, was circumspect. Reality, in this place, is certainly a curious affair.

"Where," I ask, "did the allegations come from?"

"The accusation that the abuse was not being reported came from a police officer who was talking to two kids. Two *severely emotionally disturbed* kids." Aha. Was one of the kids Mike? Was he the one who blew the whistle? Maybe he told Ann? Maybe Ann took him to the police? But where is this woman going with the "severely emotionally disturbed" business? She continues, "And the police officer took what they had said at face value and didn't understand the population or know the population, and did a report investigating and didn't find the reports which were there all the time. At the sexual abuse hot line.* There were no reports to the police because we deal with the abuse line. That's the law; that's who you call. If the child wants to call, the child can call."

In fact, what it says in the *Welcome* brochure is, "MISTREATMENT: If you feel that you are being mistreated, you may talk directly to the person who you feel is mistreating you [oh, swell] or to a staff member. [Yes? Suppose it's a staff member who is mistreating you.] You may contact your social worker or parent/guardian when you feel that you have been abused in any way. But before you do call be sure to correct any misunderstanding by discussing it with a member of the staff." Or else? This does not strike me as "if the child wants to call, the child can call."

Lydia goes on. "You have to understand the history of these children. You have to understand the history of this particular child. This was just a common occurrence. In many sexual issues—the child's very confused. Sexually. And it was probably a projection of his own wishes rather than an actual happening."

Oh, great. In spite of the fact that most kids are removed to state custody because they have been abused, Lydia is going to now pull a proto-Freudian rabbit out of the hat: The kids are just fantasizing. What she is saying is that kids who are here because they have been abused are not credible (because they have been abused) about whether they are being abused. Suddenly a kid who has been abused (against his own wishes) is, in reporting present abuse, "projecting his own wishes." "*But* . . ." Lydia shrugs.

Now I begin to understand why Lydia has only just returned from a month's (enforced?) absence (suspension?). I begin to understand why Ann looked so surprised that Lydia would talk with me.

---

* This is a hot line established by state child welfare agencies for the reporting of child abuse.

≈

Mike and Ann are still in emotional encounter as I return to the living room.

"I *told* you. The kid was touching my models. So I pushed him away and he pushed me back and then next thing I know the counselor has me like this, breaking my arms behind my back, and they put me in the seclusion room. I didn't even do anything wrong."

"You could have gone to Lydia."

"*I* know. But she never does anything. She sticks up for the people who are here."

They stop talking as Lydia comes in behind me. Ann stands. "Oh, you're finished? I have some business to discuss with Lydia, Mike. Why don't you show Louise around the house?"

Mike leads me down the hall, showing me his room first: two sets of bunk beds, four old bureaus, four metal lockers. On Mike's bureau sit two model airplanes, the finished product of his hobby.

"So, Mike, you mind talking to me about this place?"

"I'm happy to talk to anybody that can do anything about it. Basically—did she tell you about the level system? Basically, the levels are based upon the behavior."

"Lydia said you had to do something real serious to drop a level."

"That's not true because—" Mike stops abruptly. "I don't know if I'm supposed to say anything about—the stuff that's going on here—there's been stuff going on here the last three months that—hasn't been right. And I'm—I'm not gonna speak for the other kids, but I'm gonna speak for myself. The way they've been treating me—I was supposed to be out of here four months ago. And they postponed it until this Thursday. And now they want to keep me here longer."

"And they've been treating you how?"

"The way I'm being treated is—they take you away from your parents and stuff because of neglect or abuse. Okay. But then you go here and you get worse neglect and more abuse than you did with your parents. I mean when I was livin' with my father, the only thing he ever did was go out every night and leave us home alone. I mean, every average father and mother do that. Go out from time to time and leave the kids home alone at night. I was eleven and my brother was fourteen and my sister was thirteen.

"But then I've gotta come here and have people pushing me or restraining me or fighting with me or hitting me. And that's not right what they're doing, but nobody's doing nothing about it. They *say* the levels are based on your behavior, but see when you do something that they don't like, they go ahead and they do what they feel they want to do. Not what the right thing is. What they feel they want to do.

"I've been here now about a year and three months. The only thing I'm getting out of this is abuse and neglect, and there's no reason that should be going on. Why shouldn't I be home and just be left home every night while my father goes out? I'm not sayin' I'm the perfect child in the world, okay? My point is I don't deserve to be here. Some people here, they need to be in a place—not like this, but a place—until they know how to take care of themselves, or do right. But, see, me, I know all of that. Just like all my teachers tell me I look older for my age, and I'm more mature for my age. Half the people here, they don't know how to act their age."

"Do you get violent?"

"No. I've never gotten violent here, never. There's no reason for them to go ahead and force violence on me. I was never a violent child. The only reason they ever took me away from my father is he used to go out at night, not every single night, and leave us home alone."

"Mike, have you seen a whole lot of restraints used here?"

"Yeah, yeah. The whole reason is they don't use the rules like they're supposed to be used, they use them in their own ways. The way they do it is if they don't *like* something you're doing, they go ahead and give you consequence time—for something they feel they don't *like*. Even though it's not in the book.

"Okay. F'rinstance. The stupidest thing is—you know where the rec room is? Well, there's a little step off it and there's a bathroom. And outside it there's a water fountain. Well, I mean you can't go from the rec room to the water fountain—which is about ten feet away—you can't go there to get a drink without asking permission.

And that's so strict it's like saying I can't wipe my butt without permission."

Mike has, by now, more than warmed to his subject. What strikes me, as it has so often when listening to the kids, is that they seem to have such a more highly evolved sense of justice than do their keepers, who so readily rationalize the abuse of their dominance in the language of what will be "healthy" for the kids; in the unconflicted (if misguided) certainty that their might makes them right.

"And if they don't like something," Mike is saying, "okay, if they don't like the way you dress, they tell you, 'You better change. You not goin' on activities with *me* like that. You better go change *now*.' And by the time you change they're sayin', 'Well, gee, I'm leavin' now, you're not ready.' They don't use the rules. Why? I don't understand. I just don't understand."

As I listen to Mike, it strikes me that these people, these circumstances, these "therapeutic" setups do indeed have the power to change kids' behavior. They have the power to teach those kids who have not already been so persuaded, that authority is arbitrary, dictatorial, mean. That when people get clout this is how they use it. And that if you behave this way, you too can have clout. Why shouldn't these kids learn to moon the system? (Anybody got a reason?)

"What is the 'problem,' " I ask Mike, "that they see you as having?"

"I don't see me as having any problem at all," he says. "Except that I'm here and I shouldn't be here. But the way they look at it is, well, 'This kid's here. The reason he's here is because he has a problem.' "

Everywhere and always: Nobody's in foster care for no reason. Nobody's in a "treatment center" for no reason. Nobody's in a psychiatric hospital for no reason. We buy it, wholesale. That there are expert life-deciders, psy pros (like golf pros) who know how to get the kid to go into the little round hole.

Although Mike is the only kid here in regular—rather than special ed—school, lately, he tells me, he has been getting into trouble, talking back. But how unreasonable is that when his daily life— even to drinking from the water fountain—is so totally under others' control? Yet—there is more to it, yet, than that. As I hear the drill sergeant barking orders, see the other kids scurrying to grab stuff, I ask Mike what the kids are going to do now.

"They go out on activity," he says. "Pool, or skating, or bowling."

"And you're not with them because . . . ?"

"Like I was saying, I don't particularly fit in with the way these kids act. They embarrass me when we go out—the way they act—toward ladies. Like where they go to play racquetball, it's the neighborhood around my school. The school I go to is the regular school. The school they go to is like treatment centers. So I go down there to play racquetball and there's kids from my school that live around there. Especially girls.

"And when we go down there, the kids here react upon the girls. Then, when I go to school, it's like, 'Oooh, Mi-ike, you live with this kid I want to stay *away* from!' See, my friends come around, 'Oh, hi, Mike.' And the guys start trying to show off or act bad. It's horrible."

Yes. Mike is something of a snob—a white kid, something of a redneck, while most of the others are black. (There are odd politics here: race, gender.)

Mike continues, "For instance, one time we went down there, there was a girl that goes to my school, and her mom was there and everything, and one of the kids here started sayin' to her all kinds of nasty stuff. And her mother got real mad and she came up to the staff member and started yellin'. And then her mother knows I go to school with her kids and she's: 'Don't hang around with Mike because he's just like those other kids.' "

But it is bizarre: Kids can be targeted for placement in this system precisely because they do hang around with "those other kids"— kids who are socially disruptive. Indeed, child advocates in California inform me there is now a "diagnosis" of Gang Behavior Disorder. So here's Mike, whose placement, whose "treatment" it is to be placed among such kids.

I go back to the initial question, the levels. "How often does the level board get changed?"

"Every other day." (So Lydia was right: The levels aren't changed every day; they're changed every other day.) "See," he says, "you come in on Level 3 and then you do a certain amount of things wrong and get a certain amount of consequence time and you drop to Level 3 Red List. And if you do something wrong again, you drop back another level. Then if you do something wrong again, you're down to Level 1. But see, what they've done to me is—last Monday I was on Level 4 and they dropped me all the way down to—I'm on Level 1 now. See, like I was telling you before, there's been problems that have been goin' on here—with Social Services, with police. And everything that happened—they think it's because of me. Which it is. There was a problem with certain staff sexually abusing one of the kids, a little kid, a seven-year-old kid. And I got a little tired of it, so I made a phone call.

"Ann was the first person I told. And she was the one who told all this. And then an investigation started, and it's still going on. And they know that I made a phone call."

(Remember? "If the kid wants to call, he can call"?)

"Did the little kid talk?"

"No—because he's afraid to. Basically, the staff think they can get away with whatever they want, and nobody can do anything about it."

We have drifted back to the living room just as Ann emerges from meeting with Lydia. We move out to the car, Mike continuing his pleas, Ann continuing her assurances that she is trying, Mike threatening to run, Ann telling him to just be patient. Me, wondering what the upshot of all this will be.

≈

Here is what happened:

Two weeks later, Social Services pulled all the county kids out of Res-Q Ranch. The investigation continued. The house was put up for sale.

Here is what happened then to Mike: He was placed in a private psychiatric hospital—supposedly for three or four days, until they could find him a placement. He remained in the psychiatric hospital for three weeks.

Eventually, all that could be found for him was another residential treatment center, but in another county, away from his sister and brother, away from Ann. Another version of Res-Q Ranch.

Three weeks later Mike ran away. He has not been heard from since.

It is impossible for me to know how Mike was, what he was like, when the "help" and "treatment" started. But it seems to me Mike has by now more than earned the right to be what he will, in any case, now be called: a troubled child.*

---

* PS This just in: I am informed by the legal services agency that represented him that Mike has since been located; that he passed for eighteen, got a job in a gas station; and that, amazingly, he has found his own solution to his situational problem. He is living with a teacher who appears genuinely interested in him. I am further informed that in the past year three or four of the kids that the agency represented have similarly solved things for themselves.

3

Bart Simpson

Meets

Bruno Bettelheim

ON MARCH 13, 1990, in a Maryland nursing home, the much-venerated psychiatrist Bruno Bettelheim committed suicide at age eighty-seven. Author of such widely acclaimed books as *Love Is Not Enough: The Treatment of Emotionally Disturbed Children*; *The Empty Fortress*; *The Children of the Dream*; and *The Uses of Enchantment*, Bettelheim—a refugee who had been imprisoned in Dachau and Buchenwald under the Nazis—was renowned as well for his work with autistic and severely disturbed children. He claimed an 85 percent cure rate during his thirty-year tenure at his private laboratory, the University of Chicago's Sonia Shankman Orthogenic School.

His death triggered major obituaries in the press calling him

- a "man who left to the world—especially to parents and children—an enduring vision of love, innocence and idealism" (*Parenting* magazine);[1]

- "one of the great figures in American psychology, known for the originality, warmth and wisdom he brought to the study of the minds and emotions of children" (*Washington Post*);[2] and
- a "pioneer in treating childhood mental disturbances [who left] major contributions to therapy for children" (*New York Times*).[3]

Within a year it would have been made abundantly clear to any who chose to see it that, in fact, Bettelheim was "adamant and relentless in maintaining and propagating his unproven, unscientific theory. . . . This 'refrigerator mother' [as causative of childhood autism] proved devastating to many mothers of autistic children." That his legacy to many of the children entrusted to him for "cure" was the legacy of long years of incarceration under a terrorist regime. That what he was "known for" was the stuff of his own mythology and bore little resemblance to reality, including his qualifications and his training, but most especially his "warmth and wisdom." That his self-proclaimed 85 percent "cure" rate might better be claimed as an 85 percent *survival* rate; a testimony not to his "therapy," but to the children's initial inner strength, intelligence, and health.

The crumbling of the myth began with a small notice in an alternative weekly, the *Chicago Reader*, headed SOME PROFESSOR DOWN IN HYDE PARK, and it said: "RIP Bruno Bettelheim, who apparently was understood to be a great Chicagoan everywhere but in Chicago. We appreciated the thoughtful page-one obit in the next morning's *New York Times*; from the play the local papers gave his death, he might as well have been a waiter at the Berghoff."[4] Innocuous enough on the face of it.

And then came the letter signed "Name Withheld":

". . . Several national magazines ran obituaries which portrayed Bettelheim as a smiling, warmhearted man who cured emotionally disturbed children by surrounding them with an atmosphere of love, kindness and security. That was Bettelheim's public persona, carefully constructed in his many books and articles. In person, he was an evil man who set up his school as a private empire and himself as a demigod or cult leader. He bullied, awed, and terrorized the children at his school, their parents, school staff members, his graduate students and everyone else who came into contact with him."5

How did Bettelheim get away with this?

"He cut his school off from the outside world so that nobody would see how cowed and frightened the children were. Children were allowed out only under close supervision, and were discouraged from talking to anyone 'outside,' even about the most innocuous topics. Bettelheim told the children over and over how lucky they were to be at his school, and that if they didn't do as they were told, they would end up in a state mental asylum where they would be given drugs and shock treatments. He censored the children's mail, so that they couldn't complain to anyone. The staff regularly searched the children's few belongings, so that it wasn't safe to keep any records or diaries. Bettelheim went out of his way to worsen the already weak relationships between the children at the school and their parents. He had all those little people completely at his mercy.

"I lived in fear of Bettelheim's unpredictable temper tantrums, public beatings, hair pulling, wild accusations and threats and abuse in front of classmates and staff. One minute he could be smiling and joking, the next minute he could be exploding. Almost anything I did could be construed as a form of rebellion or as a type of behavior that had to be changed. One time I made the mistake of telling Bettelheim in a quiet tone of voice, that I thought there were too many restrictions at the school. Bettelheim beat me for that. Another time, he dragged me out of the shower with no clothes on and beat me in front of a roomful of people. . . .

"How did Bettelheim make it look as though he had a high success rate? He admitted a lot of kids to the school that weren't crazy in the first place. . . . These kids were, of course, unhappy, but that was the extent of it. There were some autistic children there too, but the whole time I was there, I never saw any of these autistic children improve in any significant way. . . .

"It's agonizingly difficult to write about this. I've been trying to put these memories behind me for a long time. . . . These memories have robbed the joy from my life. But when I saw those obituaries that painted Bettelheim as a hero, I could keep silent no longer. If I may quote a letter from a longtime friend who was a teenager at Bettelheim's school when I was there, 'Isn't it frustrating to want to tell your story but be afraid to because 1) who wants to relive those years in hell and 2) who wants to announce to the world that you lived in a loony bin, even if the inmates were saner than the keepers. . . .' "

Following publication of this letter, others poured in. One, from a former counselor, Stephen T. Herczeg, defended the school, asserting that the children had been placed at the school precisely because they were "dysfunctional" (read: not credible), thus casting doubt on their present testimony. "As in real life, some children experienced more success . . . than did others," Herczeg wrote. Having thus suggested "Name Withheld" was no more than one of Bettelheim's failures (and thus still "sick"), Herczeg concluded with this curious sentence: "Those of us who have lived and worked at the Orthogenic School understand that we have the freedom and choice to perceive the School and Dr. Bettelheim as it benefits us psychologically."[6]

What can this *mean* except that it would be psychologically uncomfortable for the author to view the school or Dr. Bettelheim in other than a haze of soft light—even if that light were no more than a romantic distortion. Herczeg is suggesting that it does not matter what really *happened*, but only what it benefits him psychologically to *believe* and maintain happened. (And this from a psy pro positioned to decide whether other folks are in touch with reality?)

Other letters came from former inmates. "Winston 1984" wrote, "The public persona of Bruno Bettelheim was self-shaped by his books, some call them hagiography, describing his breakthrough treatments (as he saw them) of the most seriously disturbed, the autistic. His copious books described at length his walled fantasy world of treatment: happy, free children amidst an environment demanding only freedom and self-expression, caring, motherly, always helpful practitioners twenty-four hours each and every day: a world where every physical item, each social set-up, each minor happenstance and accoutrement, were part of a Grand Plan based on the total therapeutic rehabilitation of the child. . . ." Rather,

"Winston" writes, "the Orthogenic School under his reign was a terror-ridden place, a place of savage, painful, frequent, random, abusive and searing beatings, draggings, hair-pullings, and a whole host of malicious humiliation that would break the ego and soul of any human, strong or weak."[7]

The controversy quickly spread beyond the pages of the *Reader*. By late summer, the *Washington Post* had published an article by Washington-based writer Charles Pekow, a former inmate of the Orthogenic School. ("Bettelheim had standard lines he gave us all: we were considered hopelessly 'crazy' by the outside world and only he could save us from lives in mental institutions or jail. 'You get better here or you go to the nut house,' I heard him routinely tell school-aged children."[8])

On September 10, 1990, *Newsweek* published a piece titled "BENO BRUTALHEIM"? (on its Lifestyle page!). Under the subhead "Cult figure" we read: "Patients were not the only ones who knew of Bettelheim's explosive temper. There are indications that at least the local psychiatric community knew exactly what was going on, and did nothing. Chicago analysts scathingly referred to the doctor as 'Beno Brutalheim.' William Blau, a counselor at the school in 1949, explains the silence from school staff members by claiming Bettelheim was a cult figure for them. Another former teacher agreed. 'He created a disturbed culture there,' she says. 'If he said the sky was green, he expected you to see it that way, and many of us did.' As for the patients' silence: 'Who would believe us?' asks Pekow."[9]

So here we have the astonishing fact that Bettelheim's routine use of terrorist tactics—unprovoked, erratic, unpredictable violence— was not only *known* within the professional community, but was kidded about (Beno Brutalheim). Surely the question of why those folks knew and did nothing is more interesting than the question of why powerless children who had been labeled loonies did nothing (which is surely a rhetorical question that only serves to impugn their believability). And yet—as further stories appeared, this most interesting of facts, which would seem to go directly to the heart of psychiatry's claim, as a profession, to be a benefactor of children, to act in children's "best interests," would never appear again.

In October 1990, *Commentary* published an article by Ronald Angres, son of a psychoanalyst, and former Orthogenic School inmate (from age seven to age nineteen): another powerful indictment of Bettelheim's entirely ruthless and unpredictable verbal and physical assaults on children.[10] In November, the *New York Times* printed ACCUSATIONS OF ABUSE HAUNT THE LEGACY OF BRUNO BETTELHEIM.[11]

That, for the most part, the psychiatric community's response was restrained is perhaps unsurprising, considering that Bettelheim's theoretical concoction about toxic mothers causing autism had long been discredited (after doing decades of destruction). And considering that his claim of an 85 percent cure rate was presented without any supporting evidence. In fact, Bettelheim's most ardent public defender was David James Fisher, a lecturer in the Department of Psychiatry at the University of California, Los Angeles, and a research psychoanalyst, who had conducted two interviews with Bettelheim during the last years of his life and whose prestige would have been enhanced from the association with an eminence.[12]

Fisher and pediatric psychiatrist Rudolf Ekstein wrote in response to the *Newsweek* article. "*Severely regressed* and *disturbed patients* in psychiatric settings require firm boundaries and structures, as well as a staff treating them with kindness, tolerance, empathy, patience, and knowledge," they stated. Loftily flaunting their professional competence, they assumed the pathology of the whistle-blowers, sight unseen: "These therapists are subjected to an ensemble of anxieties, frustrations, disappointments and regressive pulls on them in their everyday encounters with patients. . . . As an administrator, Bettelheim was working with an extremely taxing patient population, a population of *inccurables*, of *individuals who had been given up on by other therapists*; he also had to contend with a spectrum of emotional responses to these paatients on the part of his care-taking staff, who may have felt driven crazy by their patients at certain moments. . . . That [Bettelheim] expressed anger, impatience, frustration, and an authoritarian tone is not surprising or out of character. To insinuate that he was a cruel or insensitive bully—a patient abuser—seriously misrepresents the record" (italics mine).[13]

Would that these psy pros had the same compassion for kids who feel driven crazy by their treaters, their imprisoners, and who express similar anger, impatience, and frustration! However. Ignoring the fact that they don't (any more than, evidently, did Bettelheim), we read, "Bettelheim remains the empathic advocate of the helpless child and of the most inaccessible of patients. What strikes us as 'abusive' and 'brutal' is this form of scandalous and debunking journalism. It could potentially damage the hopes of recovery for the severely disturbed patients currently under treatment in psychiatric hospitals, eroding their trust in their caretakers, and it also shows no grasp of the psychological difficulties and therapeutic aspirations of mental health professionals, many of whom were educated by Bettelheim's sparkling writings and inspired by his tough-minded humanity."

These, then, are the tactics of aggressive psy defense: name-calling (regressive, disturbed, incurable), along with a posture of obvious and unchallengeable superiority to the victim—the child who, in all their wisdom, they are empowered to treat. The plea that there should be sympathy, instead, for the jailer of this "extremely taxing" population is curious. But, as with Herczeg's letter to the *Reader*, it is the last sentence that is the real oddity. Why should the fact of former inmates speaking out "damage the hopes of recovery" of "severely disturbed patients currently under treatment in psychiatric hospitals"? (Unless the writers feel it likely these patients are receiving similar abuse.) And (for heaven's sake) what *are* the psychological difficulties of mental health professionals that we are failing to grasp? Surely the authors cannot mean the professionals are psychologically impaired themselves?

The implication (although I may not be grasping the thing correctly here) seems remarkably similar to the last line of Herczeg's letter: "Those of us who have lived and worked at the Orthogenic School understand that we have the freedom and choice to perceive the School and Dr. Bettelheim as benefits us psychologically." In other words, psychological difficulties set in when these annoying folks come forward with their experiential truth.

As the controversy continued into 1991, more evidence was uncovered: that Bettelheim's credentials were not what he had claimed them to be; that he had never finished his training; that his true credentials were in art history. Even the origin of his interest in and purported expertise with autistic children was not quite what he had painted it to be.[14]

As Bettelheim told it, "It really began in Vienna where Anna Freud saw an autistic American child. A mute American child. She thought it would be interesting to find out what psychoanalysis could do for such an abnormal child. But, in order to be effective, the child would have to live in a home that is completely psychoanalytically organized. One hour a week, six hours a week wouldn't do it: it would have to be day and night. Through a complicated configuration of circumstances, this mother then came to us, my [first wife, Gina Weinmann] and I. We took this child into our house as an experiment for a few months; this experiment lasted for seven years till the Anschluss. It was a fascinating experience to live and work with this child. I tried to help her to begin to talk and learn in school. . . ."[15]

Bettelheim's first wife, Gina Weinmann, however, remembers it differently. " 'I was studying at the Kinderhaus. Anna Freud began there her work with disturbed children,' Weinmann says. 'I have a diploma from the school. Patsy was the child of a wealthy American family and was about seven when she came to me. She was in my care from about 1931 on. But, after all, Bruno and I, we were man and wife, we lived together and the child lived with us. This experience is naturally the basis of what Bruno called milieu therapy [the belief that a therapeutically controlled environment can bring about improvement in a patient's condition]. But he did not treat Patsy.' "[16]

≈

The person who started all this, who first broke the silence—the original "Name Withheld"—is Alida Jatich. After firing the first salvo, Alida quickly went public and quotes from her, her signed letters of response to stories in the press, pepper the coverage that followed. A computer programmer, she is now in her thirties—with a clearheaded, very direct, and no-bullshit tone of voice. Placed by her Ohio parents in the Orthogenic School at twelve, she remained there for the next six years.

Why, I ask her, was she sent there in the first place?

"It was never all that clear," she says. "My parents were overly strict to the point where—I would stay up at night and read?—they'd beat on me for having a light on. And beat me for going to the bathroom at night too many times. Or if I said something they didn't agree with. They'd give me a three-hour lecture and then I might say something back and I'd get beaten for it. It got to the point where I couldn't stand it anymore. I started to fight back—because their way of exerting power over me was hitting me all the time.

"I wasn't difficult in the usual sense. I'd never broken any laws, no use of drugs or anything like that. It was just—for lack of a better word—I was more of a Bart Simpson type. I said things people didn't want to hear. I think that was probably most of it.

"And see, I was two grades ahead in school. And the other kids were older than me and bigger, and they'd tease me and pick on me, and they'd hit me a lot. And the school would not do anything to protect me at all. And they would just as soon I was not there. Because I was the source of disturbance—just by being different. I was a gifted kid, and they didn't have anything for gifted kids, so they just didn't want to bother with me. So I ended up getting put away just for having a mind of my own."

In the course of the published back-and-forthing, several former inmates wrote testifying that the Orthogenic School wasn't all that bad; that it helped them. I ask Alida about that, and mention I've been told I will always hear those claims made—by former inmates of every institution, every treatment program, every school with a treatment component. Why, I ask her, would that be?

She answers that it is the ability these places have to convince the child that he or she is nuts, is hopeless, is unwanted by anyone else: to convince the child that, whatever is done, it represents the only chance of social survival the child has. "A lot of the kids who insist they really were crazy, the place 'saved their life'—even though they'll still admit all the bad things happened—they say it was a bad thing but it was good because they were hopelessly crazy. The thing is, the kids who stayed there weren't.

"But see, they ruin a person's self-image. If you're a kid and somebody tells you you're crazy and that person's some big expert and your parents think so too and all the other kids there are crazy too—they *say*—and in six to twelve years you're never exposed to anybody who says there's nothing wrong with you—then you find it hard to believe that anything else is possibly true. And then at the end, if you had to realize the whole thing was a lie, then you'd have to say that a huge part of your life was basically a lie and shouldn't have happened. There's an awful lot of grief there. If you grew up in a place that was basically founded on a lie and was an embodiment of a lie, and everything that happened to you was an expression of that; if you are the product of an environment that was just vile—what does that make you?"

This, of course, makes sense. And it is a sense we recognize when the environment is a home, a family that repeatedly inculcates in a kid the "fact" that she is bad or stupid. Why would there be reluctance to recognize it here? Think of Joey, how readily he accepted his "diagnoses." And the potential for the brainwashing is explicit in Delia's testimony about her much briefer confinement as well.

Alida would seem, then, to be entirely correct. And it is this brainwashing feature, this feature of breaking a kid's will, her sense of self, that led so many of those reporting on Bettelheim's school to muse on its affinity with the concentration camps that Bettelheim suffered in.

Indeed, Bettelheim himself acknowledged that he modeled his "therapeutic milieu" on his camp experiences—the breaking down of the will and the self; the complete disempowerment (only with the additional claim that he would use this for positive change).[17] And, frighteningly, within the concentration camp experience can be found the same kind of conversion phenomenon. In a review of the book *Children of the Flames: Dr. Josef Mengele and the Untold Story of the Twins of Auschwitz*, the reviewer writes: "One especially disturbing aspect of the book is the fact that some of the victims remember Mengele as a charming father-substitute in whom they yearned to place their trust. There are glimpses of Mengele joking with the children, taking them on outings, hugging them. One survivor insists he was gentle; another flatly states that he 'loved little children.' "[18]

Bettelheim's break-the-will formula is also what led to the frequent use in the reports and stories of the word "cult." Whether or not a regime such as Bettelheim's meets the strict criteria for a cult, it certainly shares techniques used by cults: a charismatic male leader exercising complete control; a profession of messianic mission; and the capricious dispensing of paternalistic warmth and brutality.

If both cults and the Nazi camps infantilize people, deprive them of will and control, how much easier it is when the people in your custody are, in fact, infants and children—who have no psychological choice except to believe you, and to believe you mean them well.

Chuck Marks was an inmate of the Orthogenic School from 1955 to 1971. That is sixteen years of his childhood. If he left the school at twenty-six, as Alida has told me, he would have been *ten years old* when he was placed. Here is his testimony: "On one occasion my mother came to Chicago to visit with me. For three days we stayed at the Knickerbocker Hotel, during which time my lateness coming to breakfast greatly angered my mother. She declared that she was 'fed up' and would report me to Dr. B. after returning me to the school.

"Later that evening, as Dr. B. was making his rounds, I feared for what he woould do to me as a result of my mother's report. He told me that he had spoken with my mother, and that in his opinion she was making a big to-do over nothing. It felt great to have him on my side."[19]

From this child's perspective, then, there was kindness, or perhaps, as Alida proposes, gratitude that he was *not* being beaten. What he could not have known, however, is that it was incidental kindness. Whatever Bettelheim's true feelings were about children, his feelings about mothers were unambivalently stated when he determined they caused autism in children: mothers were viciously pathogenic.*

---

* ". . . I would stress that the figure of the destructive mother (the devouring witch) is the creation of the child's imagining that has its source in reality, namely the destructive intent of the mothering person" (Bruno Bettelheim, *The Empty Fortress*, [New York: Free Press, 1967], p. 71).

"And there's another matter," Alida is saying. "Some kids just aren't cute. I think that's part of the reason I got sent away. You get some ugly-looking kid, they get treated a lot worse by everybody. Or if they're physically awkward, which I was. I had motor problems. And that's a physical problem, and not caused by me having anything emotionally wrong. People just thought I was being careless. But I was called a 'spaz'—if you've ever heard that word? A derogatory term for somebody who falls down a lot or doesn't move smoothly.

"Also I was put two grades ahead—so a kid who's put two grades ahead, and they're little and they're real awkward and not much to look at—and you know what the bigger kids are gonna do. They're gonna tease the kid. They're gonna beat on the kid. And that's probably the reason why the school people, after a while they just said they didn't want to keep me there. Instead of figuring out some way to protect me, which would have been the simplest thing to do, they told my parents to put me someplace else."

Alida is appalled by her parents' credulousness when faced with psy and educational authorities; but, as all of my listening led me to realize, it is a credulousness that many, many among us share. How, I ask Alida, did your parents get you there? Did they tell you where you were going?

"Well, I didn't know until after I was there it was a mental institution. Otherwise, I would have found some way to avoid going. My parents claim now the school system told them it was a school for gifted kids. But then when they took me there, Bettelheim was sitting there, saying I was a paranoid. I certainly wished later they had taken me right back home. But—they were the kind of people that would slavishly follow anybody who they think is an authority or expert."

And so we hear it again—the grip that psy "expertise" holds over adult America, the authority we vest it with, is what facilitates its unchallenged territorial dominance over children, only culminating in the psychiatric incarceration of reasonably normal, certainly average, kids.

What, I ask Alida, was the worst part of being there?

"If you want my opinion, the single worst thing about being put there is that you're deprived of your dignity. I think most of the bad part is being confined anyway, being incarcerated—under the label of being mentally ill. And anything further in the way of abuses—he was legendary for his temper. But that just made it a very frightening experience. At the same time, the humiliation did not come from that, it came from being there in the first place. Under that label.

"As for the other kids, I did not get the impression they were eccentric at all. They just seemed very ordinary and very dull and boring people. The only thing that was unusual about them was that they'd been there since they were quite small, so they had been raised in an institution. And it seemed like they just accepted whatever happened—as if it was normal. It seemed they had adjusted to being institutionalized. And they said, 'Well, we are crazy and we belong here because we are.' But the ones that said that—none of them actually were crazy. The only crazy thing about them was the fact of thinking they were crazy. I would say, 'None of you *act* like it.' And they would say, 'But we are.' "

Scary. Truly, to my mind, the realm of science fiction: psy-fi.

"Now there were some who were brain damaged," Alida says, "and it was very obvious. However, when you talked to them, or listened to them, or saw them, you did not get the impression that it was caused by abuse. These were people who were wired up wrong. And it was obvious to me that these people were never going to get it together in that place."

Certainly, from what Alida is saying, there is a lot more going on here than can be accounted for by insurance companies covering inpatient psychiatric care for kids.

Alida continues, "But once any kid's labeled, the label sticks. And you don't see anybody protesting it because everybody's too ashamed of the whole thing. Even if the family afterwards agrees that the whole thing was bad, you don't see them standing up and saying anything. They don't want people to think they put the kid there because the kid was crazy, and they don't want people to think they put the kid there wrongly. Either way makes the family look bad. And then the hospital just goes and snags some other kid on the hook. But in my opinion," Alida says, "if these kids get out and are able to make a decent living—*they're* gonna—put their *parents*—in some *na-asty* places."

This is such a Bart Simpson thing to say. I laugh.

"I know that's blunt," she says, "but that's my way of speaking. That's what got me in trouble in the first place, if you want to know. You may think what I said is funny, but lemme tell you: The Bart Simpsons of this world do not wind up in the cartoons. They wind up in the hatch."

≈

Ultimately, the net effect of the Bettelheim uproar was—not much. As with the media accounts of kids placed in private, for-profit psychiatric hospitals, the story played out in a conceptual vacuum, without context. Thus, the public was not asked to question the fundamental underlying beliefs that make such things not only possible, but likely; not asked to speculate on their assumption that psychiatric intervention (other than the blatantly brutal) can't hurt.

So a story that could have and should have served to raise a far larger issue came to rest as no more than a single-instance curiosity.

Alida says, "That's right. As far as its effect on other institutions, the effect has been none, absolutely none. The thing is, everybody says, 'Well, I read this thing in the paper. I would never send my kid to quote-unquote that kind of a place.' And they send them someplace else. Because they think that this story only applies to the one place. They think, Well, that place was run by somebody who was basically a fraud and a cheat—but this other place is run by wonderful people who have a loving atmosphere. And they're gonna fix my kid up good as new, and he's gonna come out of there looking like Pat Boone or Shirley Temple. They're gonna look like Theodore Cleaver when they come out. Instead, they come out zombies—helplessly dependent, with no spark; the kid is no longer part of his parents' family and harbors a lot of hidden anger."

≈

It was Bettelheim who imported "milieu therapy" into this country. In keeping with his background as an art historian, Bettelheim's milieu emphasized decor. "Every detail of the building, action, attitudes, is a carrier of symbolic meaning," he wrote.[20] There were statues in the garden, an antique rocking horse, a Victorian doll-house in the lovely book-lined waiting room. . . . According to the school's current director, Jacquelyn Sanders, "The idea that a place should be beautiful is Bruno's. He filled the place with artwork and put chandeliers and real china in the dining room so the children would know by their surroundings that they were valued."[20] (Since the children seldom got to spend time in either the garden or the waiting room, an equally likely goal was that the parents of prospective students—no longer, as before Bettelheim, the children of the poor, but rather extremely intelligent offspring of affluent families—would feel the place compatible with the hefty "tuition" fees.)

Beyond classy aesthetics, though, what does milieu therapy *mean*? "The theory behind the use of a therapeutic milieu is that control, conditioning, or modification of the person's environment can have a beneficial effect on his course of treatment, the alleviation of his deviant behavior, or his capacities to learn to become socialized."[21]

Well, that certainly seems pretty straightforward, even obvious. What is most astounding about it is that it qualifies as a whole *theory* in psychiatry. Whereas it is simply something taken as a given by every citizen conscious of the malevolent effects of living in roach-plagued, rat-infested, crack- and violence-ridden neighborhoods.

The only significance to be derived from that definition, in fact, is what is *implied*—agency. The agent who holds the control does the conditioning. As one perspicacious critic wrote, "the successful therapeutic community is, at heart, a benevolent autocracy."[22] But who is to define success? As the Bettelheim story shows us, a milieu's "success" requires no more than its progenitor's *claim* of success (and all subsequent critics relegated to the school's small failure pile, a *reasonable* failure pile, given that the inmates were "severely disturbed"). And who will, himself, say he is not benevolent?

Bettelheim *insisted* that his milieu be called a school (although, according to Charles Pekow, in keeping with Bettelheim's policy of inconsistency—as evidenced by the abrupt and violent eruptions

Alida described—he once hit a kid for saying he lived in a boarding home instead of a mental institution).[23]

There are many schools around the country that could be said to derive from the Bettelheim tradition: private schools, charging big bucks, claiming a "therapeutic milieu." Often, as with the Orthogenic School under Bettelheim's regime, they are headed by males whose personalities lean toward the flamboyant. They tend to arrive on the "helping" horizon like gangbusters. Touting grandiose schemes for child saving, their charismatic heads tend to spew cosmic, if secular, theologies about What Is Wrong with Children Today. They appear on television and are the subjects of admiring articles in the press: They TURN DISTURBED TEENS AROUND. They MEND SHATTERED LIVES.

Sometimes, abuses are reported.

In the case of the school we shall call the Bumble School (let's call the director Anthony Bumble), these abuses, reported to child and licensing agencies, included (verbatim):

- Unhygienic eating situation (kids ate with the pigs in the pen): "Kids say pigs mob them and they are forced to give pigs the food to leave them alone."
- Kids are forced to go out without a coat in the snow and in temperatures below thirty-two degrees Fahrenheit.
- Kids were denied sleep during group sessions designed to resolve problems, regardless of how late it was.
- Some of the veteran students were allowed to hit and restrain other students who were causing trouble.
- Students were pushed into freezing water while wearing sneakers because of unsatisfactory work. "Reporter states that J. said staff person threw him against the wall and has done this to other students. On Christmas Eve the students were digging trenches and one child did not dig the trench straight and was pushed into a creek and made to stay in her wet clothing and dig the trench until it was straight." (On *Christmas Eve?* Is this Dickens, or what?)

Also: Children must restrain each other; required to cut grass with scissors for as much as thirteen hours; kids not allowed to write to parents—school officials tell parents that kids won't write; girl tried to commit suicide, was treated at the hospital, and her doctor told the parents not to take the child back to the school because he felt she would try again. They took her back anyway and she jumped off the roof and is now paralyzed.

Ah, therapeutics. Ah, treatment milieu.

Such abuses, reported, however, are seldom heard beyond the walls of state agencies—for two reasons. One has to do with the weakened credibility of children presumed to be severely troubled (or else they wouldn't be at those schools). The other is that the passions of the founding charismatics extend to combative libel litigation against any outspoken critic. (Thus, I am using a pseudonym for the somewhat disguised, but entirely existent, Bumble School.)

At eighteen, Katie's a pert, lively, outgoing young woman, her personality entirely consonant with the popular cheerleader she was in the seventh, eighth, ninth grades. Occasionally, even during those years, according to her mother, Katie would sometimes wake up and say, "I can't go to school today." Although her mother, Paula, says, "I thought it was just immaturity," Katie did get sent for counseling. Paula says that at that time (as now), "Lots of people were sending their kids to therapists—or starting to." It was when Katie began to lose interest in cheerleading, in being popular, however, that Katie's parents became seriously alarmed. (Whatever impact the women's movement may have had, it apparently has done little to diminish the benchmark status of cheerleader throughout the country.)

As Katie explains it, "All of a sudden I didn't want to deal with the things that go on in high school. I didn't want to deal with the pressure, the drinking and drugs and everything that was going on with all my friends. And I think my way of getting around having to be popular and do all those things was by saying I didn't want to go to school."

Isn't that interesting? Katie didn't want to go to school or be a cheerleader because it equated with being popular, and that, in turn, equated with pressure to drink and do drugs. In essence, what happened to Katie—being first institutionalized (placed in what her mother refers to as "the lockup") and then sent to the therapeutic Bumble School—happened because she didn't want to do the things kids do that make them vulnerable to being hospitalized (and sent to places like Bumble).

Katie says, "I think I would have worked it out on my own. But it scared my parents to death."

"But Katie," I say, "if you weren't that much different from the other kids you knew, why *your* parents and not everyone else's?"

"My parents—I don't know—*cared* too much? My dad especially. He wants so much for us to do well and be well. He did not like the idea of therapy at all. But all his friends were kind of saying, 'Well, maybe she needs therapy.' And he just said, 'Okay.' And they sent me over to the university hospital. Which I think was a big mistake."

As Paula tells it, they took Katie to see the head psychiatrist there, "And he evaluated Katie and recommended that we put her in as soon as there was room."

How, I ask, did they convince Katie?

"You don't convince them," she says. "You take them over there. You know what's gonna happen. You know that they're gonna be put in there and locked up."

"But they don't?"

"They don't. And it's hard. It's very awful. When she finds out she can't leave."

More and more it begins to seem wrong to say that parents are "dumping" their kids in psych hospitals (although no doubt some are). Much more accurate is to say they are responding as they have been admonished: seeking and obeying what they have been convinced is *medical expertise.*

Katie was on the locked ward for six weeks. I ask, "What were the kids like, Katie? What was the place like?"

"My best friend was anorexic. And there was a young girl who had tried to kill herself several times. Both girls were there less time than I was. And both girls wound up going home." How strange.

As for what the place was like, Katie says, "You got up in the morning and took a shower—of course we weren't allowed to have any belongings. We were not allowed to touch each other. Just constant surveillance. I think hospitalization was the biggest waste of time, the biggest waste of money."

"The youngest kid was . . . ?"

"Steven. He was ten. I was fifteen, turned sixteen while I was there. But I didn't see the sun for six weeks. Literally, I learned how to play pool. We played cards. We didn't do anything. Had a session with our doctor once a day—for about thirty minutes."

"During which what occurred?"

"Nothing, as far as I was concerned. My doctor was the type who, if you didn't speak to him, he didn't speak to you. Very arrogant man. He's the one who sent me on to Bumble School. I don't remember anything except his telling me if I didn't shape up, this was going to happen to me or that was going to happen to me."

"And you didn't leave the ward?"

"We didn't leave the ward. It was a locked ward—a very, *very* locked ward. I couldn't have a hairbrush. I couldn't have fingernail polish. We had to put all those things in a cubby. And they watched us shower—so we didn't drink the shampoo. Thinking if I wanted to kill myself, I would drink my shampoo. What we did mostly was sit around and tell stories about ourselves—amongst each other, never in front of the nurses. And when I look back on it, none of the kids had done anything out of the ordinary. A lot of the kids didn't come from very much money at all. A lot were being paid for by insurance. And I remember a lot of kids would have to leave because their insurance wouldn't cover them anymore.

"No tape recorders. No cameras was a big thing. We made good friends there, and when someone left, we wanted to have pictures of our friends. And they said no, because if someone became famous, I could show evidence that they were crazy at one time. They never put it in those terms. We were never really told anything about why we were there. But they did say you could use the pictures to show someone was once *institutionalized*.

"Most of us would talk about running. You got to a certain level, they would let you go out with your parents for an hour at lunch.

And we'd talk about—if you ran away during that hour. It was like jail. We sat around and talked about ways of getting out."

"Did your parents visit?"

"They visited twice. They would come to these meetings. And if the child started to cry in the meeting, the parents were sent home. I don't know how they'd expect you—when you see your parents and you really want to go home—and the parents walk in—to just not cry. I just about started to cry saying that. Just now."

It was not just if the *kid* started to cry. . . .

Paula says, "I remember going over there to visit her after she'd been there a week. And of course we had already gotten long letters cussing us out about putting her in there, and we didn't know what was going on there. And we went for our first visit. And I remember I teared up and the nurse made me leave."

"Why?"

"Because you were to show resolve."

"Resolve?"

"That she was going to stay there and going to go through the treatment. And nothing that she could do was gonna convince us to get her out."

As much as anything, this curious regulation—most particularly applied to a girl like Katie who had done nothing more egregiously nonconformist than not want to go to school, than be upset (she had not run away, not been into drugs, not gotten in with the "wrong crowd," not lied, not stolen)—again points up the real motive of punishment lightly veiled by the word "treatment." (In fact, the more emphatically "treaters" stress the new psy understanding of biological, neurological, chemical imbalances as causative, the less logic connects the purported cause to the practiced response. If some kind of faulty machinery was believed to be driving Katie's behavior, what sense would such hard-nosed rules—which seem to imply willfulness; too lenient parenting—make?)

Paula says, "That's the way the program runs in the lockup ward in the university hospital. Under the top professional you can get. The most expensive situation you can find. Katie stayed there six weeks because that is all the insurance we had. We ran out. It was time to do something. We had to move her. We didn't have any more money to pay for the hospital situation.

"And so the psychiatrist recommended the school."

Again and again one hears this curious symbiosis between schools and psychiatry: schools recommending the hospital evaluations that so often lead to placement; psychiatrists recommending particular "therapeutic" school placements. . . .

Katie says, "So what happened was my parents came to me with a brochure of a boarding school. It was the doctor's idea. They said, 'You're going to come home for two days'—which confused me because I didn't understand why I couldn't be home and recover from *this* place. And they said, 'Then we're going down there.'

"And I looked at this flyer for this boarding school where you just ski and play tennis and volleyball all day. . . .

"It was never brought up that this was a 'therapeutic' boarding school. It was never brought up that there were no vacations, there was no summer, there was no Christmas. So we packed my bag. We went down. And I never came back."

Not, that is, for the next nine months.

"I really felt betrayed by my parents at that point. It was awful. And Tony Bumble and the staff were very, very good at what they did, very manipulative, very smart. From the minute I walked in the door, Tony Bumble was there and—when I went in I had on a little Deadhead-looking outfit. And he said, 'Oh, do you like the Grateful Dead?' And I said, 'They're okay.' And he said, 'Oh, I know Jerry Garcia really well.' That sticks out in my mind because it just gave me a different idea of what was going to be going on. That he knew Jerry and I would get to see all these wonderful things here. . . .

"My parents walked around with me for about four or five minutes, and then they left. And then—I was in shock for about a week."

"What was this place like?"

"They had this thing called a tether system. The first thing they think new kids do is they run away. I was too scared to run, but—I was tethered for about four days. Which means I had a Level 3 with me all the time. It takes about a year to get a level, so most of these Level 3s had been there about three years. It takes a *long* time to earn a level. So when you're tethered, a Level 2 or Level 3—they're with you all the time, all the time. Like you can't get up in the morning until your tether picks you up.

"At that point they were hand-holding me, which means I had to hold a Level 3's hand all the time. Couldn't take a shower, they had to be in the shower with you. Couldn't leave your class. They had to pick you up after class and walk you to the next class. It's a very prestigious award to be given a level, so then they can do whatever they want to. They can tether other people."

This is simply not the world as we expect it to be: In fact, it is the kind of mind control dictatorship, the kind of autocratic imperial society Americans expect to find only in works of imaginative or speculative fiction. I am feeling . . . perplexity; incomprehension. As with "escorted" and "dragged," with the "eight-foot ban"—kids "tethering" other kids? "How's that again?" I ask.

"Let's say I acted out an abuse—just said something bad, or 'did one of my issues.' "

"Did one of your *whats?*"

"Issues. Like there was one girl whose issue—she was a real bitch. She bitched to everybody. She wore a ton of makeup. So they took the makeup away and said, 'No more makeup. You cannot wear any more makeup.' And she got caught wearing a little bit of foundation. Well, she would get tethered.

"Another guy, he was nasty to everybody, very snobby. Say he was nasty to someone—another kid could tether him. And the person who holds your tether is responsible for all your actions."

By now I am frowning deeply as I grope for some way to think about all this—except as a controlled experiment in social fascism; social facism with a psy name: positive peer pressure. Katie takes my silence as a cue to elucidate:

"Say I had Level 1 and *I* could take *his* tether. Say he was nasty to somebody while I held his tether. But then *I* would get tethered. Because I let him act out. The whole thing with that school is the tighter you get with the faculty, the more power you get. The more power you get, the more freedom you have."

"You mean freedom to take power over other kids?"

"Exactly. Exactly. It was happening in the faculty. It was happening with the students. It was crossing over, until they were just getting out of control with this power."

Out of control. In this context, within the frame of the picture Katie paints, the phrase gains, for the first time, the ring of authentic meaning.

"There were always crazy things happening," Katie says. "And if one thing happened, the whole school would be involved. Like we had these things we called TAs. Tell-alls. That means if you do anything wrong, you come into your dorm meetings or you go to a faculty member and you tell them what you did. I had huge TAs at one point. If you turn yourself in, you still lose your level and you get tethered, and it takes about a month to win the community back over. The biggest threat was that the community would turn on you.

"And if the faculty thinks you have TAs and you don't come forward, they put you in a room and don't let you out until you've done every single one of your TAs.

"And if you don't do *your* TAs before somebody tells about *you*, then you're in big trouble. And usually kids are around together. So when somebody goes into a room to do their TAs, everybody—all these kids—go running to do *their* TAs so they don't get busted. The whole school—every time somebody got put in a room, everybody ran for a faculty member to do their TAs."

Where are the *parents* (the reader may be wondering)? It's tempting to feel somewhat smug at this point; to be thinking, Well, if it were *my* child, I would simply go down there and pull her out. Katie's parents knew some (far from all) of what was going on. Why didn't they? Why didn't others?

Katie's father, Dave, is a seemingly reasonable, caring corporate executive. He says, "For the parents? The school made you feel like shit. They would constantly remind you that they had complete control of your child and it was none of your business." After all, the implication is *you* failed. Or she wouldn't be here. "And if you gave them any grief at all, they said they would just kick her out. And most of the parents were scared to death their child was gonna get kicked out—because then they wouldn't know what to do with them if they got them home."

And so we are looking at the phenomenon of middle-class parents who act initially out of genuine concern, responding to the general cultural belief in psy help, imbued with the general cultural belief that anything "therapeutic" *can't hurt.*

Dave continues, "For example, Katie had—one of the first things that she did down there that she was not supposed to do was apparently have sex with one of the boys. And I can remember— every conversation I would have for the next three or four months, when I would ask, 'How's Katie doing?' the first thing that would come out of their mouth is, 'Oh, your daughter's the one that had sex.' Constantly remind me of that, sort of to keep me in control.

"And when we went down there, you were only allowed to see the kids under certain conditions. One time my wife and I went out there to visit—drove all the way—had told them ahead we were gonna be there and wanted to take her out for the day. Not for an overnight. You couldn't do that. And I remember we got there about ten in the morning. We were required to sit in the lobby—the size of a half bath—for about two and a half hours. While a lady sat right in front of me, trying to get enough time to talk to me. Then, after about two and a half hours, she said, 'Now what can I do for you?' I said, 'I want to take Katie out.' And she said, 'Oh. Okay.' I just felt they really abused the parents. But. The parents were so afraid of their own children that they didn't know what to do. And remember. They had your money."

Correct. The terms of admission required full payment for the year up front (about thirty-five thousand dollars, Dave says, before extras). Nonrefundable, by contract, under any conditions.

"And," Dave says, "the fellow that ran it ran it with an iron hand. He was the god."

Recalling the word that was used about Bettelheim's regime at the Orthogenic School, but not wanting to escalate beyond reason, I ask gingerly, "Anything about all this seem to you close to a cult?"

"Pretty close! I never thought of it until you said that, but I think it was pretty close! The kids hated it, but they bought into it. They didn't have a choice. They were scared to death. They were absolutely petrified of him, and of the people that ran the school. It was to where they would tell on each other—even though they would hate doing it. Yeah. It was like a cult, now that I really think about it. Once you walked into that place, you didn't question anything because you were scared to."

In fact, although schools like Bettelheim's and Bumble's probably do not meet strict criteria for being called *cults*, they meet enough criteria to be called cult*like*: They are a closed group; the kids are cut off from family or anything *other;* the authorities do not brook challenge or inquiry; they employ rank as privilege to keep the inmates/members policing each other. . . .

Katie says, "And there were captive dorms. Which means—Tony believes that nobody runs away without telling somebody. So if somebody ran away, if you didn't pick up on the fact that someone was gonna run away, the entire dorm was tethered. Some dorms stayed tethered—which means that every single person in the dorm has to stay together all the time; you have to hold hands— sometimes a dorm would stay tethered for a month. The entire dorm would be out of classes for a month."

This too was something I was to hear repeatedly: the use of school as a privilege; its withdrawal as punishment. When so many kids are initially placed because they hate school, cut school, are failing in school—it is hard to know whether this is comical or lunatical. "So," Katie is saying, "if the dorm then wasn't making any progress tethered"—meaning if no one confessed to having known of the runaway's plan—"you became a captive dorm. Which meant you couldn't leave the dorm. The staff would bring your food and you'd sit in meetings and deal and deal—which means every single person has to deal and deal in some way until they change."

No, I don't know what dealing and dealing is, nor do I ask.

"It strikes me," I say to Katie, "that there are two ways kids can go under this kind of totalitarian regime. They can band together into a little guerrilla action. Or allow themselves to be co-opted. Obviously here the school was skilled enough to co-opt kids."

"Unbelievably!" she says. "There was a lot of brainwashing involved. You've got people telling you that you've got these problems. You tend to believe it. It takes a while, but it sinks in. And the only way to deal with Bumble and not live miserably was—because people were on you every second—was to rise above, and be one of *those* people. It's a lot of manipulating, a lot of therapeutic talk. When I came home, I was driving my parents crazy. Analyzing every little thing they did. I could back them into a corner because they did not know how to use the terms. Once you start to use these tools, it gives you a lot of power over other people. It's very much power."

Between themselves, Katie's parents had resolved to let her finish the school year (so at least she would not lose the credits). And then, in the spring, they would pull her out. Doing so, however, was not going to be easy. It was Bumble's intention, like Bettelheim's, to keep these kids for years.

As Katie's mother tells it, "The weekend we went to the final parents' weekend late in the spring, we admitted in the whole therapy session—"

"Therapy session?"

"At the school. They put all the kids and parents together and they're supposed to talk about what's going on. Supposed to be an open kind of . . . And we admitted that we were gonna take Katie out."

"*Admitted?*"

"Yes, admitted. Then from then on, we were treated with an absolute cold shoulder, and no one would speak to us. No one was allowed to speak to us."

"But *why?* What was the fear?"

"You were just manipulated awfully by these people. You were made to feel so stupid. You were made to feel as if you were harming your child—if you took them out."

"Why," I ask, "do you think some kids get caught up in this, and some other kids with equal or even greater problems don't seem to?"

She pauses, then, "I don't know."

"What do you think makes parents susceptible?"

Again she reflects. "Well—we just cared. We really cared. And we got into it. And—I don't know—there's a great deal of love there when you will go to these extremes to try to help your child. And not just say, 'Oh—just—get out of the house.' Or whatever."

"Doesn't that make you the perfect—patients, clients, however you would put it? Because when you walk in you already feel guilty or lousy or desperate or . . . ?"

"Yes."

"So maybe an 'expert' could sell you anything?"

"Oh, sure! But we did not think the psychiatrist at a university hospital would have recommended this school unless he felt it was *good*."

"You suppose he ever visited it?"

"He never *did!* We found out after we put her in there that he had never been there. And he never went down there to check on his patients. And he had two, maybe three there at the time. We were upset to find that out. And we had every reason to trust him.

"But you don't know the feeling of helplessness when your child is emotionally strung out and you don't know what to do about it. I just didn't know what to do."

As for Katie: She returned home. She chose to go to a different school, a true boarding school. She enjoyed it and she did well. And she got into three colleges. She chose one, then—had second thoughts. . . . Last spoken to, she was determined to go back and finish at a different college.

When I last heard from Katie's mother, she said, "I don't know. We took her to a psychic reader about a month ago—we take that with a grain of salt. But he told Katie that if she didn't get engaged on a manic affair, and end up in a trailer with three babies, in time she could probably graduate with more than one degree."

Maybe she will. (Given what we are looking at here, I am not inclined to pooh-pooh psychic readers.) If so, it strikes me, it will be distinctly despite—not because of—what was done to "help."

4

A Brief Business Trip

THE POPULATION of the four counties that comprise Little Rock, Arkansas, is roughly 513,000. According to the Research Department at the University of Arkansas, state data show that of this number, 135,076 are under eighteen years old.

In my hotel room, during a lull in my interview schedule, I pull out the telephone directory and look in the Yellow Pages under "Hospitals." Here, in a full-page ad, I find Living Hope Institute.

- "Treating the physical, psychological, and spiritual needs of each patient."
- "We have a team of Christian professionals who care about you and the needs of your family."
- "We offer both inpatient and outpatient treatment programs."
- "We offer hope & health for psychiatric and substance abuse problems."

Arkansas Children's Hospital ("Where love can move mountains") offers Turning Point, a "Child & Adolescent Medical/Psychiatric Unit." And with facilities for treating children with learning disorders, behavior disorders, mood and anxiety disorders . . .

The BridgeWay ("New Starts Start Here"), a seventy-bed private specialty hospital ("Free Assessment"), offering "Individual and specialized programs for behavioral and emotional disorders, depression and stress, phobias, learning disabilities, eating disorders and chemical dependency."

Baptist Rehabilitation Institute of Arkansas, which offers Recover Teen, "A short-term psychiatric program for teenagers with behavioral & emotional problems in a warm, caring atmosphere."

CPC Little Rock Hospital ("Comprehensive Psychiatric Treatment, part of a large national chain, offering Psychiatric Care for Adolescents and Adults; No Cost Assessment & Crisis Intervention 24 Hours a Day, 7 Days a Week, In-House School Programs, Substance Abuse Treatment for Adolescents and Adults, Covered by Most Insurance.")

Charter Hospital of Little Rock ("Private, Confidential Treatment for Mental Health & Chemical Dependency"), dealing with emotional problems, behavioral problems, school difficulties, alcohol and drug problems . . . ("Most Insurance Accepted").

Pinewood Hospital ("Complete Psychiatric Care"), which is in Texarkana.

Shadow Mountain Institute for Children and Adolescents ("JCAHO-CHAMPUS Approved Psychiatric Acute Hospital & Residential Treatment"), which is in Tulsa, Oklahoma.

And—the one I have been invited to visit—Rivendell Psychiatric Center,* "Located on a 20 Acre Secluded Setting."

If you recall J. R. R. Tolkien's *The Hobbit*, you may recognize the name Rivendell, the elfish place where Bilbo Baggins, Gandalf,

---

* This institution's real name (as are the others, as listed in the 1990 Little Rock Yellow Pages). Since the Rivendell staff were the most direct, open, honest, and *intelligible* of all my site visits, I feel comfortable using its name. (There is nothing to be served, on this issue, in attacking or targeting any particular facility when what I am questioning is the entire ideology.)

and Thorin found temporary respite in the Last Homely House, belonging to Elrond: where "Their clothes were mended as well as their bruises, their tempers and their hopes. Their bags were filled with food and provisions light to carry but strong enough to bring them over the mountain passes. Their plans were improved with the best advice."

≈

I have completed my Rivendell tour: the bedrooms, the classrooms (in one, a blackboard bears the mysterious chalked inscription "How the government spends our $?"), the seclusion room. . . . I am in the conference room with Liz Rainwater, staff member of Arkansas Advocates for Children and Families; Scott Williams, director of marketing; and Charles E. West, senior executive director.

Rivendell, I am told, was first started in 1985 as a unit at Saint Joseph's Hospital in Memphis by Robert Wood, a Ph.D. psychologist, and six other psychologists and an administrator.

What, I ask West, was their idea? By 1985, after all, the private, for-profit psychiatric hospital boom was well under way and the big guys like Charter and Psychiatric Institutes of America were deeply into the game. . . . What was their shtick?

West says, "I think the innovation was that they took a lot of different things from different places. I don't think there was any part of this that hadn't been used by somebody. I think their model was a behavioral program with a strong peer hierarchy. Kids earn a certain badge level—that gives them more responsibility. It's like a family structure. In other words, you've got all the kids on a particular team—we use red, blue, and gold for that reference. We call them teams. They used to be called families. But the whole connotation of that was that as someone was here and did better, they were given increasing responsibility. And that's a peer hierarchy system. The kids are taught to be responsible and to manage the team-running, and through that they learn the responsibility that you have in any family."

Again I feel I am drowning in language of no particular content. What is being said here that couldn't be said to be the philosophy of a Boy Scout camp? And what is it about this idea of "peer hierarchy"—the doling out to kids, by adults, of power over other kids—that rankles? I decide—I am, after all, speaking with an administrator, a businessman—to see what, eventually, I can learn about the *business*.

But first I ask, "What was the founders' vision?"

"They decided after a few years of running that unit that they would form a corporation, Rivendell of America, and build these facilities. The vision was to go across the country."

Currently, West tells me, there are eight Rivendell psychiatric hospitals—one in Bowling Green, Kentucky; one in West Jordan, Utah; one in Billings, Montana; one in Butte; one in Panama City, Florida; one in Saint Johns, Michigan; one in Seward, Nebraska.

"Quite frankly," West says, "you asked about the founders' vision a while ago. [That] vision was that any child that ever came here would be able to have access to our care. No matteer whether they could pay or not. And that was just kind of company philosophy. And—very utopian.

"But," he says, "unfortunately—not very fiscally sound. And what happened over two or three years—we had a lot of success with this facility, and Bowling Green started off pretty well. But then, as they started opening the other ones, they didn't do as well. And financially they started having problems." A new president was brought in. And after he was here several months, he and the chairman of the board just decided they'd buy it all out. "We opened with sixty-four beds and we've recently done a major renovation project and expanded to seventy-seven."

I am starting to quite like West's candor, and I'm recalling another conversation I had, with the marketing director for a major chain, in which she kept talking about "serving community needs" and then occasionally substituting the word "market" for "community needs"—before quickly reverting to "community needs."

"Your economic base?" I ask. "Third-party insurance?"

"It varies from state to state. Arkansas has a pretty active Under-21 Medicaid program. Medicaid pays two hundred fifty-five dollars a day. Our charges right now are running pretty close to eight hundred dollars. We're one of the lower facilities in charges, within Rivendell. It just depends on the market." (Why does that word seem soothing?) "And I think you can say that for all the facilities."

I realize suddenly that I *understand* all this talk of markets. Not that I am particularly business literate. But, compared with psy-speak, there is something ineffably coherent about profit and loss. And—so far at least—we are not talking in circles!

I mention that I have noted in the phone directory that Little Rock seems virtually ringed by child and adolescent psychiatric hospitals; that it seems like a harder place to get your appendix out than to get your kid out.

"Well," West says, "of course six years ago, when we first opened, we were one of the few games in the state. All of our history, we stayed just about one hundred percent occupancy. Until the past year, year and a half. We still stay fairly full, but at times we have some open beds. The reason being—the competition's just unbe-lievable."

This is fun. It's as if we're talking about hotels, the problem of the tourist business dropping off.

West continues, "For many years there was a Certificate of Need law in Arkansas, as there is in many states. [A Certificate of Need law says that in order to build a new facility you are required to prove the need for the additional proposed beds.] And so when we built this facility, we went through the whole Certificate of Need process. They [Arkansas] subsequently got rid of it. Most states have gotten rid of it. So what you've got now—it's free enterprise. Any-body that wants to can build a hospital anywhere.

"What's happened is all these major chains like Charter and CPC have come in. You see, a lot of these companies for several years have had tremendous growth. But finally, it's like any other industry—they've built and built and built. Until now there's so much that—it's like our market. With CPC coming in, and Charter coming, just in the past year—you'd have to question that we're not overbuilt in central Arkansas."

Isn't this refreshing? I am actually becoming interested, in-volved, *sympathetic* to the business problem here.

"How," I ask, "do you go about competing?"

"We advertise. Scott Williams will show you some ads later on.

He's our professional relations director." From across the table, Williams smiles and nods. West continues, "Then we have professional relations representatives. And they actually cover the state and talk to referral sources. Most parents aren't going to refer someone. Most referral sources are professional psychologists, psychiatrists, social workers. So we've—from day one—tied in with them." Makes sense. "We let them know we were not coming into Arkansas to be competition for them." Makes sense. "Because they provide the outpatient component." Right. "We've always worked with all the community mental health centers in the state. So they've been a real good referring source for us.

"And the first three years we were here, we were pretty much a secret to the general public—because we didn't advertise. And especially over the last two years, as the competition's really picked up, we've started doing TV, newspaper advertising."

Makes sense. (I am really getting into this.) "Would you say," I ask, "the profitability is down significantly? Or just stabilized?"

West says, "This facility's always done real well, and we're continuing to do real well—but it's like anything else: If you've got a gas station on one corner, then you build one on the other corner, they're gonna take some of the business."

I like the metaphor: kids as cars: kiddie cars: psy guzzlers. (What I do not know at this point is that this automobile feature will keep cropping up again and again.)

"We're still profitable," West says, "but it's tougher. I don't know that we're unlike any other business. I've given this a lot of thought, because you know the health care industry's under a lot of attack. Mental health care in general. The federal government's looking at why are the many billions of dollars rising so quickly. And I think, in health care, we tend to be a microcosm of what most businesses feel. We deal with so many different variables that are brought in, and a ten percent or a five percent increase here or there—it all kind of landed together on us. That's why our inflation's higher than other industries'.

"Of course, our labor costs are significant, 'cause that's your big cost in the health care industry. And the state of knowledge has increased, and people have become more specialized. . . . I'm not sure anyone's actually making as much as they did a few years ago."

"Are all the Rivendell hospitals run with the same treatment philosophy?" I ask.

"No. There've been variations over the years. They all started basically the same way we did. Now some of them specialize in certain tracks. Building design, those kinds of things, are cookie-cutter. What we've found is this particular design is real conducive to a psych setting. A lot of thought was given to that. So if you went to Rivendell in any of the states, and up to the front, it's pretty much the same."

Hmm. Like McDonald's. "It would seem to me," I say, "that in a strained market the people at the top would begin to think about adaptability. Doing something different with the facility."

"That's what I meant by saying that as all these Rivendells have opened—the original concept was what we were doing here. That was the original program of Rivendell. Over time, for one reason or another—their market is already saturated, or it wasn't as accepted in one place as another—they've had to adapt and develop a different program."

So it's *not* like McDonald's—a Quarter Pounder here is not necessarily a Quarter Pounder there. But to understand how refreshing West's frankness is, listen to the senior director of marketing at Charter Medical Corporation in Macon, Georgia, Joanne Neely: When asked whether—in their eighty-five psy hospitals in the United States (plus two in London, one in Switzerland)—they have specialized programs, she said, "That depends on the needs of the community. For example, it's not surprising at all to know that we have one of the most sophisticated gambling addiction programs— in Las Vegas, Nevada. It's *the* gambling addiction program in the Las Vegas area. Macon, Georgia, there's probably no need for a gambling addiction program. We have eating disorder programs in certain major cities—in cities where people feel compelled to have a certain physical presence. We have sexual abuse programs in certain locales of the country where maybe it's the family dynamics or such that maybe sexual abuse is more common. So there are treatment tracks based, again, on the needs of the community. To help communities with problems that are maybe unique to one part of the country." By comparison, West strikes me as an astute businessman, who *knows* he's in business and not a paragon of charity "serving the needs of communities."

He says now, "We were talking about the original philosophy. I think what happens is—your Charters and CPCs are in business to make money. Just like any other corporation is in business to make a profit. The original intent of Rivendell, as far as I know, wasn't to make a lot of money. The original people truly, truly wanted this to be a place where someone came to get help and payment was not the overall.

"But you know, like any other business, you have to figure out a way to stay in business and survive financially. So that's been part of the modification. Because each facility had to modify to meet their market to be successful.

"And in Utah, there've been seven different facilities built in a two-year span—all the different companies in the Salt Lake City area. The point I'm trying to make to you is seven different companies came into the Salt Lake area in a two-year span, and built. And it was such a glut that Rivendell really had to get into some different things out there. So in Utah now, Rivendell is really a different animal. It's really an RTC [residential treatment center]. *We're* licensed as an acute care facility. We could just as easily be an RTC. In fact it's easier to be an RTC. The thing is—nobody pays for an RTC.

"And I think people have started to take this up. I got an announcement from Hickfa [Health Care Financial Administration] saying that they're gonna instruct the states—where they've always had Medicaid in the past for the Under-21 psych program—to also start looking at criteria to pay for RTC. In the end, that's gonna save the federal government a lot of money. Because a lot of facilities that are treating a lot of these kids acutely could be being RTC. It's a lower price. Certainly I think that with government agencies looking for ways to cut expenses and it being such a big political topic now, and with the glut-of-overbedding situation in so many areas, I think RTCs are gonna become much more viable."

"So that might be an adaptation?" I ask. "You convert to an RTC, drop some staff, make adjustments that would save you some money?"

West says, "You don't have to drop staff. I think you would . . ."

Liz Rainwater says, "Change staff."

West says, ". . . revamp some of the departments."

Suddenly I have a thought that pops my enthusiasm for all this problem solving. "It strikes me kind of like there's this pool of unpopular kids, like toxic waste. And we just occasionally, either because of scandal or because of economics, change the name of the kind of place we dump them in."

This seems, even to me, a somewhat outrageous thing to say, sitting in the conference room of a psychiatric hospital in the presence of its executive director and director of marketing (or professional relations). Liz Rainwater jumps in: "I think the key to what-all you just said is 'unpopular kids.' There's a real rap, I think, this industry's taking for these kids being institutionalized by so many places. Because all these kids have been hopped around to ten different places. And that is opposed to what our original philosophy was." *Our?* For a second, it strikes me odd that she, as a child advocate, is identifying with the hospitals—until I remember that Liz used to work at Rivendell (which is how I've gained access to this meeting). She goes on about the original idea: "What it was, you bring someone here and it'll take six months, and we keep them until we really work the problems out. And what we're finding over time—we've had to modify that because of payment sources."

"And," she says, "don't let anyone fool you. Everybody's tryin' to say, 'Oh, no, payment doesn't drive it.' That's b.s., you know. Payment—I mean every physician will tell you, 'Oh, no, I keep 'em however long they need to be here.' But they keep them here as long as they get paid for it."

"Known as the miracle cure," I say.

"Sure it is," she says. "It's that way everywhere."

Of course. That's why it's known as the health care *industry*. And why so many people advocate for national health care. But the problem here is deeper than the question of who pays for what—it's a question of what the what is.

West says, "The thing we try to do, as corny as this sounds, is to really try to fix what the problems are. And I think the more the system's driven by the money, you get less and less fixed. Because it cuts everybody down to thirty days or less time. All you've got then is these kids are institutionalized. That's all you got. You can't fix 'em. It's too quick."

"Fix what about them?" I ask (again). "Are we talking about changing conduct? Behavior disorders?"

"You got on my favorite topic, right there," he says.

"Why?"

"Conduct disorder has always come under a lot of attack. But I've seen too many lives changed here to say that conduct disorder is not a psychiatric illness."

Okay. I won't argue that it is not possible, or sometimes desirable, to act to change a kid's behavior. I certainly will not argue against helping a kid, or befriending a kid. But why does that prove that the lousy conduct is a psychiatric illness? Because you're making the change in an institution called a psychiatric hospital?

So here we are again. The land that linear thought forgot. Kid misbehaves. You put him in a psy facility. Maybe, for one reason or another (including wanting to get out), his behavior changes. And that is how you know he had a psychiatric illness.

"Yeah, sure," West says, "it's the environment they're havin' to live in or something like that. I can tell you, we've taught 'em how to cope with that. And I think a lot of their lives are better today and we turned a lot of kids around. And sure, a lot of money's been spent on that. Our last study showed approximately seventy percent of our kids had not afterwards been in any trouble with the law, or reinstitutionalized. The group that was here the first two years we were open. But the thing is—and I don't feel good about this—but you do follow-up on the second two years, it's gonna be a lower percentage. Because our length of stay has dropped so bad I know we didn't do as good as we did with the first group."

"Is it true," I ask (hoping to get back to *business*), "that diagnoses change to suit insurance?"

He says, "I guess the best way to answer that is when acute care hospitals went to DRGs [diagnostically related groups]—well, there were several computer companies that made millions of dollars the first year DRGs came in line. Because what they did is they sold physicians in hospitals these computer diagrams that told you, 'With these symptoms, this is the best combination for the most payment.' This is how they work it. Psychiatrically, we haven't had to do that yet, because we don't have DRGs. But sure. I'd be kiddin' if I didn't say that we look at the particular diagnosis as far as payment. And just to say someone is a strict conduct disorder is not as popular today as it was a few years ago. Let me just tell you that everyone tries to hide behind that old saw that payment doesn't drive treatment. And it's just baloney. We might as well admit that it does. It does in every health care institution in the United States."

Liz signals that it is time for us to be going. We're going to be late for our next appointment. As I'm packing up I say to West, "Have any of the kids actually read *The Hobbit*?"

"Yeah, some of them. We've been showing the movie on VCR. But we don't play it up anymore. You know—we had Bilbo Baggins's parking space out here for years, until recently. That was just kind of some quirky stuff—that the founders were into."

Bilbo Baggins's *parking space?* And the kids are the patients here?

≈

As we drive off I find I am still considering Rivendell's business interests: After all the murky psy-speak, it seems so restful. Maybe, I am thinking, they should specialize in substance abuse. Public passion about that is not apt to diminish. Nor, in the prevailing climate of conservatism, is the power structure's posture of assault on the drug problem. That's it, I decide. These guys should get into substance abuse.

Several months after leaving Arkansas, I find this in the *New York Times*: LITTLE ROCK SCHOOLS INSURE DRUG TREATMENT. [1]

"School and city officials in Little Rock, Ark., are providing full insurance for treatment of drug and alcohol abuse to all the district's 20,000 students, a program that the officials say is the first by a public school system.

"The coverage pays up to 100 percent of the cost of treating students referred by the school district to 10 local psychiatric hospitals and counseling centers, which have agreed to reduce rates for students in the program. . . .

"Officials plan to pay the carrier, Blue Cross and Blue Shield of Arkansas, the $267,000 annual premium for the plan through donations, although so far they have only raised a quarter of that amount." Said Frankie Sarver, executive director of Little Rock Fighting Back, " 'This city has no treatment program for children under age 16 unless they can afford private care. . . . This program will place treatment at private psychiatric hospitals, which can cost from $6,000 to $30,000, within the reach of any student who needs it.' "

Goddamn.

5

Sad

(But Interestin')

JOHN HAS BEEN in Rivendell.* He has also been in Shadow Mountain Institute (in Tulsa); also in a goodly assortment of other facilities listed in the Little Rock phone directory. In fact, John has been in a lot of different places in his fifteen years.

It was John's experience, for the first nine years at least, that his life was out of everybody's control.

As his adoptive mother, Linda, has written me, "In 1984, we learned that John, our great-nephew, and his sister, whom we had been told had been adopted in Oklahoma, had actually been in foster care since leaving Arkansas in 1978 [when John was three, his sister two]. The father's rights were not terminated until 1983, and the mother's rights had then not been terminated at all, though beginning steps had begun for same.

"We brought the children home with the understanding with the Oklahoma courts and the Department of Human Services that when the mother's rights were terminated, we wished to adopt.

---

* Again, I will ask the reader to understand that I use this facility's real name here *because it was one of the better, more forthright institutions I visited.* Whatever one may find wrong, or doubtful, the wrongness or doubtfulness derives from the underlying ideology, not the shortcomings of this single place.

"The adoption summary was that these were very wonderful children, who just needed a good home, and love. We felt we fit that need. Love is something we had plenty of, and we felt we had been successful in our first children. They were grown, and loving, productive, useful citizens that we had thoroughly enjoyed raising. We had no fears of the empty nest, but also didn't have any fears of having more little ones. We enjoyed parenting, but have always realized that they were ours for a very short while."

As it turned out, John and his sister had been through some twenty-three moves in foster care. As it turned out, they had all the problems one would reasonably expect, given their experiential reality. Linda details them as: "using very vulgar language, no table manners, verbally lacking, sexually acting out, stealing, sneaking food, educationally very behind, impulsive, fighting, manipulative . . ." About John, Linda has written that he "gorged himself on whatever food was available, never seemed to be sorry if he hurt others, wouldn't or couldn't sleep, would cry for two or three hours at bedtime . . ." They hooked into therapy, and their voyage in psyland began.

≈

The hotel has forgotten my wake-up call, so I come to consciousness with Linda's voice on the phone from the lobby, announcing she and John are here for our appointment. Begging five minutes, I scramble to dress and throw the bed together, mind scrabbling to approximate readiness. Five minutes to the second, they are at the door. Linda comes in first, a slim woman in her fifties; outgoing, gracious. John—solidly built and seemingly reticent—follows, perhaps inevitably seeming to be in tow.

I want to order coffee (badly). I offer them breakfast. Linda says, an instruction to John implicit, "John has already had breakfast." Then, "Haven't you, John?"

Well—but still—you've both been good enough to come here, and I'm ordering anyway. . . . And you'd like coffee, Linda? And if John wants anything . . . ?

Linda appears to relent. I hand John the room service menu.

"Why don't you have eggs?" Linda says.

"Okay."

"Eggs how?" I ask.

"Fried."

Linda, glancing at John: *"Please?"*

John says, "Please."

(As I recall this now, I am thinking how tempting it will be for the reader to slip into the psy-chair, evaluating and diagnosing Linda or John.)

The order placed, there wants somewhere to begin. "John, I understand you were in Rivendell a few months ago. I was there yesterday, and I passed their seclusion room. I don't know how it would feel to be in a seclusion room. . . ."

John smiles. " 'I want to go home.' "

"They claim they don't use it much."

"When I was there they used it a lot. They used it a lot. If you have a problem with somebody, or start calling people names, you get sitting time out. If you don't want to sit, you get standing time out."

I try to interpret this: You say to the kid, "Go sit over there." The kid says, "I don't want to." You say, "Fine. Go *stand* over there." John continues: "Then they take you out of standing time out and they put you in the seclusion room. That's called open-door seclusion. The door's open so you can see out.

"But if you're acting wild, wilding, hitting the walls, bangin' around, cursin' everybody, or even running out of the seclusion room, they'll put you in and lock the door for a certain amount of time. And then after that, if you keep banging on the walls, they see you're gonna cause harm to yourself in there—actually, they take your shoes away from you, your belt, things that they think can harm people—but if you keep banging your head and hurting yourself by hitting the walls, they'll put you in restraints.

"There's five-point restraints. They strap your wrists down to your bed and they tie your waist and your feet down to the bed. They have little slots in your bed where they do that, strap you down. Then, after that, they put you in this little program where nobody can talk to you, and you can't talk to anybody. They isolate you. Your roommate moves out so you're all by yourself. And they bring your food in to you. And they have the door closed so you can—until you respond to their things and tell them why you did this."

In the parent packet I have been given at Rivendell is a form: Authorization for Treatment Techniques that Remove a Patient from Environmental Stimulation When Other Forms of Intervention Fail to Assist the Patient Maintain Self-Control:

"Rivendell environments provide techniques to assist patients when they are unable to regain emotional control. These techniques are used only when the patient's behavior could be disruptive to the therapeutic environment." It is hard to know whether to take this assertion as deliberately opaque. But it certainly *could* be taken as an imaginative premise for a work of psy-fi: The "environments" provide techniques? And they do so in their own defense (when the patient's behavior could be disruptive to them)?

"1. Time out from positive reinforcement—a short time interval (approximately 15 minutes) spent in a quiet area where the patient can calm down and regain control of his/her behavior and emotions.

"2. Open-door time out—a procedure implemented when a patient cannot regain emotional control in the therapeutic environment and needs the quiet of a Time Out Room where he/she can pace, move around, and ventilate until a calm state is achieved."

Then there are "Special Treatment Procedures," which are "techniques used for patients whose behavior makes them dangerous to themselves or others. These techniques are used *only* when ordered by a physician for a limited, specified period of time or until the patient regains control.

"1. Time Out with Help—is defined as the brief physical holding of a child to prevent him/her from harming him/herself or others. Its purpose is to allow the patient an opportunity to regain control of intense emotions. In general, this interval of holding is for no more than approximately 10 minutes, but it will vary according to the clinical needs of the child." The thought suggests itself that, were these "clinical needs of the child" being met in an identical way in a facility labeled juvenile justice, there might well be public fuss about brutality.

"2. Seclusion—is defined as the confinement of a patient from the therapeutic environment to the seclusion room." (Never mind the English. Is this "confinement from the therapeutic environment" for therapeutic purposes? Or is it, again, the therapeutic environment acting in its own defense? Answer: both.) "The behavior *must* create a serious threat of harm to the patient, others, or be a serious disruption to the environment.

"3. Restraint—is defined as the removal of a patient from the therapeutic environment and the application of mechanical restraints in order to prevent behaviors that threaten harm to self or others. The behavior *must* actively create a serious threat of injury."

It is important not to be romantic about this. As we will learn, John's behavior can be extremely vexing and even scary. But one would suppose that it is precisely when his behavior is vexing that he would most benefit from a "therapeutic environment" (were there any content to that phrase), and not from being ejected from such. If the only "therapeutic" intervention is a show of greater force (the use of physical restraints, one way or another; or an assault of chemicals), it becomes difficult if not impossible to distinguish "treatment" from "punishment." Most important, perhaps, for that portion of the population that is suffering because they've been brutalized by parents, or surrogate parents (as in foster care), this "treatment" is no different from what they are used to.

It is my opinion that there is no *idea* here (certainly not one that is helpful). But even were one to argue that there is an idea buried somewhere in all this, an idea that might serve some refractory children, I doubt one could argue that same idea would serve the entire hodgepodge of "disorders." It's like suggesting that no matter what is medically wrong with you, you're going to get your leg set.

Concluding this document is a gesture of outright deception. It asks that the kid sign to "agree and authorize that the procedures described above may be administered to me (the patient). If a physician so directs, other clinical staff, consultants, and/or contractors of Rivendell may also be involved in these techniques." It goes on: "I certify that I have been read the above and that these techniques have been explained to me in language that I understand and that I have had the opportunity to discuss my concerns or have answered any questions I may have. I also acknowledge that there are no physical conditions/limitations that prevent my (the patient's) participation in the activities/treatments agreed to in this consent form."

Disregarding the interesting question of what physical conditions might prevent a kid's "participation" here, this all certainly sounds like "I" (the kid, the patient) am being asked to voluntarily enter into this contract, this agreement. Ha. "(If the patient is underage or has a guardian appointed by the court, this release must be signed by the patient's parent or guardian.)"

If the patient is underage? In a psychiatric hospital for children and adolescents?

Linda's distress at the idea of restraints seems real; her rush to defend their use is congruent with the necessity that one trust the institutions one is advised by professionals to turn to for help. She says, "They monitor them at all times. I felt that—there are times when it's necessary. If you have not lived with a child who is totally out of control, whom you can do nothing with . . .

"John was in restraints, once. I think that was the only time. And he, after that point, did much better. It was like it—got his attention. And they're very careful that the child is not—hurt. You understand, they have to be. Otherwise they'd have a lawsuit like *that*—even though we signed all those papers." Linda is rueful. "It isn't an ideal situation for anybody to be in. Nobody could hate it any worse.

"John, I think, can tell you: He had no intention of doing anything they told him to do. He had been in another program, where he got to call all the shots. Including not seeing us—whatever he wanted to do was it. But this whole thing was very structured. And he didn't like it a bit. Did you? *Un-unhhh.*"

John starts to say something.

Linda continues, "Let me tell a little background real quick."

John says quietly, "She doesn't have to know."

Linda says, "She doesn't know anything about you, okay?"

My coffee comes (and Linda's, and John's eggs). Hallelujah.

"First of all," Linda says when the room service person has left, "John is adopted. When he was nine years old. And I have found out quite a few things about his past that—I feel like a lot of his

problems are caused by this." The subject/object, John, has removed his attention from us to his eggs. Briefly, I flash that I am
serving a purpose here, this scene is serving a purpose, but the
coffee has not kicked in. "He was first abused at one month. He
remained in a very abusive situation, very neglected situation, until
he was twenty-one months old. He was in foster care for seven
years. Nine placements that they'll admit to. I was told verbally
there were twenty-three moves. That's not easy for any kid.

"At seven months they found him, and the parents had separated.
The mother was pregnant again. His mother had cerebral palsy and
was very handicapped. She really could not take care of him. Even
to pick him up. She had one good arm, and she would yank him by
one arm and plop him in her lap. There was no bonding, you know.
And at seven months he was found dehydrated beyond being able to
cry. Human tooth bites on his arms. And the social worker got a call
about him being there and she went to the hospital. But they put
him back in the home.

"This abuse and neglect continued and the parents signed the
papers for him to go into foster care. And that's just a little of what
I've found out. I've been more successful in Arkansas than in Oklahoma. Oklahoma's very secretive about what went on."

What must it be like to know this about your early life? And why
would one expect, as a result, anything other than someone troubled by it? Social norms, social expectations, are not predicated on
abusive childhoods. And yet recent estimates of abusive childhoods
for girls are as high as one in four for sexual abuse alone.* What this
means is that huge numbers of kids are being taken for deviant/
disordered simply for adapting and surviving as best as they can.

"John," I say, "what do you remember about your childhood?"

"Well, my mom kept marryin' people and divorcin' people. Every
time I went to visit her, a new guy was there. This one guy she
married, his name was Phil, and he beat us a lot. I remember one

---

* Indeed, in "Incest: A Chilling Report" (*Lear's*, February 1992, p. 52), Heidi
Vanderbilt, using statistics from Diana Russell's 1977 study, *The Secret Trauma:
Incest in the Lives of Girls and Women and Sexual Exploitation: Rape, Child Sexual
Abuse and Workplace Harassment*, estimates one in three.

time I got beat because I was tryin' to untie a knot in my shoe and I didn't. And he beat me for it. He'd told me to untie a knot in my shoe.

"But there were weird changes of places. We were goin' from place to place. Which was kind of sad because—you got fond of some people, where you'd stayed for a little while. And some places you wanted to leave real bad. So what I'd do is—I took something. Then they'd want me to leave. And so—it was kind of interestin' with all these different places. And it was kind of sad. Sad and interestin' at the same time. I have one sister. She went with me most of the time."

Linda: "Like he said, he was tryin' to get bounced. He worked real hard at gettin' bounced. He worked real hard at gettin' bounced from my place. And he's good at it. Real good at it. He knew how to get bounced. And his sister would have the choice to stay or go with him, and she always chose to go with him. She adjusted much better—Lanie got something John didn't get. Part of it is, she's not as shy as John. John always hung back, was more reticent. But Lanie would get in and get the attention.

"Now—she also would get the attention at John's gettin' in trouble, if necessary. She had a lot of inappropriate ways of gettin' attention. And we caught it real fast. I saw this happen: She would hit John—there happened to be a mirror and I saw her hit him— then she ran into where we were. Well, John was going to hit her back. There was no gettin' around it. We saw he was goin' to hit her back. But she'd learned where we would see only that John was hittin' her. As I say, I caught it real fast. But no tellin' how many times that wasn't caught in these various places.

"And Lanie did things like—lie down on the sidewalk and then start screamin' she fell. Anything for attention. Where this is not John's style. And I'm sure that a lot of times he just kind of got pushed to the background. And I understand that. And it had to be hard. And he is very into the control issue. He likes to control things."

So (I am thinking) does Linda. (And so do we all; and so, most emphatically, do the professionals in the psy sector. And why would a kid whose entire childhood was out of control *not* want to achieve some control?)

John, then, is part of that population of children whom early severe and repeated abuse and disruptive, apparently random shifting around has traumatized. Is this a mental "illness"? He did not, after all, *imagine* that life could not be trusted to be benign.

If someone gets punched in the stomach, pain and bruising may occur. Does this suggest that the stomach was defective to begin with? But it is not John's *feelings* that have brought him into the psy world. It is his *behavior*. And that, in itself, tells us that what we have here is a social judgment (and one made in a contextual vacuum, at that). ". . . [A]nti-social behavior is the precipitating factor that leads to mental treatment. But at the same time the fact of the illness is itself inferred from this behavior; indeed it is almost true to say that the illness is the behavior for which it is also the excuse. But any disease, the morbidity of which is established only by the social failure that it involves, must rank as fundamentally different from those with which the symptoms are independent of social norms."[1]

"John," I say. "You remember thinking that coming to Linda's was 'just another placement'? Or . . . ?"

John says, "I was told people wanted to adopt me. Relatives."

Linda interrupts (again). "He'd been told a *lot* of people wanted to adopt him. But he didn't believe it. Coming home, he was whining and crying and not wanting to do what we said to do. We just thought the kids were frightened. I mean—we were a little frightened, too.

"See, John's birth dad was my husband's nephew. Okay? When the kids left Arkansas in 1978 and went into foster care, we had asked about what we could do. And we were told they were going to Oklahoma to be adopted. The next year we were told they had in fact been adopted. Turned out not to be true." Eventually, however, through whatever tortuous winding of events within Arkansas Human Services, the system found there were relatives, Linda and her husband, and contacted them.

"And my husband and I talked about—you know, we were pushing fifty. But—it was something we wanted to do. Because—they were ours. We have love in our hearts, my husband and I, it comes very naturally. And we just told them that we would take the kids until they could terminate the mother's rights. With the understanding we would be able to adopt them.

"But John, from the time he came home, was wantin' to leave. Looking for la-la land—where you never have to mind. There's no authority over you. Where he doesn't have to go to school, he doesn't have to mind any rules. He's getting much better now, though." This last in that slightly louder tone that signals she is talking *to* as much as *about* John. "He has learned to control himself when these things are necessary."

It's annoying, this talking both to and about John. And some readers may by now be well on the way to identifying Linda's shortcomings. To focus on that, however, is to assume there is, for John—somewhere out there—an ideal family circumstance; one that he would embrace and then all would be magically well. It is to forget that, absent Linda and her husband, John and his sister would undoubtedly still be drifting around somewhere, lost in Oklahoma's (or Arkansas') child welfare melee; with John, at least, almost predictably winding up in some long-term residential treatment facility, with no one paying attention. No, Linda cannot reasonably be held accountable for John's hurts—by us, that is; the psy system can and does do as it pleases.

She continues: "We knew immediately that we had our hands full, and we hooked into therapy—right away. Not only for their sake, but for our sake. 'Cause it felt like there should be some things we could do to help them adjust.

"Frankly, I was very disappointed in the first two places we went to. There was a lot of: 'If you only loved him enough.' A lot of blaming, guilt—that we weren't doing enough. And—I didn't know what an unbonded child was. I really expected the kids to—um—be grateful. And I realize now-w-w that that was un*reas*onable. But at the *ti*-ime—after all, hindsight's wonderful. I thought they would be really glad to have these folks that wanted to take care of them, help them grow up. Go to college. And that they would understand that we really loved them. And"—she laughs—"John wasn't at all grateful."

Naive? Of course. (Had she known what she was in for, would she have gone forward? Would John and his sister be any better off?)

"What were you going through, John?" I ask.

He says, "I wanted to be someplace where I could sleep when I wanted to, eat when I wanted to. I was thinkin' I'd like to get out of there and go back to the shelter. 'Cause there I did whatever I wanted to do."

"The shelter?"

"In Oklahoma," Linda says. "It's a lockup facility where we picked him up. They were only supposed to have them for two or three weeks between placements. But they were real nice—they let John and Lanie stay there from March until September because they'd been in all the foster homes, and they had no place to put them."

"Nice people," John says.

"He didn't have to go to school," Linda says.

"We went to school. They had a school there," John says.

"A couple of hours a day," Linda says. "Not actual school, either. They were very educationally regressed, very. Lanie was going to first grade for the third time. John had been passed, but he couldn't count to a hundred."

John says, "I couldn't count to *two* hundred—because when I got to a hundred . . . Because—you know how it goes twenty-nine, thirty? It was a hundred, and when it got to a hundred and nine, I thought it went to two hundred."

Think about it. There's a certain logic to that.

≈

"We build the mind and heart, as well as the body, during the early years of a child's life," Linda has written to me. "And very often we channel the course of the mentality of the young toward failure when they are not given the love and care each child deserves. John is such a child. I don't know that he was ever given what he needed. I don't know if we have done enough. It hasn't been easy for us. But we do love him, and we don't want to give up on him. We want him to have every opportunity to be 'well.' We didn't realize what a serious problem we had on our hands."

For a while, John got by in school because—for a while—he was quiet and caused no problems. At home, heeding the therapists, Linda tried the behavior mod arsenal: positive reinforcement, point systems, selectivity about what to fight over.

"I read every book I could find or was recommended to me on parenting," Linda has written. "I just knew I had to find some answers. I read a few books on adopting older children (the ones I read all had happy endings). I was finding no answers on my own, either." But she was learning to speak psy. "I read a book called *The 60-Second Scolding* and realized I had been 'talking through the point,' and have tried to do better.

"I had set an unrealistic goal of two years and everything would be okay, and two years had come and gone, and it wasn't okay. I decided to change our therapist. The director of Children and Family Services recommended someone, said he was very good with children from the foster care system, and oppositional. Again, he said we were doing all the right things, and John might never be any better. After about a year, he suggested we might want to put John in boarding school to give the family respite and it *might* help John.

"I could not see how it would help John to be moved again. That seemed to be John's goal. He repeatedly stated he wanted to leave. In fact, after doing some things he knew would be especially upsetting to us, he would ask if he could live somewhere else, or were we going to send him somewhere else. When asked where he wanted to live, he would say anywhere but here. . . .

"The therapist suggested spanking. His idea was that abused children often did not understand anything else. Not being spankers, this was difficult, but we were without hope or other ideas. Spanking Lanie caused her to scream and seem almost hysterical. John, it did not faze, and one night I was going to spank him and I realized if I hit him I would not be in control: that I wanted to hurt him. I was physically ill when I realized this, and felt our whole family system had become dysfunctional.

"John's fifth grade teacher had worked with emotionally disturbed children before coming to our school. She told me that he was severely emotionally disturbed, the first time those words had been used by anyone."

By now, John was waging what looked to Linda like all-out war. In class he talked back, sometimes threw things when being disciplined, stole, lied, tore up things (things in the teacher's closet, one of the swings . . .), refused to do schoolwork, or to read. But he drew. What he drew were violent pictures. Even his teacher backed off.

"John would talk about killing people, and began talking about how wonderful Hitler was, and how he wanted to be like him; talked about becoming a paid assassin, being a marine and 'getting' to kill people.

"John was very insistent that he did things because he hated me. He threatened his sister more and more when he began seeing her attach to us, and he threatened our grandson many times. It was explained to me he didn't really hate me. I was just safe to hate; that he hated his birth mother and her abandonment."

The school counselor talked with John. He told Linda that John was "not bonded," had no trust in anyone; that he had serious oppositional behavior. All of this, of course, Linda could tell for herself (but now it seemed official). Just for good measure, the psychologist threw in "borderline personality" and "possibly manic-depressive." The psychologist suggested that John go to the Boys' Ranch, which, Linda writes, "took boys with no other homes, boys who couldn't stay home because of their behavior."

Now, in my hotel room, Linda says, "The straw that broke the camel's back was—he and Lanie ran away. They did call me at work to tell me they were gonna run away. What I said was, 'Wait till I get home and we can talk about this.' He told Lanie that I didn't care. He told me that he hated me. The kids wrote me a note and John signed it with his preadoption name. I guess they thought they were gonna go down to our cabin at the river, right?" Linda turns to John, who, eggs long finished, has been sitting quietly.

John says, "No."

"Where'd you think you were going?" Linda asks.

"Downtown."

"Downtown?" Linda shakes her head. "Undoubtedly they got lost. They were found not more than two blocks from home. And Lanie says, 'I want to go home.' That made John very angry. And he took off on his bike. And he was found on one of our busiest roads, terrible traffic, riding against the traffic. My husband found him."

And so John was sent to his first placement, Boys' Ranch.

While he was there his biological mother died.

"Now," Linda says, "the Ranch felt like—that caused a lot of depression and all. But he'd always been depressed. But I'm sure it didn't help any. I called the caseworker and asked did John want to go to the funeral. What she told me was that John said he really didn't know her that well and he had no desire to go."

John says, "I said, 'No.' That's what I said."

"You didn't say why?" Linda asks. "She just made that up?"

"I didn't say why."

"So she made that part up. Anyhow, things got worse. And at the end of September they called and told me that John wasn't doing well at school, and that they wanted to put him in therapy. That he was talking a lot about death. Which they did—put him in therapy. And they put him on an antidepressant."

Things continued to worsen. Linda asked for a staff meeting and went up to talk with them. "I said, 'John's now failed the sixth grade. He's two years behind in school. He is not following your rules. He's been in therapy and he's been on a high dose of this medicine. And he is not doin' any better. I'm not at all sure you're what he needs. I don't know. So—help me.' Well, the director did a lot of 'rescuing.' In front of John, how it was all the teacher's fault. Making excuses for John. And tellin' me what-all they thought they could do.

"I suggested they change therapists. Because the very first thing I ever heard from that one was how everything was my fault. Because John felt like I had abandoned him."

What we are looking at here, it seems to me, is a mess in reality, one caused by real events. There is no question that John needs some kind of effective befriending; some repair work, if you will. The current emphasis in the psy sector is heavily weighted toward presumption of neurological or genetic deficit. Yet it is unclear to me what might possibly be served by referencing John's innate biochemistry. (You can break a watch by jumping up and down on it; only an enraged/guilty two-year-old will claim it was the watch's fault in the first place.) There is also no question that Linda is not taking well to being blamed. Should she be? (And who gets to authoritatively use the should-word?)

John went with the family for a visit at their cabin, and—"There was a lot of threatenin' being done. A lot of oppositional behavior. John's always had a lot of trouble sleepin'. Couldn't fall asleep, would cry for hours when he first came. But we did take him back to the Ranch and were hopeful."

Soon after that the Ranch called Linda to say they couldn't keep him anymore unless he got some intensive evaluation. They didn't know what to do with him.

He went for a six-week evaluation at Turning Point at Children's Hospital, where, Linda said, "John did exactly what he wanted to do when he wanted to do it. He didn't want to see us, he didn't *have* to see us."

John says, "All I really had to do was set goals, do my goals, and take my medicine."

"What kind of goals, John?" I ask.

"Like—they have—you have to make your own goals. Say you were gonna make one on why you didn't like your parents. Then during the day you had to find some kind of free time to write that down, prepare that, to write down that reason. And you'd have to do that and then at nightly meeting you'd have to read that out loud."

"Did it make any difference, John? Did you find it helpful?"

"No."

"He'd tell them what they wanted to hear," Linda says. "And he can do that. I mean he *still* does this. I'll give you a real good example. Two days before Easter and the week after Easter have been our hardest time since John came back home. So we went to his therapist the fourth of April, and I said, 'John, I think you need to talk to the doctor about what's gone on with you this week.' And I said to the doctor, 'This was not a good week. . . .' "

As Linda goes on I am thinking: John would seem to be entirely a socially created result. It does not require science to inform us that infants require infant care and children require child care. The question raised is this: When the state intervenes and takes children into custody (as it did with John and Lanie), does it not then have an implicit obligation to provide for them the kind of stable care the parent they have been removed from was not (they assert) providing? And does it (should it) not then have a liability/obligation to repair at its own cost whatever damage it does? (I guess I am asking: Is there no warranty here?) Twenty-three moves may be, in John's words, interestin' (and sad; kind of sad and interestin'). But they can only exacerbate, not resolve, the kind of normal original rage the smaller John would have felt: The "help" can only do damage.

Linda barrels on: "He went into the therapist's office and he manipulated the doctor completely. He went in and started talking about my grandson, Kevin. He did not talk about any of his feelings. He made a big thing about Kevin."

"I *did?*" says John.

"And even when I pointed it out to the doctor that he was being manipulated, it seemed to upset the doctor that I said it. John probably does not even remember what he said that week. I probably remember better than he does, because I've been keepin' little notes, et cetera—not that I have a wonderful memory—he's so bright— I'll tell you, he'll tell them what they want to hear. . . .

"I will say this—that I haven't been there. I don't really know. John knows. He has been in there. I look from the outside. That's not the same as living there. But I will say this: Because Turning Point did no good, he went back to the Ranch and became even worse. Okay? I mean the Ranch called me again and they wanted him out of there. They got him an emergency hearing, and he went to Rivendell. And then Rivendell recommended longer treatment. And he went to another facility. Which is where he came home from this past November. Not because they thought he was ready to come home, but because there was no money."

Although Linda's insurance had kicked in once the adoption was formalized, John's stay at Rivendell had exhausted the coverage. And John's threats of violence to the family, his sexual aggression against his sister, made the idea that he could simply go home untenable. And so there had begun that frantic scramble for some funded alternative to which so many families testify. Medicaid finally covered his stay at Shadow Mountain, but it was not inexhaustible. Although Shadow Mountain felt he would need a stay of twelve to eighteen months, after 137 days Medicaid denied further funds.

Kids like John—kids who have been vastly and profoundly wounded both before and after state intervention—constitute a discrete knotty portion of the kids who fall under the domain of the psy sector: kids for whom something must be done; kids whom, in many ways, society *owes* restitution. (Or, to put it in a more politic manner, kids whom it is in society's best interest to assist.) Just because both Mike and John have been removed from parents by the state does not mean that they are similar—yet both have been in psychiatric hospitals and thus both, as a matter of record, are classified as "emotionally disturbed," and both contribute equally to the alarmism about the alleged epidemic of psychiatrically needy kids.

They are not at all the same, nor were they in the same places (nor, even, in the same part of the country)—and yet the "treatment" that was given them was cookie-cutter: coercive conformity. Kids like Delia are not even in John's neighborhood, or in Mike's. And yet the "treatment" she received was—again—coercive conformity. To put a kid like Delia in eight-hour isolation for accepting a cigarette from a friend is bizarre and outrageous. To put a kid like John (who Linda has told me was routinely locked under the porch in one foster home) in isolation seems vicious.

To describe John in terms of his "emotional disturbance," in terms of "psychiatric diagnoses," is to suggest that John's rage, his volatility, are somehow perverse, "sick." It's to suggest that a "healthy" child similarly treated would not suffer as John does, or behave as John does. In fact, given the severe abuse he was subjected to virtually from birth, it would make at least as much sense to suggest the somewhat more frightening idea that, given what happened to him, John is perfectly normal; to dignify his real experience, and to put some of the bucks that are currently wild-goose-chasing ever more fantastical disorders in the far more fortunate kids into a system of reparations for kids like John.

When John left this last facility, Social Services offered to place him in a therapeutic foster home. Recounting that, Linda sighs in frustration. "Now the kid's already changed houseparents six times since he went to the Ranch, changed houses once, has been in and out of three placements—therapeutic, psychiatric placements. Now you're gonna put him in a therapeutic foster home? These people don't know him. If nothing else, I know him. Okay?"

"There was fear bringing him home. He had threatened to do

bodily harm to all of us. Lanie was very frightened of his coming home—he threatened her. But he said something he never said before." Linda looks over at John and smiles fondly. "He said, 'I *want* to come home.'

"And I had to go for it. I made it pretty straight out that this was his last chance—our last chance and his last chance. We wanted to make it work and he said he wanted to make it work. That's what you go with. *But*. If it hadn't been for those facilities, would he have ever said, 'I want to come home'? I don't know if it's the medicine that's made him realize that some of these things he does are destructive to himself as well as relationships. Or if he has learned that through therapy."

Nor do I, of course. All I feel sure of as Linda and John stand to leave is that it is kids like John that a credible psychiatry would be talking about helping.

If it knew how.

6

The Disciples of Dr. Bisch

THE CRUCIBLE OF THE PSY world is *diagnosis*. On diagnosis rests the claim that treatment be reimbursed as a medical procedure. Indeed, on diagnosis depends psychiatry's authority, its assertion that it is in fact a medical specialty, a science. The naming of the diseases (disorders) stakes the claim of expertise, and the right of intervention.

This naming itself has a name. Nosology. To the uninitiated ear it may sound like the study of proboscises. What it means, in fact, is the classification of diseases. A disease (my dictionary tells me) is any departure from health. (Health is, in effect, any departure from disease: "physical and mental well-being; soundness; freedom from defect, pain, or disease . . .")

Disease is, for one thing, "a particularly destructive process in an organism, with a specific cause and characteristic symptoms." But it is also "an evil or destructive tendency or state of affairs: as, 'bigotry is a *disease* of society.'" In other words, disease can be a specific material occurrence—or it can be a metaphor.

In terms of physical diseases, this ambiguity is fairly clear. We can speak of something being a cancer on the body politic, and few will be so literal minded as to suppose the next step involves actual

131

surgery on all citizens, or mass ingestion of chemicals. In terms of psychiatry, the ambiguity is almost entirely unclear. When you call someone sick, crazy, bonkers, weird, nuts—are you saying something literal? When a newspaper described former President George Bush as "hyperactive," was that literal? Whatever validity there may be to the concept of psychiatric illness, naming, in the psy world, has always been an expression of social opinion. "Giving the name has been the starting point for social labelers. The power to give the name has been a core element in the social control nature of mental health professionals and institutions."[1]

The *Diagnostic and Statistical Manual*[2] is, for psychiatry, the Book of Naming, the Book of Judgment. It is taken for doctrine, but can it be that it really is dogma? That the DSM, which when first published in 1952 listed sixty types and subtypes of mental illness, by 1980 contained more than two hundred, finally in 1987 including even tobacco dependence, along with school learning problems, adolescent rebellion disorders, and sexual dysfunctions,[3] certainly suggests that what is being named here are not so much diseases as social judgments made in congruence with shifting public moral postures.

Reading about the evolution of the DSM, to its third *revised* power, is somewhat like reading the history of the Balkans: ongoing border wars, eruptions, skirmishes, the odd assassination, uprising, overthrow . . . From between the lines of this Manual, which proudly trumpets itself as being atheoretical, ooze the passions of professional combat and bloodshed. Battles fought, blood spilled, over—theory.

To read about the evolution of the DSM is to know this: It is an entirely *political* document. What it includes, what it does not include, are the result of intensive campaigning, lengthy negotiating, infighting, and power plays. Psychiatric *physicians*, passionately committed to locating underlying causality in biological, genetic, or neurological deficits, warred with Freudian acolytes; both fought invasions of psychological clinicians: Those whose worldview was determinist/behavioral peered armed through tall grasses, on the lookout for sneak attacks by those whose worldview was sociopsychological.

Put more mildly, "Diagnosis is often the location in the psychiatric world where both lay and professional critics fight over the roles and functions of diagnosis. These struggles are ample proof that scientific discoveries are not the result of an ongoing 'march of science' as much as of political battles."[4]

Up until the 1980s the DSM had been dominated by the analytic movement: by 1980, the antipsychoanalytics—the bios and neuros—had mobilized to stage an "atheoretical" putsch.

Then, artillery was aimed straight at the psychoanalytic heart: at *neurosis!* By the time DSM-III appeared, neurosis, the concept, lay slain in the field. Neurosis, which had been the word that explained, that identified, that accounted for; neurosis, with its explanatory rationale ("etiology") set securely in apparently factual complexes and drives—how could it be that it was simply done away with? Declared not only dead, but dead wrong?

How could that which millions of Americans had embraced in themselves as being *there*, and spent millions of hours grappling with, wrestling with, struggling to tame, and sometimes—finally—declaring conquered thanks to psy intervention, suddenly be said never to have been there in the first place?

The ostensible goal in advancing beyond DSM-II had been to develop an empirically grounded manual that would be theoretically neutral and thus, as a reference work, a peace treaty. Instead, what the task force at work on the manual had on its hands was a professional riot.

As one insider, Theodore Millon, wrote: "[T]he exclusiveness of the analytic interpretive model could no longer be sustained in light of equally plausible explanatory and empirically demonstrable alternatives: for example, a 'snake phobia' may stem from repressed conflicts in which residual anxieties are symbolically displaced; it may also reflect directly conditioned or generalized avoidant learning; also possible are constitutionally low biological thresholds for a highly prevalent 'instinctive' response."[5]

Armies massed on both sides of this conceptual Maginot Line. Millon writes: "[T]o avoid what was anticipated to be a brutal and potentially destructive confrontation, the task force proposed that the issue be cleverly finessed by separating the concept 'neurotic disorder' from that of 'neurotic process.' Neurotic 'disorder' signifying mere descriptive properties, could then be introduced as a formal DSM-III designation without necessarily connoting the operation of a neurotic 'process,' that is, a sequence in which intrapsychic conflicts are resolved unconsciously via various defense mechanisms, as well as being expressed symbolically in symptomatic form."[6]

But the finesse was no go. As one of the scores of memos that poured forth impatiently put it, "To respond to this sort of unscientific and illogical, but psychologically understandable pressure [to reinstate neurosis] . . . is unworthy of scientists who are attempting to advance our field via clarification and reliable definition."

All I can say is—ask anybody who sought psy assistance in the fifties, the sixties, the early seventies: They were told with no uncertainty that neurosis *was* clear, that it was a reliable definition (and if they didn't *believe* it, well, that sort of denial was what they were in the psychiatrist's office to deal with).

A second pandemonium episode was triggered when, in a May 1975 task force meeting, someone suggested that maybe it would be good if the forthcoming DSM included a definition of the term *mental disorder*. There is nothing in the record to indicate that this suggestion was anything more than someone doodling out loud; nothing to suggest that it was intended as a guerrilla tactic deliberately calculated to set off the ensuing explosions. In fact, at the time it must have seemed a remarkably good idea. A definition. Hmm.

Everyone was sent home with the assignment to draft a proposed definition. As it turned out, only one member was able to actually attempt a definition, and it apparently wound up winding back and around itself, ending up in the neighborhood of the laboriously loquacious and abstruse.

The task force chair, Robert Spitzer, was then faced with a dilemma. Everyone had agreed that *mental disorder* should be defined. The alternatives seemed to be to accept the one attempt that was handed in, or to concede it had been an impossible assignment in the first place, or—to bite the bullet and cobble one together yourself. With another task force appointee, Spitzer gave it a go. Included in their proposed definition was the apparently simple statement (surely in keeping with the goal of receiving medical insurance reimbursement) that "mental disorders are a subset of medical disorders."

Oops.

As word of this pro-bio heresy got out, the uproar was immense: The bio-neuro-psy camel once again had its nose in the nosological tent. A former president of the American Psychological Association wrote that "to attribute marital conflict or delinquency . . . to a biological defect, to biochemical, nutritional, neurological, or other organic conditions . . . is to sell our psychological birthright for short-term gain."[7]

Psychological *birthright*?

An amended statement was approved by the task force in April 1979. However, that was editorially modified, without task force approval, to say, in effect, that although there was no definition of mental disorders, here is how we think about what we think about when we think whether something is or is not one of them, more or less:

"No precise definition is available that unambiguously defines the boundaries of this concept. (This is also true of such concepts as physical disorders or mental or physical health.) However, in the DSM-III each of the mental disorders is conceptualized as a clinically significant behavioral or psychological syndrome or pattern of an individual that is associated, by and large, with either a painful symptom (distress) or impairment in one or more important areas of functioning (disability)."

DSM-III, and subsequently DSM-III-R, was then hoisted to the shoulders of the psy parade and acclaimed for, among other things, its pioneering role in—for the first time!—defining mental disorders.

No longer could it be claimed that psychiatry was an "unidentified technique applied to unspecified problems with unpredictable outcomes . . . for which long and vigorous training is required!"[8]

Or could it?

Even as the psy authorities continued to assert that the definition of mental disorders actually defined what we were talking about, the literature continued to reflect confusion and dissent. A committee appointed by the Institute of Medicine at the request of the director of the National Institute of Mental Health (NIMH) published its *Research on Children and Adolescents with Mental, Behavioral and Developmental Disorders* in 1990. Here the committee says, "No term is wholly adequate to convey the range of psychopathology. The term 'disorders' has achieved acceptance, as a broad rubric without theoretical implications about etiology. The term 'illness' may convey an implication that the troubles being discussed are like medical diseases or have a clearly established biological basis. 'Diseases' conveys a specificity and pathological implication which is inappropriate for most childhood mental disorders. Terms such as 'conditions' or 'problems' appear frequently in the report and are usually synonymous with disorder or syndrome.

"The term 'mental' is not quite right, either, since it seems to split the child into 'mind' and 'body.' In some circles 'mental' is derogatory, and there are advocacy groups, such as the parents of autistic children or those with Tourette's disorder, who feel that having these disorders classified as 'mental disorders' has an etiological implication which slights their biological foundations. The triad 'mental, behavioral, and developmental disorders' conveys the spectrum, but it may also mistakenly imply that there are conceptually clear distinctions among these categories. There are also semantic concerns about whether the field of inquiry should be called 'mental health' (as in the National Institute of Mental Health) or 'mental illness/disorder' (for which individuals come to treatment)."[9]

Just as I occasionally found myself diverted from the overall ethical and moral issues and drawn instead into the private psychiatric hospitals' business and marketing problems, so—as I probed, poked, explored the DSM—I found it possible to admire the pluck of those who had set out in a rowboat to make a definitive chart of dark waters that they could not actually see and on the wetness of which not all of their colleagues agreed, nor even on the nature of the body (pond? lake? bathtub?).

Another much-touted feature of DSM-III was its alleged high rate of what it termed "inter-rater reliability." Meaning "the extent of agreement between two judges."[10] In fact, to begin with, inter-rater reliability was not particularly high. What was needed was training, a way of drilling psy practitioners to make sure they were behaviorally programmed to respond to certain cues with the same response. Mirowsky writes: "It is only necessary to get the judges to consider the same information and follow the same decision rules. The pieces of information do not have to be related, and the rules do not have to reflect anything more than the ability and willingness of the judges to use them. Take the medieval diagnosis of witchcraft as an example. Several highly respected inquisitors agree that witches may be known by three or more of the following signs: talking to animals, foul breath, avoiding churches and men of the cloth, walking on moonlit nights, and dancing alone. To validate the diagnostic category and criteria, we only need show that any pair of trained inquisitors using these signs and the three-or-more rule will agree on who is or is not a witch more frequently than expected by chance. The more the inquisitors follow these guidelines, the more they will find themselves in agreement, which will bolster professional use of the diagnostic system and public confidence in the professional determination."[11]

Some of the early attempts to explain DSM-III in language that would ensure everyone had the same understanding fell prey to what I would diagnose as the Bisch Disorder.* Louis E. Bisch, M.D., Ph.D., was a professor of neuropsychiatry at the New York Polyclinic Medical School and Hospital and an associate in educational psychology at Columbia University. In the 1930s he wrote a book, *Be Glad You're Neurotic*. This work may have lost currency with the vaporization of *neurotic*, but Bisch's place as a historical footnote was nonetheless assured by the writings of James Thurber.[12]

Indeed, Dr. Bisch (as memorialized by Thurber) expressed in the 1930s the very difficulties of contemporary diagnosis—of conflicting interpretations—by portraying this hypothetical case:

---

* There are eight possible criteria to look for in diagnosing this disorder. The primary indicator is: Attempts to be deadly serious invariably result in unintended comedy.

Three men "start across a street on a red light and get in the way of an oncoming automobile. A dodges successfully; B stands still, 'accepting the situation with calm and resignation,' thus [Thurber writes] becoming one of my favorite heroes in modern belles lettres; and C hesitates, wavers, jumps backward and forward, and finally runs head on into the car."[13]

As Thurber tells us, Dr. Bisch then recounts what the McDougallians* would say ("Instinct!"), what the Freudians would say ("Complexes!"), and the behaviorists ("Conditioned reflexes!").

Since, even back then, there were the neuroscientists to consider, Bisch also "brings in what the physiologists would say— deficient thyroid, hypoadrenal functioning, and so on."[14] As Thurber tells us, "The average sedentary man of our time who is at all suggestible must emerge from this chapter believing that his chances of surviving a combination of instinct, complexes, reflexes, glands, sex, and present-day traffic conditions are about equal to those of a one-legged blind man trying to get out of a labyrinth."[15]

Dr. Bisch's partiality evidently lies with the Freudians. About their take on poor Mr. C, who ran headlong into the car, Bisch writes, " 'Sex hunger,' the Freudians would declare. 'Always keyed up and irritable because of it. Undoubtedly suffers from insomnia and when he does sleep his dream life must be productive, distorted, and possibly frightening. Automobile unquestionably has sex significance for him . . . to C the car is both enticing and menacing at one and the same time. . . . A thorough analysis is indicated . . . it might take months. But then, the man needs an analysis as much as food. He is heading for a complete nervous collapse.' " As Thurber sensibly remarks, "It is my studied opinion, not to put too fine a point on it, that Mr. C is heading for a good mangling, and that if he gets away with only a nervous collapse, it will be a miracle."[16]

Bisch states, "An automobile bearing down upon you may be a sex symbol at that, you know, especially if you dream it." To which

---

* I have no idea who they are, which just goes to show the ephemeral nature of psychiatric certainties.

Thurber lends his contention that "even if you dream it, it is probably not a sex symbol, but merely an automobile bearing down upon you. And if it bears down upon you in real life, I am sure it is an automobile."[17]

Perhaps inevitably, elucidation of psy language leads professionals to the invocation of anecdotes (case histories), and they run the risk of showing symptoms of the Bisch Disorder. This happened to the author of a 1982 book, *The New Language of Psychiatry: Learning and Using DSM-III*.[18] The author refers to symptoms as "cardinal manifestations" (which puts me in mind of Margaret Rutherford as the medium in *Blithe Spirit*). "Vandalism, theft, juvenile delinquency, running away from home, unusually early or exceptionally frequent casual sexual relationships and recurrent physical fighting are cardinal manifestations of mental disorders."[19] Moving on, he says that yet another cardinal manifestation of a mental disorder would be a degree of personal hygiene that is not up to that of the prevailing social group's norm.[20] Other cardinal manifestations that he brings to our attention include coldness, aloofness, a lack of warmth or an inability to express tender and warm emotions.[21] Even: "a lack of a true sense of humor is another manifestation."[22]

Either the author suffers profoundly from this last-mentioned manifestation, or he suffers from a phobia that has made him assiduously avoid any information connected with the concept of sexism. He offers the following case illustration:

"A thirty-year-old woman whose dutiful husband left her two weeks ago because she has always been jealous and suspicious and hounded him constantly about his whereabouts is brought into the emergency room after trying to cut one of her wrists with a dull pen knife. She inflicted a laceration on the left. She is drunk after drinking a half bottle of scotch and the examining psychiatrist believes that her state of mind before and while intoxicated with alcohol is related to the specific life stress of being left by her husband."[23]

Now we are told that before DSM-III this woman's diagnosis might have been nothing weightier than simple adjustment reaction and alcohol intoxication."[24] Which might seem to the ordinary person like enough considering what she'd been through (dutiful husband my fat fanny).

However, "In DSM-III she would be said to have an adjustment disorder, codable on Axis I, paranoid personality traits codable on Axis II, alcohol intoxication coded on Axis I and a lacerated wrist coded on Axis III." And that ain't all. "Because so much of what happened to this woman is related to being left by her husband, specifying that life stress on Axis IV would help the other health professionals who look at this diagnosis to understand what the psychiatrist meant when he listed Adjustment Disorder in her diagnosis."[25]*

At the risk of seeming naive, I ask: Wouldn't it be simpler just to write down "left by husband; got drunk"? (Or better yet, skip the writing down, commiserate with her about the bastard, and send her home for a good night's sleep?)

To be fair, on the copyright page of Levy's book is a note telling us the book was not written or endorsed by the American Psychiatric Association. Rather, there appeared an APA-endorsed training guide[26] and an APA-published casebook.[27]

In the *DSM-III-R Training Guide*, the authors may have intuited a potential Thurber among their readers: They say, in effect, to anyone who might snicker or giggle that *it is not funny*. And if you think it is, that's only because you are unqualified to read it in the first place:

"Unsophisticated readers of DSM-III-R commonly misunderstand it to be a 'cookbook' of psychiatric diagnosis. While its format promotes the misconception, and even some pseudoclinical 'computer diagnosis' programs use it to sales advantage, it is not intended for such use. . . . Similarly, DSM-III-R has been called a 'phenomenological' manual [actually, we are going to be lucky if it is any kind of logical] but careful reading of the criteria and accom-

---

* If the reader is perplexed by all this "Axis" business, that is as it must be. Although we will learn more of *what* it is shortly, *why* it is, I fear, will remain blurry. All the author of *The New Language of Psychiatry* can tell us is that "[a]n important change that came with DSM-III is that a patient's psychiatric diagnosis will *look different*."

panying chapters discloses encouragement of a comprehensive clinical approach to evaluation and diagnosis."[28]

And this further disclaimer:

"Anyone using DSM-III-R to carry out clinical, statistical, research, legal, or reimbursement purposes related to accurate diagnosis should first be fully trained in the clinical fields relevant to each of the five axes. This implies a biopsychosocial foundation for assessing the medical, emotional and social characteristics of the patient; interviewing skills; and expertise at obtaining and interpreting information about the patient from other sources (e.g., family interviews, medical history, physical examination, specialty consultation, psychological testing, laboratory procedures). It further suggests, with no prejudice intended, that individuals with incomplete biopsychosocial background or training may be inherently limited in their use of this diagnostic system."[29] Here, then, is the classic psy assertion of not only dominance but exclusive and certain knowledge about human *being*: Only the initiates can know what the gospel means. To challenge its meaning is, in their eyes, to challenge the profession's anointment. It is also proof that you don't know what you're talking about.

As the axes suggest, the DSM is set up like an unusually complex Chinese menu: one from Column A, one from Column B; also, one from Columns C, D, E.

"Column A" (Axis I) and "Column B" (Axis II) are meant to record mental disorders (or even not-mental disorders—known as V codes—that are nonetheless "suitable for treatment"). These are the top limbs on what is called the "diagnostic tree."

Axis III is where the clinician lists all the patient's medical/physical disorders or conditions.

What you wind up with so far looks like this:

Axis I:	295.35	Schizophrenia Paranoid Type
	305.0	Alcohol Abuse
Axis II:	301.20	Schizoid Personality Disorder (premorbid)
Axis III:		Liver cirrhossis [30]

So far, all one seems to need to get along in this diagnostic world is either a willingness to believe in the meaning of the named disorders, or a will to belong sufficient to suspend disbelief. It is with Axis IV, however, that it strikes me the authors begin to fight heavy headwinds. Axis IV is an attempt to codify "social stressors." It is used to describe how much environmental stress the patient is under in terms of how much stress an average person would be under in the same situation.

Social stressors are things I personally happen to feel familiar with. Without meaning to be argumentative (and no prejudice intended), I don't think anybody really requires clinical training to know the proverbial automobile bearing down when she sees it. Nor do the authors, actually. What they arrogate the need for expertise to is the Severity of Psychosocial Stressor Scales (1-None, 2-Mild, 3-Moderate, 4-Severe, 5-Extreme, 6-Catastrophic).

Here, they tell us, "The evaluator must remember certain guidelines prior to rating the severity of psychosocial stressors. First, rate according to how an 'average' individual, with similar sociocultural values, would react to a particular stress."[31] Now, imagining oneself into another person's culturally average values—the capacity for empathy—is not something that has come up in the DSM literature before. Including it is an oblique way of accommodating those critics who have long argued that psychiatry is imposing middle-class standards on poor and minority groups.

The authors, however, bend over backwards to avoid consideration of that particular class scenario. In doing so, I am not sure the example they do use helps them out: "For example," they write, "a 25-year-old distraught man presents for evaluation. The primary stressor is a reduction in this individual's spending allowance from $1,000 per week to $500 per week. For the 'average' individual, having $500 per week for miscellaneous expenses would not be stressful; therefore, in spite of the strong reaction of the individual, the degree of stress rating on Axis IV would be none."[32]

This strikes me as just as arrogant and insular as would be a judgment pronounced on a ghetto kid. I do not think the authors have quite got the hang of the "average" individual in whose sociocultural circumstance it is customary to receive a thousand dollars a week for odds and ends and who suddenly finds that cut in half. Rather, they seem to be speaking from the viewpoint of the "average" psychiatrist-parent, still sore from years of allowance wars, who doesn't think a twenty-five-year-old should be getting any sort of allowance at all. There's some basic disapproving lip pursing going on when they say, "in spite of the strong reaction of the individual." The judgment strikes me as understandable (and one many of us outside the "average" of the sociocultural ambience in question might share), but it shows them blind to what the young man who has just walked into the psychiatrist's office probably expects, considering he feels sufficiently stressed out by the event to want to pay the psychiatrist $150—nearly a third of his slashed weekly take—just to get it off his chest.

What he probably does not expect is to be told that he's lucky to get half. (That may well be just what his parents said.) From the standpoint of what is practical for the "average" psy practitioner, it seems bullheaded as well. The young man will no doubt quit the office on the spot, take his $150, and go out and join the woman whose devoted husband left her high and dry. (From the young man's standpoint, of course, it may be just as well he got out of the psychiatrist's office before further misunderstandings occurred.)

There's a lot of muzziness here, some clear reverse class bias (3-Moderate), and a lot more left unexplained. Granted, this young man's story is a tiny part of the diagnostic whole, but it reveals exactly the pervasive social biases it purports to deny exist in the "objective gaze."

It further illustrates that inter-rater reliability simply depends on those entering the psy world sharing the same social biases to begin with, or being willing to be trained into those biases as the trade-off for membership in the judgment club. Those who differ and do not defer are simply said to have "incomplete biopsychosocial background or training" and are thus "inherently limited in their use of this diagnostic system."

The more the DSM-III-R tries for the kind of specificity that will eliminate diagnostic variation based on subjective judgment, the clearer it becomes that this cannot be done. For example. The diagnostic criteria for Adjustment Disorder in DSM-III-R are:

"A. A reaction to an identifiable psychosocial stressor (or multiple stressors) that occurs within three months of onset of the stressor(s).

"B. The maladaptive nature of the reaction is indicated by either of the following:

"(1) impairment in occupational (including school) functioning or in usual social activities or relationships with others

"(2) symptoms that are in excess of a normal and expectable reaction to the stressor(s).

"C. The disturbance is not merely one instance of a pattern of overreaction to stress or an exacerbation of one of the mental disorders previously described.

"D. The maladaptive reaction has persisted for no longer than six months.

"E. The disturbance does not meet the criteria for any specific mental disorder and does not represent Uncomplicated Bereavement."[33]

That is the theory. What is the practice?

Consider Jimmy, who, at nine, is in a foster care kinship home (i.e., he is living with his uncle but is a ward of one of the agencies designated by the New York City Child Welfare Administration). The evaluation I am looking at was prepared by a licensed psychologist, based on a referral from his school. This is the reported "Reason for Referral and Background":

"Jimmy was referred for a psychological evaluation in order to assess his cognitive and emotional functioning. Jimmy has been disruptive in school. His foster father, who is his uncle, stated that Jimmy may have some learning disabilities. Jimmy's parents were drug addicts and died of AIDS. He then went to live with his paternal grandparents, who died of natural causes soon after his placement with them. Jimmy attends a special education program. He is reported to be attending the 3rd grade. Jimmy is seen for psychotherapy twice a week. He was suspended for two days last year, after banging two of his classmates' heads together. He is reported to flee from class when the door is opened. Foster father reports that Jimmy is worried about his uncle, foster father, dying.

Jimmy has told his uncle, 'I won't cry! My father taught me not to.' He needs to be watched constantly."

It would be hard to argue that Jimmy, as described, is not *troubled*. But how is it possible to argue that his "symptoms" are "in excess of a normal and expectable reaction to the stressors"? What is a normal and expectable reaction when you are eight and both your parents die, then your grandparents die; when the school you attend more than likely doesn't have time for you; when the norm around you is (more than likely) addiction and violence; and when you are in the custody of a large and impersonal bureaucracy?

"Jimmy experienced the most difficulty on a task where knowledge of factual information was tapped. . . . His knowledge of information was extremely limited. He did not know what a baby cow is called. . . . This deficit is probably caused, in part, by previous deprivation." That certainly seems likely. It also seems likely that Jimmy has lots of factual information about things more related to his life and environment than baby cows, if anyone had asked. "Jimmy was most successful when dealing with a non-verbal task where planning and the ability to anticipate were important. On this task he was able to perform within the high average range." It is certainly plausible that Jimmy is just as bright as he needs to be, given the chance, and that he has been pretty busy dealing with the stuff that has happened to him. Nor is the problem that the evaluator is not sympathetic to Jimmy's reality.

"The most striking aspect of Jimmy's emotional functioning is the extent to which concerns with death pervade his thoughts. He worries about his uncle's dying. He still has not worked through his parents' and grandparents' deaths. This is a youngster who feels that he could be abandoned, yet again, at any time. . . . Jimmy worries about illness causing his world to be turned upside down. . . . Jimmy relies upon the defenses of denial, avoidance and repression. His defenses tend to be quite rigid and limited. Although his reality testing is relatively accurate, his limited defenses are not capable of handling the stress with which he must deal."

Jimmy's diagnosis on Axis I: Adjustment Disorder with Mixed Disturbance of Emotions and Conduct. On Axis II: Developmental

Reading Disorder, Developmental Expressive Language Disorder, and Schizoid Personality Disorder.

Anyone even marginally familiar with the haphazard nature of New York City's foster care system will agree that Jimmy's appraisal of the potential for disruption in his life is entirely realistic. With all this diagnosing on his record, should any of the disruptions occur, Jimmy is brought one step closer to being a candidate for a residential treatment center. The upshot of the interview is that Jimmy be referred for a psychiatric evaluation in order to assess the need for medication. Should he be put on medication, the "need" for that will become part of his record as well, further validating the "illness."

The problem is not that either DSM-III-R or the interviewing psychologist is deliberately setting Jimmy up. Indeed, it is fairly clear that the interviewing psychologist does not even believe that Jimmy's symptoms are in excess of the normal, given the circumstances. Given that, what is wrong here is identifying Jimmy as having a *mental disorder.* Joel Kovel, psychiatrist and professor at Bard College, writes: "Paradoxically, it is when DSM-III tries to become most rational and humane that it succeeds in becoming most irrational and dehumanizing. This contradiction inheres in its most fundamental concept, enshrined in its very title, that of the 'mental disorder.' The mental disorder is the object wrought by the objectifying gaze: It is not so much what the gaze sees as what it constructs. And without a coherent notion of mental disorder, DSM-III collapses like a rope of sand. Unless mental disorders exist and more to the point, exist discretely, so that they can be bounded and clearly differentiated from each other, there is no point in measuring them complete to the second decimal place."[34]

It is not atheoretical to pin on Jimmy a label that does not validate and dignify his real-life experience; it is cruel. It does not require a theory to ascribe Jimmy's misery to actual circumstance. It requires only that you are not committed to colonizing all human *being* under your psy-think system. The kind of system you use will dictate the kind of information that is considered weighty: When the system is one of grouping mental disorders, weight is given to Jimmy's deficits as though they existed independent of his reality.

In the *DSM-III-R Casebook*, several things stand out when one turns to the section on children and adolescents. One is the number of cases that are school counselor–prompted or teacher-referred. Equally impressive are the number of cases included that do not include any sort of mental disorder at all (but nonetheless receive some diagnosis). For the most part, anyone looking for concrete and graphic illustrations of what is (and is not) serious illness in children will come away knowing no more than she (or he) did.

First, we get "Don't Worry"[35] (the cases are all given little names, à la Freud). In this one, a worried psychiatrist and his wife have consulted their pediatrician about their three-year-old son, Aaron, who has been getting stuck on words and first syllables. When they realize the pediatrician has a slight stutter, they decide—for reasons we are not privy to—that he's no one to judge. They flee to a speech therapist. The speech therapist tells them, in effect, to calm down and stop harping on it and it will go away. That, in the end, is exactly what happens.

Nonetheless, Aaron is given this DSM-III-R diagnosis: Axis I: 307.00 Stuttering. Why? The speech therapist has predicted whatever it was would go away, and it did. Even the DSM, which makes ominous weather out of stuttering, recognizes that "Stuttering must be distinguished from *normal childhood dysfluency*, an intermittent speech dysfluency with no associated features occurring around age two. The clinical features are virtually indistinguishable from Stuttering. Therefore, most speech pathologists consider stuttering behavior when it occurs before age three to be 'normal childhood dysfluency.' "[36] Okay. Aaron was three. Still, the outcome was known: What seems in evidence here is an obsession with the mechanism of diagnosis that is overriding all interest in common sense. There is only one reason to write down that Aaron has a mental disorder (Stuttering). The reason is reimbursement.

If, as we have been firmly and candidly assured is the case, psychiatric hospitalization is a business, insurance-driven, reimbursement-driven, this is true, as well, of the entire psy sector if it is to have available to it customers beyond the limited range of the wealthy, if it is to extend its purview, its prestige, and its dominance. Insurance is the sole thing at issue—be it private insurance or Medicaid/Medicare. In order to justify medical insurance, clearly you must speak of health and disease in order to qualify as *medical*.

This is the single compelling reason to be speaking of diseases/disorders. It is further the single most compelling force in support of the neurological-biological-genetic model or hypothesis or conceptualization.

While for practitioners the fact that this is so is hardly immaterial, nonetheless, to the best of my knowledge expediency is not meant to equate with science. (And therein lies the fault line on which the entire edifice rests.)

And what about Ed (of "Ed Hates School")? He's nine and a half and is failing arithmetic, spelling, and science. He's had more tests than I will bother enumerating here. But the Peabody Individual Achievement Test, for one, has him scoring 10 years, 3 months for reading; 8 years, 6 months for math; and 9 years, 2 months for spelling. "Examination revealed a quiet, but personable boy who expressed concern about his schoolwork and 'just really hates to go to school.'" While the teacher and the school psychologist seem all fussed up about Ed, the psychiatrist authors conclude that "The extensive achievement testing consistently reveals that he has the most difficulty with arithmetic, and it is only in this one area that both his school performance and test results indicate a level of achievement significantly below expected levels. This suggests a diagnosis of Developmental Arithmetic Disorder."

Why is it a mental disorder to hate to go to school? To hate math? It is not. It is a Developmental Disorder. On Axis I, we get "No Diagnosis or Disorder." On Axis II, however, we get "Developmental Arithmetic Disorder."[37]

Diagnosis means always having to write down something.

There are other, similar cases, where we learn how to diagnose Developmental Expressive Language Disorder, Developmental Reading Disorder . . .

And then there are cases like Jeremy ("No Brakes"), age nine, a

kid with a "bad attitude." In school—school again—he's been repri-
manded for kicking other kids, tripping them, calling them names.
Jeremy doesn't like one of his two teachers (and, one surmises, she
doesn't like him either, which is what has brought him to psychiatric
scrutiny). "Despite this, his grades are good, and have been getting
better over the course of the year, particularly in arithmetic, art,
and physical education, which are the subjects taught by the
teacher with whom he has the most difficulty." At home, he sometimes has to be told several times to do something, and he picks on
his brother. According to his mother, sometimes he tells fibs ("His
mother also comments that he tells many minor lies, though when
pressed, he is truthful about important things"[38]).

The envelope, please!

313.81 Oppositional Defiant Disorder, Moderate (citing DSM-
III-R, page 57).

Oppositional Disorders and Conduct Disorders, along with Adjustment Reactions, were the diagnoses most often used to account
for the psychiatric hospitalization of juveniles in the 1980s. Public
outcry about this incarceration for treatment being in fact punitive
did no more than bring forth the revised psy diagnosis that these
disorders were actually symptoms of something else: underlying
depression.

Kids, of course, have no access to the political process that determines diagnosis. Nor do child advocates, who are not psychiatrists
and who, even when they are psychologists, have not organized to
affect the politics that determines what is included in DSM.

Women—for the most part psychologists—have organized to
attempt to affect gender issues. In one respect, when it comes to
kids their nagging shows. The result is peculiar. Take Rocky
("Dolls"). Rocky's a six-year-old boy whose parents seek treatment
because he wants to be a girl. He likes playing with girls, hangs out
with his mother, doesn't like rough play or fighting ("although," we
read, "he is well built, above average in height for his age, and well
coordinated"). He doesn't like cars, trucks, trains, but likes to play
with baby Barbie and kitchen toys. He likes to dress up and says he
wants to be a girl.

About Rocky, the authors of the *DSM-III-R Casebook* say, "There should be little question about the diagnosis in this case. This boy has a persistent and frequently stated desire to be a girl. He is preoccupied with female stereotypical activity, preferring to play with girls, and pretending that he is a girl, with frequent cross-dressing. He plays exclusively with stereotypically female toys such as dolls, rejecting male toys and activities. When imitating characters from books and TV, he always chooses female characters. He openly expresses a desire to be turned into a girl—not merely to play a female role.

"These are the characteristic features of a Gender Identity Disorder of Childhood as seen in a male. When the disorder is diagnosed in a female, the desire to be a male, because of a profound discontent in being female, needs to be distinguished from the desire merely to have the cultural advantages associated with being a male."[39]

Distinguished how? In effect, it would seem to anticipate the possibility that a six-year-old girl could engage in a political dialectic. This disclaimer appears to address the cultural reality of pervasive sexism and to declare psychiatry sensitive to it. In fact, the authors simply bring their diagnosis into verbal conformity with revised social stereotypes. It is agreeable of them to concede that in this society males are more powerful and more power aligned. (Their mystification that a tallish, well-built, well-coordinated boy would not want to fight suggests they have not fully considered the feminist conversation.) What they say here appears to acknowledge feminist expression of reality, and they seem truly perplexed that any boy would want to be female. So perplexed, in fact, that they are certain that in a boy this is a disorder. How much change is reflected here? It is not my experience that dominant males have ever had too much difficulty accepting their social superiority.

In fact, vigorous feminist activism on the diagnostic battlefield illuminates just how political this document is: the extent to which it is based on a dominant group's overall social ideology, within which various littler ideologies battle to define the dominant group's standard of health and social acceptability.

As Susan Faludi recounts in her book *Backlash: The Undeclared War against Women*, by the 1970s, "masochism" as a female personality trait had become a relic. Then, in 1985, perhaps in a bid to snare some attention away from the biology/neuroscience folks, and no doubt feeling somewhat sore that so many of their founder's assumptions had come under scathing attack by women, some psychoanalysts at the American Psychiatric Association decided to try bringing masochism back as a "new" disorder, and to attempt to include "Pre-Menstrual Dysphoric Disorder"; to get these included in the DSM. The APA came up with nine characteristics to define masochism, including anyone who "rejects help, gifts, or favors so as not to be a burden on others," or "worries excessively" about troubling others, or "responds to success or positive events by feeling undeserving." This was a far cry from the old "pleasure in pain" definition and, in fact, seemed more in keeping with the psychiatrists' wish to have a legitimized diagnostic name for their own mothers. Masochism was to be categorized not only as a disorder, but as a *personality disorder*, which purportedly reflects an underlying problem, not socially caused.[40]

Faludi writes, "Alarmed by the news of the proposed masochism diagnosis, Dr. Teresa Bernardez sent a letter detailing her concerns to Dr. Robert Spitzer, a psychiatrist at Columbia University and chairman of the APA panel in charge of revising the DSM. The panel was dominated by psychoanalysts, the subspecialty most partial to traditional Freudian psychiatry and a group of professionals who were still brooding over the last round of DSM revisions five years earlier, when vestiges of more outdated Freudian terminology were finally removed."[41] In other words, they were still smarting from the official burial of neurosis. "The masochism disorder's backers at the APA also seemed to resent the rise of the female-dominated psychology profession, which had been cutting into the psychiatry business since the '70s with its lower-cost and shorter-term treatment. As APA vice president Dr. Paul Fink groused in 1987, some psychologists 'won't be happy until there is no more psychoanalysis.' "[42]

The lines had been drawn for a full-scale battle: " 'The anger we saw was unbelievable to me,' recalls Bernardez, an Argentinean émigré who had previously seen her share as a citizen under the repressive Peron regime. 'It was really just lying there and when women pressed and didn't give up, it just all came out.' "43

The Feminist Therapy Institute threatened legal action, and Spitzer et al. agreed to give the women—but only *six* of them—a hearing.

With an obliviousness to the *reality* of what was going on that is truly frightening, given their power as reality-definers for others, Spitzer announced at the hearing that the whole purpose of revising DSM was to make diagnoses "more scientific."44 He then produced his "data": a "study" done by Columbia psychiatrists of eight patients, two of them men. The "evidence" that masochism existed (as a "scientific," validated disorder) was that the psychiatrists had each "independently" diagnosed these eight patients as masochists.45

As further proof of masochism's scientific validity, Spitzer produced a questionnaire he had sent to APA members, asking them if they "supported" including the masochistic disorder in DSM. As far as I am aware, this is the first attempt in the annals of science to validate a diagnosis, to establish the existence of a disease/disorder, by the Peter Pan method: Clap if you believe in fairies. It is also reminiscent of a "scientific" effort to hold a political *election* for a diagnosis. In this last context, it was a rigged election: "If the answer was 'no' [to the support question]," the members "were instructed *not* to fill out the rest of the questionnaire." Or to return it. "This method, Spitzer conceded, managed to eliminate half the people polled."46

When the six female therapists were able to get a word in edgewise, they argued that the masochism diagnosis "put all the blame on the patients' shoulders, without also taking into account social conditioning and real-life circumstances."47 Clinical and forensic psychologist Lenore Walker, using her extensive and intensive decade-plus of research, "told the panel how domestic violence often produces the very behavioral traits that the panel had included in its definition of masochism—opening the door to misdiagnosis and mistreatment of female patients and to the opportunity for battering husbands and courts to define the spouses' violence as the wives' problem."[48]

To this, the panel members simply replied that they hadn't looked at any of the battered-women studies—and they didn't intend to. By noon, the panel declared they had heard enough from these women. The women protested and were told they could stay for the afternoon hearing if they shut their mouths. ("Science," evidently, has moments when it is not immune to passion.)

"The feminist therapists returned in the afternoon to watch the panel in action—and grew increasingly distressed as they witnessed the proceedings. As the APA panelists discussed among themselves how to define masochism, they made no reference to research or clinical studies. They simply tossed out new 'characteristics,' and a typist keyed them into a computer. 'The low level of intellectual effort was shocking,' Renee Garfinkel, an APA staff member . . . recalled later. 'Diagnoses were developed by majority vote on the level we would use to choose a restaurant. You feel like Italian, I feel like Chinese, so let's go to a cafeteria.' "[49]

And quoting Lynne Rosewater, director of the Feminist Therapy Institute, "[T]hey were having a discussion for a criterion [on the Masochistic Personality Disorder] and Bob Spitzer's wife [a social worker and the only female on the panel] says, 'I do that sometimes,' and he says, 'Okay, take it out.' You watch this and you say, 'Wait a second, *we* don't have a right to criticize *them* because this is 'science'? It was really frightening. Because if this is the way they do it, then I don't trust any of the diagnoses.' "[50]

This, obviously, *is* the way they do it. And in its barely disguised social judgment, it is historically consistent:

Benjamin Rush, a signer of the Declaration of Independence and physician general of the Continental Army, is regarded as the father of American psychiatry. He, also, invented diagnoses for behaviors those in power found problematic. One was "anarchia": this he applied to folks who were unhappy with the political structure of the time and sought more democracy.[51]

In the mid-nineteenth century Dr. Samuel Cartwright came up

with "drapetomania." This, he "discovered," was an affliction peculiar to black slaves, and was evidenced by a strange desire to run away. Blacks were also said to suffer from "dyaesthesia Aethiopica"— an illness defined as paying no attention to property.[52]

Witnessing the antiwar protests of the 1960s, Bruno Bettelheim thus declaimed from his psy pulpit: The protesters had no political agenda. They merely suffered from unresolved Oedipal complexes, and were attacking universities as a surrogate father.[53]

In response to the women's protest over Masochistic Personality Disorder, the DSM Revision Task Force renamed it Self-Defeating Personality Disorder. Pre-Menstrual Dysphoric Disorder became Late Luteal Phase Dysphoric Disorder. And they included them in the appendix of categories needing further study, but they gave them identifying numbers, which made the newly imagined disorders suitable for treatment, and suitable for reimbursement.

In response to *that*, Kaye-Lee Pantony and Paula Caplan published a paper titled "Delusional Dominating Personality Disorder: A Modest Proposal for Identifying Some Consequences of Rigid Masculine Socialization."[54] For Delusional Dominating Personality Disorder (DDPD) they included fourteen criteria, among them:

"Inability to establish and maintain meaningful interpersonal relationships. . . . Inability to identify and express a range of feelings in oneself (typically accompanied by an inability to identify accurately the feelings of other people). . . . Tendency to use power, silence, withdrawal, and/or avoidance rather than negotiation in the face of interpersonal conflict or difficulty. . . ."[55] You get the picture. This they submitted to the DSM-IV revisions chair. Predictably enough, it did not engender even cursory consideration. Never mind, said the authors; its inclusion was not vital, "although our experiences following submission of DDPD to DSM have taught us a great deal about the highly political and biased process by which DSM is constructed."[56]

Numerous discussions of this paper were included in the same journal issue. Psychologist Lenore Walker argued for eliminating personality disorders altogether because of bias. She went on to ask,

"Why would renowned psychiatrists want to place new, untested categories in a nosological system that is already overburdened by a large number of classifications? Politics, of course. The competitive stance between the biosocial and psychoanalytic theorists demands that the analysts get equal space in the Book, and the concept of masochism is predominantly subscribed to by psychoanalytically oriented practitioners."[57] Equally telling: "The major argument in favor of LLPDD was the economic impact from encouraging all the women who buy nonprescription medication to deal with premenstrual symptoms by visiting their nearest psychiatrist to discuss their largely physiologically based symptomatology."[58]

And—remember my earlier metaphor about admiring the pluck of those who had "set out in a rowboat to make a definitive chart of dark waters that they could not actually see and on the wetness of which not all their colleagues agreed . . . ," etc.? Well, look here: According to Walker, the criteria for SDPD were "originally . . . created by two of the male members on the task force in a rowboat while waiting for the fish to bite."[59] And you thought—even *I* thought—I was being a trifle fanciful?

Diagnosis is the ammunition the psy sector, in its policing role, trains on those whose behavior deviates from the prevailing social ideology. Since the power base in the psy world is in the firm grasp of privileged white males, the prevailing ideology is most often one they themselves subscribe to. By 1985, when the psychoanalysts attempted to reintroduce masochism, a backlash against feminism, against uppity women, was current. Much was made all through the eighties of the social diagnosis of postfeminism: of women having gained all they sought, only to discover they didn't really want it: They really wanted to be feminine; they really wanted to go home; they really wanted to have babies.

The proposed diagnosis was congruent with a social regression, and it is not hard to imagine that, had the diagnosis been formalized, there would have been no shortage of individuals, male and female, to testify on television to masochism as the source of their wives' (or their mothers') or their own suffering, thus lending the diagnosis further authenticity. Whereas had this been attempted at the time when feminism and the women's movement had greater political respect, it would have seemed foolhardy.

Similarly, as the public became alarmed in the sixties and seventies by young people challenging authority, the psychiatric policing of children—especially in the schools—began to gain the legitimacy it now has. As the authors of *The Psychiatric Society* write, "Today . . . it is the school system, backed up by the family, that has become the center of an impressive and growing system for detecting behavioral anomalies and treating them medically."[60]

The political conservatism and economic hedonism of the 1980s coincided with the upsurge of psychiatric hospitalization of juveniles. While this does not necessarily imply causality, it does suggest that the climate was compatible with public acceptance.

Additionally, faced with an increasingly repressive atmosphere, exhausted by the apparent futility of efforts at social change, the public was more susceptible to the psy sector's salesmanship of personal "mental health" solutions for socially related distress. The greater the sense of helplessness in the face of oppression—in the face of real events—the greater the appeal of the distractions offered by psy-think. Greedy entrepreneurs, offering to diagnose children, to intimidate by incarceration (in the name of treatment), were no more than the agents of a more widespread snookery: a snookery entirely dependent on the medical, the scientific, authority granted to DSM-III-R.

Again and again I would return to this volume, nagged by the feeling there must be something here, something I must be missing. (Else how could so many smart people, some of them caring, take it so seriously?) By chance, early on August 27, 1991, I happened to notice that Sally Jessy Raphael was airing a show on "Borderline Personalities." Borderline! Another favored diagnosis for juveniles! And one I had thus far been utterly unable to decode.

Indeed, I had even gone so far as to read through a book by a leading authority on Borderline, James F. Masterson, M.D., *Treatment of the Borderline Adolescent.*[61]

Dr. Masterson's subject inspires in him an oratorical ebullience that is certainly a change from the rather flat tone of DSM-III-R and its related volumes.

"These patients' stories reveal in a clinical metaphor the ancient struggle of mankind against fate—his tragedy as well as his triumph. They tell of human beings condemned by birth and subsequent accidents of fate to be victims rather than masters of their own fortune; they are emotionally attacked and impaled before they have developed the resources and weapons with which to do battle." Wait. There's more. "They cannot seek for they are blind; they cannot fight for they have no weapons. Unable to face their fate, they make of it a virtue. Their claims become a halo; their way of life in all its human misery is defended as their path to salvation. . . .

"Let the reader now share the adolescent's lonely and painful struggle up through the levels of Dante's Inferno toward a new day that will witness not only survival but also even the mastering of life's blows."[62]

Gosh. Ancient struggle. Condemned by birth. Emotionally impaled. By what? Or rather—by whom?

Mother. "The distraught and doting mother of a 2-year-old calls her pediatrician to complain that her toddler follows her around the house and will not leave her side." "The worried, angry, depressed, frightened mother of a 15-year-old calls the pediatrician in despair about her son's dropping out of school and taking drugs."[63] What do these two have in common? The Borderline syndrome: a failure of individuation-separation: a distraught-doting, worried-angry-depressed-frightened mother.

Mother-blaming has of course always been a favorite psy sport: from the refrigerator mother who was said to cause autism, to the schizophrenogenic mother, to the mother who was said to inspire juvenile delinquency in her young. In 1983, Paula Caplan and Ian Hall-McCorquodale read 125 articles from nine psy journals, targeting three specific years: "1970, because it would presumably include articles that were conceived just at the beginning of the new feminist movement; 1982, because it was the last full year for which journals were available; and 1976, because it was midway between the other two years."[64] They found seventy-two different kinds of psychopathology attributed to mothers, including: avoidance of peers, chronic vomiting, anxiety, arson, delusions, depression, dependency, failure to mourn, fetishism, frigidity, hyperactivity, inability to separate from mother, incontinence, incest, isolation, loneliness, marijuana use, moodiness, narcissism, poor concentration, scapegoating, school dropout, self-induced television epilepsy, tantrums, truancy . . .

So mother-blame is not what takes one by surprise here. It is the opportunity to view the hospitalization of an adolescent from the overseeing psychiatrist's viewpoint; it is what one finds when one witnesses, in action, the (not objective, but, as Joel Kovel put it) "*objectifying* gaze."

Capsulized from Masterson's book: When Anne was ten, the maid who had taken care of her died and her mother became ill with porphyria. Anne began acting worse—was rebellious, stayed up late, slept in the daytime. She dressed "inappropriately." At fourteen she began to smoke marijuana, was taken to a psychiatrist who said she was hopeless and belonged in a state mental hospital. (Honest. It's right there on page 51.) She was sent to boarding school, became sexually active, was suspended—and was taken to another psychiatrist. Eventually, the doctor insisted she be hospitalized.

"Let us now follow what happens to Anne as she enters the hospital," Masterson writes, and goes on to describe her appearance ("striking"): "shoulder-length black hair, partially covering her eyes, pale white skin, her only makeup blue and white eyeliner, giving her an almost ghostlike appearance. She dressed either in blue-jeans with a black turtleneck top and black boots or in very short miniskirts. She wore one blouse open on the sides to the waist without a brassiere."[65] Ah. The objectifying gaze.

What Anne said was that she didn't want to be in the hospital. What she *did* ("acting out") was wear miniskirts, and adopt a negativistic, sarcastic, flip attitude toward the therapist, and *write provocative letters to her friends about hospitalization*, and phone friends, also *to make provocative statements*. Oh. And fail to keep her room clean.

"We"—Masterson says—"began . . . by forbidding miniskirts, monitoring her letters, limiting the telephone calls, and expecting her to be at school on time and keep her room clean."[66]

War was declared: a war between a rebellious teenager and an authoritarian father; a war in which Masterson et al. seem just as. frustrated and helpless as any other parent similarly situated. The difference being that they had the power to keep her locked up until she knuckled under.

"Dealing with an adolescent's testing is much like negotiating with the Russians," Masterson writes; "you no sooner have one issue under control when another pops up."[67]

They would tell her no miniskirts. She would say, "How mini is a miniskirt?" They put her on room restriction. They threatened to send the damn clothes home. She installed a red light in her room and burned incense. They said those things had to go. Finally, she smoked marijuana smuggled in by another patient, and she was put on the restricted floor. The angrier Anne gets, the more gleeful the therapists are because she is releasing her anger. When she tells them the truth—she doesn't want to be here—they tell her she is masking her real feelings. When she tries telling them what she thinks they want to hear, it doesn't help: "Now I know there is no point in my telling you what I think you want to hear, because it won't get me downstairs any sooner." About which Masterson writes, "The patient's recognition that the therapist was more or less in control of the situation was immensely reassuring."[68] I will bet it was.

Again, what is most interesting here is the use of a label meant to connote a medical condition—in juxtaposition with the treatment response which clearly presumes acts of will. One feature that sociologists ascribe to those designated "ill"—as opposed to those labeled "deviant" or "bad"—is the exemption from normal responsibilities. While there is certainly nothing *normal* about Anne's obligations while in the hospital, she has in fact been given a whole plateload of responsibilities (tasks that will prove her conformity to the rules of this intensively restrictive social order). These responsibilities could be called extra-normal or supranormal.

The second feature allocated to those cast as sick is that "the individual is not held responsible for his or her condition and cannot be expected to recover by an act of will."[69] Yet clearly Anne is being held responsible for the behaviors that are the only "indicators" of her disorder, which is precisely what gives the entire scenario the character of a particularly acrimonious household dispute.

But it is the third feature ascribed to the "sick role" that is the most telling: "[T]he person must recognize that being ill is an inherently undesirable state and must want to recover." This is exactly what seems most problematic here. The mission of the treatment is to convince Anne that she is ill (when she quite believes otherwise); to coerce her to recognize that the way she *is* is inherently undesirable. And that changing the way she is (or appearing to do so) is the only way to *recover* (in a purely nonmedical sense)—to recover what she most wants: her freedom to be who she is.

(Dizzying, isn't it?)

≈

But back to Sally Jessy Raphael. Let her ask for us: What is Borderline?[70]

Addressing us, Sally Jessy asks whether we divide the world into good or bad, black or white, or if we're too hard on ourselves or can't handle rejection. Her guests, she tells us, felt just that way and were given multiple diagnoses over the years—only to realize at last that they suffered from BPD: Borderline Personality Disorder.

First off, we meet Lisa, whose identifying subtitle reads "Personality Disorder Led to Self-Mutilation." And, indeed, Lisa describes being three or four years old and pulling her hair out in wads and, in first grade, stabbing pencils into her stomach. By grade eight, she was putting safety pins in her legs and fastening them.

When she cut herself she was not, she assures us, just doing it to get attention. "I learned to sew them up, so that I wasn't asking for their attention. . . ."

Sally, following the sequence of her notes, begins to respond to the issue of attention-getting. But then her mind picks up what her ears have just heard: *You really learned to sew yourself up?*

Lisa continues to detail her pain and her symptomology. Then, in response to a question from Sally, she rattles off some of the diagnoses she received: schizoaffective, atypical bipolar, manic depressive, cyclothymic, split personality. . . .

After a commercial break we meet Carlos ("Blamed Drinking for Personality Disorders") who manifested his disorder by beating his wife, beating his children.

So far, I do not see what Lisa and Carlos have in common, but I continue to watch, confident that Sally Jessy can help where Dr. Masterson did not.

Lisa is now delineating her compulsion for sex (a couple of times a day), her continued cutting of herself, her bulimia, her use of cocaine. . . .

Comes another break. Sally tells us that when we return we'll find out what Borderline is.

Yay.

After which Sally says that when you're not sure what the diagnosis is it might be Borderline. (Yes, or maybe it's the fish you ate.) Somewhere in my mind a bell is ringing. I see a light bulb.

Sally introduces our expert, Dr. Jerold Kreisman—on the psychiatric staff of St. John's Mercy Medical Center in St. Louis, and medical director of its Borderline Personality Treatment Unit. Dr. Kreisman has written a book, *I Hate You, Don't Leave Me*.

(Can it be? A disciple of Dr. Bisch?)

Sally now invites the audience to ask questions. The first to rise asks Lisa how she finds comfort in cutting herself and tearing out her hair. Lisa tells us it diverts attention from the pain.

The second audience member to speak, however, feels like my stand-in, asking what makes Lisa and Carlos certain that *this* diagnosis is the right one? It quickly becomes apparent that the prevailing audience response so far is befuddlement.

Lisa replies that at the hospital she was given a book, *The DSM-III*, and told to go through it to see what she thought. She picked Borderline for herself because it seemed to describe what she was going through.

Omygod! She picked it herself! Her own diagnosis!

Now Sally turns back to Carlos, who talks about not having trust in relationships, how it's hard, how you have to learn to trust. . . .

And I wonder: Am I the only person who still does not know what it is we are talking about? Or rather why we are talking about these various things as being the embodiment of a single thing, a diagnosis called Borderline? No. I am not the only one.

Another audience member expresses *her* frustration: Are we talking about a chemical imbalance? Something mental? Family problems? So, comfortingly, I am not the only person who still does not know what it is we are talking about, or rather why we are talking about these various things as being the embodiment of a single thing, a diagnosis called Borderline.

Dr. Kreisman reiterates that a borderline is someone who divides the universe into good and bad, black and white (which suggests to me a twelve-year-old in full cry, or a president declaiming on the "evil empire"). Kreisman says, "They love beyond measure on Monday those who they may come to hate without reason on Tuesday." (It sounds like twelve-year-olds and presidential foreign policy to me.) Kreisman explains that the disorder is most often seen in adolescents, but allows that some people suggest that the term "Borderline Adolescent" may be redundant. In fact, he tells us, "Borderline" can be identified by extremes: the adolescent who cuts his wrists, who runs away from home, who gets into heavy drug use. . . .

So once again it is the behaviors that speak of disease (as surely as the stars and the tea leaves speak of the future?).

The problem is that the same behaviors may speak of many things. It is common psy currency as well that girls who have been sexually abused by fathers and stepfathers frequently turn to cutting themselves. And sexually abused and physically battered kids run away from home. And get into drug use. If the *behaviors* are the leading determinant and play the dominant role in the diagnosis, then diagnoses have virtually no reliable relevance to experiential truth—even if enough psy practitioners have been similarly indoctrinated so that you can show they agree. Faced with this, any reasonable child may stand ready to shout that the emperor has no clothes. But if, given psy power, a kid does shout this out, it is less apt to result in a professional or public epiphany than in a prescription for psychotropic medication.

Again my confusion is echoed by the audience (I am starting to feel very warm toward this audience): "Both of your guests seem like they have been diagnosed with the same problem. But their backgrounds seem very different. Their symptoms seem very different. It's just very hard to—I don't get it."

Drumroll, please. Let the doctor try his center ring highwire act.

What they all have in common, he says, is self-damaging "impulsivity" and identity problems. "They're Democrats with Democrats and Republicans with Republicans. But at 2:00 in the morning, they're unregistered." Whoa, good one.

I am impressed: One's general impression of talk show audiences is that they will laugh, cry, clap, and nod on cue, the goal of attending the show seemingly less the seeking of information than emotional sport. But piling language on in this case seems not to be working.

After the next break Sally is moved to go back to square one. She acknowledges that the audience does not seem to understand "Borderline" and that perhaps we at home may not understand it either. She asks the doctor for guidelines.

Kreisman attempts again to explain: "The name Borderline Personality has been around for 50 years. And up until 1980, before it was rigorously defined in the DSM . . . it was this wastebasket diagnosis, where you put people you didn't know what to do with."

"Frequently," he says, "it was also a diagnosis if one of the therapists was just ticked off and aggravated at the patient. If they called me in the middle of the night and manipulated me and kept going to the hospital and aggravated me to death, they're a dirty, no-good Borderline, too."

What a remarkable thing to say. But Sally does not have all day here. She wants us to have some guidelines we can take away with us so we can know if our kid or our brother-in-law is a Borderline.

Kreisman says "Well, all psychiatric diagnoses, these days, are defined very clearly in the *Diagnostic and Statistical Manual.* And every few years, wise psychiatrists go up to Mount Sinai, talk to God, and define all psychiatric illnesses. If you're a manic-depressive, you have three out of these five or four out of these seven. Borderline Personality Disorder is defined by having five out of the eight criteria."

There was, once upon a time, another book from which this kind of scientific certainty was derived. It was the *Malleus Maleficarum*.

The certainty then was about who was a witch.*

* The witchcraft/Inquisition allusion derives originally from the pioneering work of Thomas Szasz, *The Manufacture of Madness* (New York: Delta, 1970).

7

Believing in Bio-Psy

ENID PESCHEL is the president of NAMI-CAN [National Alliance for the Mentally Ill; Child and Adolescent Network] of Woodbridge, Connecticut. As well, she is codirector of the Program for Humanities in Medicine and assistant professor (adjunct) of internal medicine at Yale University School of Medicine. In a generous effort to help me understand the revolutionary impact she feels science is having on psychiatry she has sent me her writings about neurobiological disorders (NBD) or biologically-based brain disease (BBBD)—in children, adolescents, and adults.

Among these NBD she includes: manic-depressive (bipolar) disorder, major depressive disorder, autism and pervasive developmental disorders, schizophrenia, obsessive-compulsive disorder, Tourette's disorder, anxiety and panic disorders, and attention deficit hyperactivity disorder (ADHD). She advises me that the best scientific book available on this subject is the nearly 2,000-page volume *Psychopharmacology: The Third Generation of Progress.*[1]

She has further informed me that to be scientifically accurate a classification system for severely disturbed children should include at least four different groups: 1) Children with scientifically-defined neurobiological disorders, which are biologically-caused disorders: *physical illnesses.* 2) Children with 'mental health' or psychological problems, which are sociologically- or environmentally-caused problems. 3) Children with severe disabilities who have elements of both #1 and #2. 4) Children with severe disabilities with as yet unknown etiologies.[2]

This certainly sounds reasonable. But does it really help? We still do not know what qualifies precisely as "severely disabled." What determines whether children in #2 will be shifted to #3— especially when it is a presumption essential to pharmaceutical intervention. Remember our nine-year-old ghetto kid who'd lost both parents to AIDS, his grandparents immediately thereafter, who was having school and behavioral difficulties—and who was recommended for evaluation with an eye to medication? The problem with the #2 comes in where it carries the presumption of #1.

Peschel is certainly correct when she writes in the summer 1991 *NAMI-CAN News*, "All 4 groups of severely disabled children need—and deserve to have—proper care and support. Therefore, all institutions must develop *specific & effective* programs for *each* group. Above all, it is illogical & scientifically unacceptable to apply the same programs and policies to all 4 groups."[3]

The major thrust of NAMI and its affiliate NAMI-CAN is to address issues of long-term chronic problems such as autism and schizophrenia, issues such as parents having to give up custody of their children in order to get them services from the state, and they are major supporters of NIMH and of pharmaceutical research: biological research. Research that will identify a funny gene or chromosome or whatever. NAMI itself is a highly controversial group; a powerful lobbying force, it has been known to attack psychiatrists and others who disagree with the neuro-bio ideology.*

It is, I think, important to distinguish between the NAMI leadership and its hundred-thousand-plus membership. Those mothers I met in my travels who were NAMI-CAN members did not appear to

---

* In 1987, NAMI brought a complaint against Peter Breggin's Maryland medical license because he had criticized psychiatric drugs on Oprah Winfrey's national TV talk show. Breggin writes, "NAMI is closely connected to establishment psychiatry, and its leadership supports everything I have been criticizing for years: biological and genetic theories, involuntary treatment, heavy reliance on drugs, electroshock, and even lobotomy" (Peter R. Breggin, M.D., *Toxic Psychiatry*, [New York:

have much in the way of information about or interest in the broader politics or alliances of the leadership, or in NAMI's role as participant in what Peter Breggin has called the "psychopharmaceutical combine."

Indeed, Peschel's writings suggest she identifies the problem as one of failure to make distinctions (albeit she does not address in her categories the 65 percent of kids in private, for-profit psych hospitals who simply *do not need to be there but are given severe-sounding labels nonetheless*). Because Peschel, and NAMI, include such things as attention-deficit hyperactivity disorders (and its concomitant learning disorders), along with "serious emotional disturbances" (themselves ill-defined), inevitably NAMI-CAN, like NAMI, drags a polyglot group of supporters in its wake.

If it makes eminent sense that parents of a biologically handicapped child should not (as has been true in the past) be regarded with suspicion as themselves causative, it is also true that parents who have in fact been cruel would be equally attracted by the posture of "Don't blame me" inherent in the idea of inborn defect. Most especially, as with the case of the nine-year-old kid in foster care, the idea that something is biologically wrong with the children allows the state to divert attention from a system of social cruelty, and reduces the chance that the greater society will bother with action for change.

As I listened to mothers around the country, I was fascinated (and initially appalled) at the relief they expressed at "discovering" their child had an inborn biological defect or chemical imbalance: It was relief bordering on delight. As John's adoptive mother said to me, "For a while we thought—since John's mother was disturbed—that it was something genetic, something biological. And we thought, 'At last we've found it!'"

Barbara and her husband, for example, were foster parents who

---

St. Martin's Press, 1991], p. 425, n. 1). Breggin was completely exonerated by the Maryland Commission on Medical Discipline that same year. The fact that the group would seek without qualm to suppress free speech suggests, on the part of the leadership, a zealous and authoritarian (as opposed to caring and inquiring) mind-set.

adopted four kids who had been variously abused, dumped, moved, sexually violated, locked in closets. She is a NAMI-CAN member. From what she describes, though the kids all came from different birth circumstances, they were all in the John-category of kids who have been so maltreated by both the original parents and the intervening system that the results really seem quite expectable, quite normal—in terms of what the "average" infant and child so treated would become.

Yet she is very high on the idea that these kids are neurologically impaired, that the cause is inborn, although, she says, it's an idea that might "be too radical for people right now."

"Help me understand," I say. "Horrible things had happened to these kids. Why does it require a biological explanation?"

She says, "A kid who has been abused doesn't necessarily have cause and effect. Doesn't have any conscience. Doesn't learn the impact of what they do on someone else. And that's where genetically it becomes a problem. Genetically and biologically. So there's a treatment—in other words, what works and what doesn't work.

"What happens is when they're younger, they are so needy, yet if you provide the need by your normal techniques—such as hugging—it creates almost a reverse psychology, a reverse cycle. You give them that thing that you think they need and what it does is create anger. And it is directed back to you because of the pain—almost like a déjà vu. So what happens is you have to systematically—when they're babies—you have to almost decrease the stimulus. You hold them, the back to you, facing away from you.

"And as they get older, they do everything conceivable to relieve that anxiety of that closeness. In a family situation— I'll give you an example. My son gave me a hug good night and because of the strategies that I have to use, I had told him, 'This is a level of closeness that we need to be at in order to survive in the family. Please don't give me a hug good night. Just say good night to me and go to bed.'

"Now you would think these kids would need more hugging and more touching and—well, they do, but on a very systematically scheduled time. And only in a very programmatic way. Or else the very following things will happen: This kid came up to me and gave me a hug good night. And I said, 'Tony, in order to survive in the family, right now, because of your identity problems, because of all the things in the past . . .' He understands that—that this is what he needs to do."

"But," I say, "that's not biologically altering, that's behaviorally altering."

"Right. But there is no cure-all medication for these kids. Personality disorder, there's no cure. Sociopathic, there's no cure."

"So you're suggesting that, if it's genetically based, if you eliminated the abuse, you would still have a problem?"

"Yes, to a degree. Actually, genetically, biologically, neurophysiologically, the probability of all the kids is that these kids had parents who were mentally ill and not treated. In the case history that I read there was mental illness. Grandfather had epilepsy. Grandmother and grandfather had mental illness. So it's almost like the mental illness was a precursor of this abuse."

"Lots of people abuse kids. Are we going to call it a mental illness if they do something they shouldn't do?"

"Well, I don't think it's a mental illness, but I think sometimes there is a connection with the two. Connection meaning during the manic phase is when the abuse occurs."

My point in recalling here a brief bit of this conversation is simply to illustrate that once biological, neurological, genetic language becomes the basis for talking about all the ills and the stages that kids are heir to—including severe mistreatment and social deprivation—many citizens will begin believing they know what they are talking about when they are actually speaking in tongues.

≈

Shifting the ground from experiential concepts to scientific concepts, biological concepts, has inestimable potential for danger; it portends an even greater investment of power in designated experts—a power that can well serve the interests of the state. History speaks to us of eugenics, of attempts to determine "scientific" inferiority based on race or sexual preference. No similar evidence exists in the past for the use of so-called brain science for benign purposes.

Additionally, when the conversational level shifts from feelings to neurotransmitters, most of us are effectively barred from credible voice.

Nonetheless, it is necessary to examine the neuro-bio position if only because it is undeniable that there is such a thing as brain damage. While I am not willing to even go near the two-thousand-page *Psychopharmacology* (or indeed to deal at any length with the brain-disabling properties of psychotropic drugs, which have been so convincingly detailed elsewhere), it is worth taking time to briefly review the book edited by Peschel and her husband, Richard (professor of therapeutic radiology at Yale University School of Medicine), and by Carol W. Howe (chair of the National Alliance for the Mentally Ill Children and Adolescents Network) and James W. Howe (former president of NAMI).[4] It is a work of extreme conviction, even zeal.

The editors write: "The list of severe 'mental' illnesses in children and adolescents that are characterized by neurochemical malfunctions or neuroanatomical malformations in the brain or both includes autism and pervasive developmental disorders, obsessive-compulsive disorders, Tourette's syndrome, bipolar and major depressive disorders, attention deficit hyperactivity disorder, anxiety disorders, and schizophrenia. Because of the irrefutable scientific evidence that is being accumulated, we have used the term *neurobiological disorder* (NBD) to describe these severe, chronic 'mental' illnesses that have a physical, neurochemical, or neuroanatomical basis." Leaving aside for the moment the plausible question as to whether all of these things truly belong in the same basket, the editors go on to say, "Because of the incidence, severity, and chronicity of these neurobiological disorders, these NBD represent a greater public health problem than either childhood leukemia or all childhood cancers combined."[5]

Indeed, the authors of the chapter on attention deficit hyperactivity disorder state that it is "the most commonly diagnosed behavioral disorder in childhood. Between 2 and 20 percent of all children are estimated to be affected." They write that at least 25 percent of children diagnosed with ADHD "also suffer from a communication or learning disorder. Another 40 percent exhibit patterns of behavior that include starting fights, stealing, lying (conduct disorder), or persistent disobedience, defiance and rule breaking (oppositional defiant disorder)."[6]

It is the main thrust of one chapter, "Individualized Services for Children" (John E. VanDenBerg), that there must be individualized, need-based services delivered to majorly brain-damaged or genetically damaged children. Obviously, the smaller the identified population the more manageable such a proposal would be. The severe limiting of the category would be pragmatic as well in securing more adequate medical insurance coverage. As the chapter on reforming insurance law tells us,[7] " 'Mental health' benefits, which include the treatment of serious mental illness (NBD), have low levels of reimbursement, high copayments, and very low annual and lifetime limits. Such limits have been imposed because counseling for emotional problems is subject to what insurance companies call *moral hazard*: the fact that people overuse discretionary services when they get them for little or no money." (Moral hazard, we are told, "is high in the area of mental health care because psychotherapy is very 'price sensitive': when consumers must pay for it, they do not buy much of it, but if they can get it at low cost, they use it a lot.")

It is obviously expedient to critically restrict claims about what is biologically based, what constitutes the category. Contradicting the earlier claim that NBD represents a massive public health problem, the author of the chapter "Reforming Insurance Law" writes, "NBD are serious—*but very rare*—disorders. Thus, the cost of adequately covering NBD is low. In March 1991, the Coopers & Lybrand accounting firm, commissioned by the California Medical Association Access to Better Care Task Force, calculated the financial implications of extending unlimited inpatient and outpatient coverage for the treatment of schizophrenia, bipolar disorder, autism, and pervasive developmental disorders. [Note: not inclusive of ADHD or anxiety disorders.] This extension of coverage would treat these serious "mental" illnesses the same as other physical diseases included under the major medical benefit. Coopers & Lybrand concluded that the cost of extending unlimited coverage for these specific NBD would total only $0.78 per month per insured person. To achieve this increase at only $0.78 per month per insured person would require at least two million people in the insurance pool to control for adverse selection."[8] But what happens to the $0.78, now, when pride of problem ownership (or whatever it is) leads you to include in the equation the up to 20 percent of all American children said to be suffering from ADHD alone?

Perhaps the most peculiar thing about this volume is its combination of authoritative trumpetry of bioneurological revolution and its rather modest documentation of supporting evidence. Take the statement in the chapter on brain development that "There is abundant evidence that autism represents a failure—*probably* a relatively subtle one—in brain development. [Italics mine.] We might wonder at how a disorder as clinically consequential as autism could warrant the term *subtle*, but in terms of neuropathology, the description is accurate. Autopsies of brains of autistic individuals dying of other causes have failed to show evidence of structural brain abnormalities that could be consistently observed by large numbers of researchers."[9]

We are then asked, "How can we reconcile this? On the one hand, we have a neurodevelopmental disorder leading to profound clinical dysfunction; on the other, a brain that, with our current tools at least, looks perfectly normal." The proposed answer? Either "we . . . do not have the right tools to see what we are looking for," or "We do not really know what we are looking for."

Indeed, the author of the introduction, Thomas Detre, notes that "It is most encouraging . . . that the scientists who have contributed to this volume fully expect and, indeed, hope that, once biological markers are identified, these preliminary hypotheses will be revised or altogether abandoned and that the descriptive diagnosis system currently in use will undergo substantial changes."[10]

But hey! Wait up! The *temporary* certainty about the nature of things dictates the use of psychotropic medications that substantial and credible studies have shown can have permanent brain-disabling effects, as Breggin has documented in his book *Toxic Psychiatry*. If they don't know, okay. But they *act* anyway. And the introduction makes the claim that "The publication of this volume provides convincing evidence that psychiatry—accompanied by its two traveling companions, neuroscience and neuropharmacology—has returned from its self-imposed exile into the mainstream of medicine and biology." And that "advances in neurobiology and genetics, assisted by novel imaging techniques, have dramatically changed the ecology of psychiatric research and of patient care." And that "new scientific findings, the products of laboratory experiments and controlled clinical trials, have replaced the prophetic, nonscientific pronouncements of the past that senior mentors had enunciated with great conviction."[11] (Remember the fate of poor old neurosis?)

Clearly, the building of a powerful lobbying group such as NAMI requires a more broadly based support than could be gained if it limited itself to that which is "rare."

And it is no wonder that the neuro-bio ideology's main selling point—that of nature over nurture; the removing of parental blame—overwhelms women with relief. "The 'who done it' approach has been dislodged by careful studies on genetic vulnerability and investigations designed to reveal the biological mechanisms by which stresses and other environmental insults affect the developing organism in general, and the central nervous system in particular."

Women, so long the victims of accusation under the flagship of nurture, are now offered the apparent exoneration of nature. It is a gift horse that, I believe, requires careful oral scrutiny—if only because in changing the conversation from (as it were) the unique and puzzling genius of Leonardo da Vinci to one about the physical properties of the ceiling of the Sistine Chapel and the chemical properties of the paint applied, tens of thousands of children are being told that it is not what they may *do* that is wrong, but that what they *are* is wrong.

And because it leads to such strenuous leaps of thought.

≈

Deborah is trim, intense. As a psychotherapist for children and adolescents, she has placed kids in psychiatric hospitals. As a mother, she has placed her own son.

Beginning in the more neutral territory, I ask what leads her to seek incarceration for a kid. She speaks of the laws that give children too much freedom; of the southern California culture; of the social forces that give kids too long a leash.

"Hospitalization, over the last few years in particular," she says, "seems to be almost the only viable option. Children will get to the point where they're unsupervised, they're out of control. There are no authority limits that can be established with any degree of efficiency.

"The schools are afraid of the children. The restrictions on the teachers and on authority people in general—in this area particularly—is very great. [For example,] 'consequencing'—requiring that children come in on Saturdays, for instance, and sit in a classroom and do homework if the kid consistently refuses to hand in his homework, or is truant or acts out in class. They have laws, which were backed by parents, restricting the amount of academic work they can require of a kid on a weekend. What it turns out to be is a real fun experience where kids meet all of their buddies that they've been truant with. There's little supervision.

"The second option, if a kid has been consistently truant—he's suspended from school, which really does abdicate right back to the parents who are at work and having trouble establishing the structure of the home anyway. The third, of course, is expulsion—which leaves the parent in the predicament of having to provide for the child academically, but yet the public school systems are not accepting him.

"In California particularly there's been a real dilemma: The courts don't want the kids. The 'system' is getting real frustrated with the kids. And they're giving all the responsibility back to the parents—which I understand is appropriate.

"But then when the parent comes in to me and says, 'This kid is thirteen years old. I know he smokes dope. He sneaks out at night. He will not go to school. I need to have him hospitalized.' Okay. Let's say he's fourteen. The advocacy system gives the child the right to voluntarily admit himself or refuse admission. And the hospitals are mandated by law to advise the child—that you have a right to a hearing; that you have to sign yourself in voluntarily. [To say,] 'If you refuse to sign yourself in voluntarily, we can keep you for seventy-two hours. But here are your patient rights. Here is the number of the patient advocacy.' "

"So," I say, "you're suggesting that you refer kids to hospitals because . . . ?"

"They're totally out of control. And as far as a forty-five- or fifty-minute session once or twice a week—the whole family is falling apart. The parents need to have support on an almost daily basis. The parents need to understand the secondary gain for the child: What is he getting by doing this? And how are you reinforcing it? The roles need to change. And there's so much of that. I mean good families fall into this totally overwhelmed position. It sneaks up on them. You have educated, caring, really quality people who are raising children—who may have managed one or two successfully—suddenly finding themselves with a kid who's been using drugs for years. They had no idea. I think the parents, generally speaking, the parents I deal with here, for the most part are not the abusive indifferent. There are those, of course. And they do produce children with emotional problems. Those are the kids that, more often than not, end up in residential placement. Because they don't have the support of parents and because the schools do have to step in. They do have to provide the funding. Those parents don't have the insurance. They just totally abdicate."

Much of what Deborah will say to me circles back on itself. These kids need to be hospitalized for behavioral problems, for being "out of control." But, I ask, what would happen if you just let them alone? "That's a good question. I'd really like to do some follow-up, some stats, on when does hospitalization make a difference. You can see the immediate short-term difference. But then how long does that last? And how much does it depend on the parents and their tasks and their follow-up? And what happens to the kids who just end up trying to con the system?"

Further along she ruminates out loud: "I guess I'm coming from a place where I've seen that therapists who take on adolescents, which is a specialty all by itself, and which requires a lot of experience—you have to know what's going on with kids today. You can't just come from a psychoanalytical/clinical perspective. And look at kids' behavior and make a judgment." Meaning?

"There's a test called the MMPI [Minnesota Multiphasic Personality Inventory]. It's used in courts a lot. I don't know any adolescent they've ever given that test to that by adult measures doesn't come out 'schizophrenic,' 'manic-depressive,' 'social pathology.' And that's just the way it is. . . ."

So then, are we speaking of adolescence itself as the pathology dictating incarceration?

Not exactly, of course. "That's not what I'm referring to. I'm referring to them having the adolescent swings and the problems—but also having no coping mechanisms; having self-destructive or self-defeating mechanisms, such as drugs and alcohol abuse and escapism, and violence. That combination leaves a kid really lost. In terms of how in the world is he going to be able to mitigate this very difficult period of adolescent growth and discovery."

She seems content that the distinction she is making contains a clear difference.

If Deborah is a passionate defender of the justifiable helplessness of parents in the face of the wayward youth she hospitalizes, that is only natural.

Explaining what led her to hospitalize her son, she says, "He had a lot of factors operating against him. His natural father has a long list of problems, all of which are transmitted genetically, such as chronic depression. There's manic-depressive psychosis in his family. There's paranoid schizophrenia, alcoholism. All of these things tend to be transmitted—especially father to son—the predisposition. I had a long and extended labor. They gave me a lot of drugs, which they don't give now. They had to use high forceps. He came into this world pretty beaten up, with what they considered to be soft neurological brain damage. Kept in the hospital, jaundiced, depressed at birth. Didn't attach. Was diagnosed at two as possibly having separation anxiety or attachment disorder. Real 'come here, go away' kind of behavior. Where he'd want me there constantly, and then if I'd pick him up, push me away."

Diagnosed. At two. If women over whom psychiatry/psychology has gained sway are indeed predisposed to seek intervention, even acute intervention, for their kids, then surely women who are themselves therapizers for other people's children would be that much more "at risk." Deborah has just given us the bio-tech analysis of her son's problems. She goes on to give the experiential ones:

"And then he was molested, without me being aware of it, by a big strong black kid that I thought had befriended him. That came out at a later time. His father, my ex-husband, was chronically depressed, just had a real bad time coping with life. And that even intensified his push-pull, because when little boys grow up they really need to separate from the mother. They need to be able to connect with a strong male figure, identify with him. And he didn't have that in his life.

"I took him to therapy—and he was so angry and so hostile, and so incapable of dealing with his impulses. I sought out the best. And they gave him every diagnosis—from sociopathy to thought disorder, attention deficit disorder, conduct disorder. I just—and of course each one of those diagnoses requires a different kind of focus."

In the face of this, one can only wonder what kind of Jesuitical heroics were required to allow her continued profession of psychiatric faith.

"So—I probably would have been better off and maybe my son would have been better off had I just given him all the love and affection without all the knowledge."

"Why?"

"*Why?* Because—when I first heard the diagnosis of thought disorder, I *know* how devastating this is. An eight-year-old kid who's psychotic? This means this is a serious impairment for the rest of their lives. This causes major problems in growth and development. It's a very somber diagnosis.

"If I had just been a layperson I'm sure I would have said, 'Well, what does that mean?' And they would have said, 'Well, it means that sometimes he tends to tune out from reality and you just need to get him into some structured therapy.' I wouldn't have been so— so vigilant. Of his progress. I wouldn't have been able to put together all the contradictions in everything I was hearing."

But, on the evidence, even she did not "put them together," but rather reacted like a racquetball in heated play.

"As soon as I would feel there was a contradiction and I would check it out, and he would get another diagnosis, I would change my approach to him. Based on what I knew was therapeutically appropriate. So I was a chameleon. I was wearing all these hats, and in the meantime my husband at that time would check himself into UCLA. He was gonna kill himself. Anyhow, I think I would have been a lot better off had I not been so well trained."

Or had she, perhaps, been more skeptical; less thoroughly indoctrinated.

"But I didn't have to be a therapist to see that nothing was working. And that he was getting more and more hostile. And it seemed like he was targeting me in particular, and I understand that. I was the strong parent. I was the woman. His father was the man. He said at one point, 'Why don't you just wear slacks? You're the man of the family.' And the weaker my husband would become, the stronger I would become and the more hateful he would be against me. Everything that went wrong was always my fault—because I was the strong one. That's typical: She's strong enough to handle this; she can make everything right.

"He stole my car at the age of thirteen. Got picked up by the police. They released him in my custody. Got sent to court. Lots of fines. Later on that summer he was arrested for throwing firecrackers in the next-door neighbor's yard.

"A few weeks after that, he sneaked out of his father's house, snuck into my house, knew I was gone, had an all-night party. With alcohol. Was arrested for that. But the system was very willing to just release him. If the kid is under the age of sixteen, they feel, well, it's just adolescent stuff, and the parents can get him treatment.

"The terms of probation were that he get into some kind of day treatment or private facility. So I took him to a hospital in the day treatment program, which was nonrestrictive. He would be picked up by a limousine in the morning. He would be brought back by limousine at three in the afternoon. And he was able to go through the units. He's very bright. No sign of a definite learning disability. They haven't been able to pinpoint neurological damage other than to say, 'It's just a minimal brain dysfunction of some sort.' But they can't see it in the testing. His testing scores vary widely—twenty to thirty points—on two things: The scanner goes up and down depending on his moods. So this would suggest that it's really more of a mood disorder than it is any kind of actual impairment.

"So I put him in day treatment. I satisfied terms of probation and got us through the units. I kept hearing 'treatment-treatment-treatment.' And I kept trying more, more. I tried everything from an M.D. to a Ph.D. . . .

"At one point, I remember, I was told by a therapist, 'You've got to sit on this kid, whatever his emotional problems or his physiological problems are. You can't be so concerned with him as having a disease. You have got to look at him as any other mom would look at a kid who was being so obnoxious. You're telling this kid that—because he has problems and because he's different from other kids—he has a right to write his own ticket.' So he says, 'He needs residential placement. He's getting too big. He's out of control. You can't handle him.' He said, 'Let the court system go through due process. We can use the probation to get him into one of the residential facilities.' But the court system didn't want to get involved. And insurance does not pay for residential placements.

"So—I tried contracting. I tried consequences. And I tried power plays. And—what precipitated him being hospitalized this last time—he was drinking, he was coming home drunk. I would wait up for him. And of course he would get very combative when he was drunk. It was impossible to have any kind of intelligent conversation.

"The next day I would take away his stereo. He would fight me for it. He would put holes in the wall. I would try to confiscate all his clothes. I would come up with any possible imaginable consequence. And he would just—'Fuck you'—walk out of the house.

"He had been missing school. He was not going to any of his classes. Staying out all night, two and three days at a time. Would attack his sister. I came home from work and she was hiding in the closet because she was afraid that he was gonna kill her. And he was up in his room, smoking cigarettes. And that's another house rule—you're not allowed to smoke cigarettes.

"He was restricted to his room, put on 'room status.' And—he was aware that was against the law. The police had informed him that I had no right to involuntarily restrain him to his room. That it's called 'illegal imprisonment.' "

Suddenly I am struck by what seems to be garish—California-style—humor. In this state, it is illegal for a parent to impose room restriction—but entirely legal for the same parent to hire a "service" to restrain the kid and transport him to a facility where the parent's surrogate can legally place the child in restraints, or in locked isolation.

Deborah is continuing, "The police department is very child oriented. There's a great deal of focus on child abuse. They try to give the children their rights, and protect the child. My son knew I couldn't restrict him legally. I asked the police, 'What happens if I try to physically drag him into his room and use my husband to do that?' And they said, 'Well, we can arrest you. And your husband will have to leave the home.'

"So I said to my son, 'You are just acting like a totally out-of-control, obnoxious brat. If you want—any money, if you want any allowance—I'm talking about restricting you from any kind of funds. I'm going on strike. I'm not taking you anywhere. I'm not driving you around. You get in your room and you stay in there.' Then I kept getting in his face, and he kept coming out, and I kept getting in his face. We went through that for eight solid hours. I practically collapsed.

"It escalated. After that he attacked my husband. He got the bruise on his nose then, from hitting a wall. He said he was going to smash us, he was going to kill us all. He said he was the top drug dealer in the county. That I was so stupid I didn't know his room was full of drugs and LSD.

"So I called the hospital that had seen him in day treatment. I had tried everything I know. I thought they would have some guidance for me, some direction. But I knew I couldn't allow him to tyrannize the household the way he was and I had to do something.

"So I went down to the hospital and talked to a psychologist. And he said, 'He needs to be contained. He is a danger to himself and to you.'

"I am knowledgeable, I am not uninformed. I had to agree with him. And of course—there was no way I was gonna say, 'Honey, get in the car. Let's go up to the hospital.' I thought my only option was to call Teen Shuttle. And they assured me, and my husband, that they knew how to deal with out-of-control kids.

"When the guys came to get him I was gone. I took my daughter out. I didn't want her exposed to that. My husband was not there. From my son's description, they handcuffed him, and they kicked him, and they kept him in handcuffs all the way to the facility. He claims that some doctor at the hospital who saw him right away told him that he had peripheral nerve damage because he couldn't feel his thumb. And he—had reopened the wound on his nose. His nose was bleeding. So I'm sure that it looked pretty bad—but the wound was from him attacking my husband and hitting his nose against the wall.

"We were not there, but I understand my son tried to arm himself. And they disarmed him and they got him down on the ground. And they put the cuffs on him. His hands behind his back. I'm sure that this was not comfortable. And I wish that there was any other way that I could have done it at that time."

Now I have asked Deborah whether I may speak with her son— or rather listen to him. She shakes her head. "He would simply con you," she says. "He's very smart, very charming. He would con you." Certainly it is clear from what Deborah describes that the *situation* is out of control. It is not clear, however, that her *son* is, or that this is a biological or psychological illness. It seems to me at least plausible that the constant focus on the boy's alleged defects— beginning when he was two—the reiterated imputations of illness, the total disagreement among the dozens of professionals he has been subject to, could be cause as easily as result. As Delia has told us, being under psychiatric surveillance, being psychiatrically sus- pect, for even three months can cause you to doubt yourself. To be viewed as, treated as, defective since toddlerhood? By a system of which your mother is part?

To suggest that what has happened to Deborah's son is iatrogenic—a word I encountered often in psy literature, meaning that the treatment is what's causing the problem—is not to suggest that what you have now is a kid you would cheerfully want to live with. It is only to suggest that there can be grave potential menace lurking in the seemingly benign psychiatric worldview, the notion that "treatment" can't hurt.

What, I ask Deborah, is the psychiatric hospital's concept of "treatment"?

"The hospital has a schedule of events that goes from eight A.M. till eight or nine at night. There are free periods. The adolescent inpatient program, they do have field trips. They do have their minimum of hours the kids are required by law to sit in school. They have all the special education teachers that come in. They also have study time that the child can choose—see, children earn the right to be able to have more freedom as they stay in the hospital longer.

"There's the level system. Kid first comes in—especially if we're talking about a kid who has a conduct disorder—he's on Level 1. Which means that he has to earn the right to get on Level 2—by just cooperating. Now, a kid can say, 'I'm not gonna go.' Then you don't go. There's nobody there to drag you out. 'I'm not going to breakfast.' 'I'm not going to school.' And the kid'll stay in his room. But the kid won't get off Level 1. Most kids, though, really do respond. Unless we're talking about a real hard-core case like my kid.

"The staff all demonstrate what's called good hugging, good ways to show affection. They hug each other. They're into giving positive strokes. A lot of bonding goes on in these programs."

I mentally scan Delia's story, Joey's, for hints that this is so. Fruitlessly.

"As I understand it," I say, "the level system is based on what's called the 'token economy.' What lies behind that philosophy?"

"It came from the philosophy that kids have to learn how to restructure their world with lots of assistance from the externals. Kids who get lost and fall through the cracks, especially if there's a drug and alcohol problem, which tends to be pretty common out here, have lost the capacity for that internal discipline. Because, as I say, there's been no external discipline. So they go from not having the discipline to having the discipline, structure, in terms of negative consequences that the structure offers to them—to give them a sense of how they can effectively use time on a day-to-day basis and be able to accomplish things that will increase their self-esteem. Raise their self-image."

I think what she's saying is they show the kid who's boss.

"But," she says, "it's easy to go through the levels. If a kid is cooperative, the levels don't represent any kind of deterrent."

But is it "healthy" to be cooperative with involuntary incarceration, most especially when it is called voluntary? As usual, it gets even murkier:

"As a matter of fact, you put an abused kid in the hospital setting—kids can respond to abuse either by identifying with the aggressor and being real violent themselves, or by being pseudocompliant. If you put a compliant kid in the hospital, that kid is probably going to whip through the system—'cause they bend over backwards to please the staff." Can *anyone* win this game? "I think learning to live within a structured environment is important no matter what the emotional impairment is. I'm projecting from my own experience—but just because a kid has mental illness, and just because a kid has had a lot of bad breaks, doesn't excuse that child from behaving in a minimally socialized fashion, as long as there are ample opportunities for affection and for communication and for caring and for reshaping. So I don't see anything wrong with having a schedule that you follow, and having a structure, and having them have to earn more and more freedoms."

"Then that," I ask, "is the 'treatment'?"

"No, that's not the treatment. That's the structure. The treatment is individual therapy at least three times a week. Group therapy every day. Occupational therapy. Recreational therapy."

"What makes recreation 'therapy'?"

"Well, it's being able to choose something that you enjoy. Rather than learning how to do an art or a craft that could be turned into some kind of occupational choice. Recreational therapy could be— well, do you want to go to the gym? Do you want to build up your body and lift weights? Do you want to go swimming in the swimming pool? Or do you want to do ceramics? Whatever the child would like to do that's going to build up his self-esteem and—be a channel for his outlets."

"But they do advise kids over fourteen of their rights?"

"My son read in his patients' rights handbook that he had a right to an advocate. So within a few hours he was requesting a call to an advocate. And—the hospital claims they called her within the amount of time, and left messages. She claims, I believe, that she didn't get messages, or that she was not called in the twenty-four-hour period. There again—the situation is real unique. I mean, most kids, they're given the handbook and they're advised of their rights and—they forget it. They don't want to talk with a patient advocate. But my son memorized his book." She laughs. "And he confronted them, and he said, 'I know my rights.' And, 'How can they handcuff me?' And, 'How can they do this?' And, 'I want a hearing.' And, 'I want to go to court.' He's very skillful. I mean, he's therapy-wise. His mom's a therapist. He's been in therapy most of his life. He prides himself on being able to outmanipulate therapists and to totally frustrate them. So he knows the jargon. He knows the laws. The kid would be a great criminal attorney.

"He said, 'I want to know the criteria for involuntary placement.' And she told him—I think it's an extreme mental condition essentially. Just bad behavior is not a criterion or just having what's considered to be normal emotional reactions to certain circumstances won't justify it. You have to have a DSM-III diagnosis as having some kind of mental disorder that is seriously impairing you. So he was fighting it on the grounds that he did not have a mental disability.

"Well, I talked to the advocate. I said, 'We have testing reports that go way back. This kid has been given many diagnoses, all of which are serious. Plus, his behavior is totally out of control and we can't handle it because he is self-destructive. How can he possibly build a case on the fact that he doesn't have a mental disability?'

"But they called in a psychiatric evaluator, a psychiatrist, and she evaluated him independent of the hospital. She's an independent contractor. And we had the hearing. And my son was claiming—his position was that he had a hard time adjusting to his stepfather, that it was simply situational, that it was a reaction to the divorce and to the change in life-style, and it's all within the norm of what would normally be expected. And—it sounded great.

"It's the independent psychiatrist's job to just objectively review whatever material is there. And to give whatever tests are necessary, and to make an independent evaluation of what she sees going on. She doesn't have to prove that he's not impaired to get him out. All that she has to do is have any kind of evidence to suggest that a less oppressive environment would be helpful. Well, the thing was—he'd been in day treatment, which is the step down. And even though he made his thirty units, it's because he was sat on. But they did not consider his stay in the day treatment center successful. As a matter of fact, when the psychiatrist discharged him, he told me, 'He's gonna end up in jail or dead.' He says, 'Nothing's gonna help. You've been to every therapist in the world.' He said, 'It's extreme depression, which he refuses to look at. He's got extreme anxiety, which he refuses to take medication for. And he's angry. He will not let anybody close. He will not talk about his problems. And when you have that combination, it's just pretty much guaranteed that he's gonna end up just burning himself out in a self-destructive way.'

"So they had all this. They had all the evidence that a less oppressive environment was not effective. And—for the first time in his life the kid had a group of professionals and adults that he couldn't con. And—was shocked. His mouth dropped open. He said, 'What? I have to stay? You're telling me I have to stay?' He was just beside himself. And he started to cry. I felt so bad.

"And the advocate immediately said, 'Let's go up from here. Sign right here and we'll go to court on this and we'll get a writ.' "

What is interesting here is the impression Deborah seems to share that SB 595, a kid's right to an "independent" review, is in any meaningful way about a kid's due process rights, his liberty interests. In fact, it is a *clinical* review. Not only is the word "independent" specious when applied to the review—(the psychiatrist can be, and often is, affiliated with the hospital)—but even without the potential for corruption there is bound to be legitimate nervousness on the part of the reviewer. If he or she were to say that the kid did not need to be in the hospital, would there be liability should something happen? The parents, after all, often are in alliance with the hospital psychiatrists.

The truth, according to a report by the local patient advocacy program, is that among the 891* admissions reported in San Diego County between January 1, 1990, and November 30, 1990, only four minors were found by the reviewer not to meet the admission criteria.[12]

The San Diego report challenges the process: "In those cases where a review does take place . . . the question must be asked as to whether any rights are legitimately protected and what the benefit is of such a lengthy, elaborate, expensive, and intrusive process."

Is the process misleading to minors? the report asks. "Because the minor is told that they have a *right* to a review and because an advocate comes in from the outside to 'represent' them, does this not create a perception that the minor is choosing a legal type review and not a clinical one? If so, what effect does this have on the minor? Is this an honest approach?"

Is the process potentially detrimental to minors and to families? "The SB 595 process requires that minors privately disclose personal, intimate information to a total stranger and then participate in a meeting where family, hospital staff, a psychiatrist, and an advocate openly discuss all the problems that led to their being hospitalized. One must ask what impact this has on the teenagers' self-esteem and what the effect is on the family. One must question whether any purpose is being served."

The hospitals are the ones that introduced this legislation, and they are perfectly happy with the review process. Why? "Hospital staff have indicated that minors often do not get involved in treatment until after the review process is over and in that sense they feel the clinical review process is of value." In other words, as in Delia's case, a sort of public degradation ceremony is enacted in which it is brought home to the kid that there is no way out, no one able to be effective on her behalf. "However," the report notes, "one

---

* A number far below the projected estimate of 1,757 over eleven months, which was based on the *actual* number of admissions in 1988. Investigation showed a significant number of admissions were simply not reported. A review of medical records at five of seven facilities in San Diego County showed a slight *increase* in admissions over 1988, not the 49 percent decrease suggested.

must ask whether the actual intent of SB 595 was to produce compliance with treatment or to provide a legitimate review of the appropriateness of these admissions."

Over lunch Richard Danford, director of San Diego's patient advocacy program, says, "What's tragic is that the providers will say, 'These review hearings are good things because the kids are rebellious, not involved in treatment, may be on suicide precautions or unit restrictions because they're contesting being in. And they sit and they listen to the hospital tell them why they have to be in the hospital, and psychiatrists tell them why they're so sick, and why they need to be in the hospital. And then to have this decision made that they have to stay in the hospital. And they say that after that they're 'more compliant' and they're 'ready to get invested in treatment.'

"It's an absolute joke that it's called an 'independent' clinical review. We had a follow-up hearing after that thing became law. At the capital. And we had all the lobbyists there and the psychiatric association. And I just stood up and said, 'Who is kidding who?' I said, 'I've had to publicly speak on this issue because one of my responsibilities as patients' rights advocate is to educate the community about all the requirements of the law.' "

Danford continues: "And every time I speak, without influencing what I want my audience to think, I describe this process. When I tell them it's an 'independent clinical review' conducted by a psychiatrist on staff of the hospital, I get laughter. This is unbelievable what we're trying to do. It's a lie. You make the kid think that it's due process. You tell them they've got a right to a hearing. They're advised of it, that there's this advocate from the outside that's gonna come in and represent you. And it's a lie. Because all it is is a second opinion by a psychiatrist on the staff of the hospital.

"There's no reason whatsoever to dress it up this way unless you're trying to make somebody think it's something other than what it is. And at that point I recommended that if they insisted on going forward with it, that it be amended—that the advocate be eliminated from the process: that I didn't want to participate in this any longer. I felt dirty when I did.

"In fact, our focus became just trying to make sure the kid

understands all of this, to minimize the damage. So when it's all over with, they're not pissed off because they thought they were getting something else. And also to maximize— We were able to save the writ language in 595, which says after the hearing's over, minors retain all writs including the writ of habeas corpus [a writ or order requiring that a prisoner be brought before the court at a stated time and place to decide the legality of his detention or imprisonment; safeguards against illegal detention or imprisonment]. In some counties, kids don't have rights to writs—so they're up the proverbial creek without a paddle. In this county they do, so after they've been through this process you can say, 'Oh, there's something else you can try.' Most of them say, 'Go to hell.' Those who do request writs get out. The vast majority do."

In other words, when kids get a legal review—as differentiated from a clinical review—the majority get out. And they get this legal review *after* losing at the clinical review. What Danford is saying, what is happening here, is that in the majority of cases, a true independent hearing, a listening to the kid and the circumstances, will contradict and overrule the psychiatrists.

Deborah's son, however, did not file a writ. In a sense, Deborah conned him out of it.

She says, "I worked out a deal with him. I said, 'All right. I will let you out if you show me that you can comply with rules for one week.' He said, 'That's too much. I'm not gonna do that. I can't smoke in here.' 'Well—that means you have to quit smoking for a week.' He said, 'That's crazy. I can't do that.' I said, 'Nicorette gum. They'll prescribe it.' I said, 'That means you have to go to all your individual therapy sessions. You have to attend school. And you have to go to group, and you have to participate. I want to see that behavior for one week, and I will let you out. Seven days.' He said, 'I'll file a writ.' I said, 'File the writ. But you'll be in three or four weeks if you file the writ.' I was conning him. He could get out in three days.

"He said, 'You're shittin' me.' I said, 'No. No. I really believe that we would get an attorney and we would represent ourselves. You can do it the easy way: Give me one week of compliant behavior— and I'll let you out.' Well. He tried it. But he snuck cigarettes in. So they busted him down. He was almost on Level 3. I mean he went from Level 1 to Level 3 in a matter of five days. You can do this, easily. So. They found him with cigarettes. They busted him. And he was fully expecting to be let out. Good old Mom was gonna buy the—'Oh, Mom, I *tried*. I did a pretty good job.'

"So I came on Friday. I said, 'You broke the rules.' 'For what? I went to school. Didn't I go to school? Didn't I talk in group? I didn't even call the therapists assholes once.' I said, 'I'm sorry. Those are my terms.' So he threw a temper tantrum. He screamed and yelled—and I had to walk away from that. Which is hard. But I did. And I said, 'Let's try this next week.' So he did. He quit smoking, he got on the Nicorette gum. He got points. He earned a half credit in school. And I said, 'Okay. Fine. Let's sit down and make a contract. So I made a contract. The therapist reviewed the contract. He said, 'Okay. You agree to do this, you agree to do that, and your mom will let you out. . . . You know that Mom can always call Teen Shuttle if things get really out of control.' He says, 'You can always call those guys to come beat me up?' I said, 'If I can't stand you being at home and being this violent, disruptive.'

"So—he came home. He doesn't go to school. He gets hostile. But he's not been violent. He's not hit anybody. He doesn't drink anymore. Which I think is—great. I think it's absolutely great. But he's still a mixed-up kid. He's got a lot of problems."

In the end, despite having detailed all her son's deficits from birth, his biological predisposition to mental illness, his earlier childhood rape, Deborah places blame on social forces.

"I just don't see there's a firm delineation between what the schools can offer, what the courts can offer, what the parents can offer. Parents don't know how to be strong. And then they try to be strong and they end up doing it wrong. I think everybody's confused." And here it comes, the in-my-day. "When I was growing up, right was right and wrong was wrong, and there were things that you had to do and it may have been too oppressive—and I think my generation was very much into fighting the oppression and 'do your own thing'—but it was definitely a reaction against something that was very defined. Today there's so little definition. What is right? What is wrong? What is preferable? What is cool? So kids are defining in their ways, in a way that is really demoralizing. Even my good kids that I see that are just having normal family problems are ashamed to be seen with a nerd. A nerd is defined as a kid who does well in school. So they're struggling to find their own definition and to find values and morals. I don't know what happened to the strong morality factor. Kids do not want that much power. They want to be told how to behave and how to be adults and how to grow up.

"They need something to rebel against."

As I take leave of Deborah, I am musing: But maybe one way of thinking about it is that her son *might indeed* have something to rebel against, and rebelling against it he is: The oppression of having since childhood been seen as a psychiatric case; of—because his mother is of the psy world—having been under twenty-four-hour psychiatric surveillance ever since he was born.

8

The School
Connection I

In "A CRITIQUE OF DSM-III," Joel Kovel writes of the celebrated diagnostic handbook the *Malleus* that it "described its socially deviant objects with even more unanimity than do the psychiatric practitioners of our time. . . ." He says, "[T]he *Malleus* was perhaps the first distinct precursor of DSM-III—a systematic compendium of forms of deviance, artfully constructed by men who were considered representatives of order and reason, and who devised their system to enforce submission to the prevailing reality principle. Viewed with centuries of hindsight it appears bizarre and perverted in the extreme, a sadistic attack on an entire gender carried out with a repellently fanatical degree of repression. We must also be prepared to admit, however, that the *Malleus* was also a careful and intellectually sophisticated, even elegant system that embodied a kind of rationality which in turn derived from and lent legitimacy to a dominant worldview." And he adds, "Nor can its high degree of rationalization be separated from the barbarity it enabled."[1]

While it might seem hyperbolic to equate the present level of psychiatric policing of children with the scientifically legitimated murder of thousands of women diagnosed to suffer from what might now be called Biologically Based Witching Disorder, it is sobering to note that the severity gap diminishes considerably once social norms are taken into account: The greater degree of witch-directed barbarity is in keeping with then-prevailing norms of rough justice. The fifteenth century was a more raucous time all around, and there was not much evidence of the nicety of feeling that inspires us now to finely debate the propriety of capital punishment. (*Peine forte et dur*—torture—was then a routine legal prescription, not something to be reported to Amnesty International.) And—there were not then those psychoactive substances that so effectively reduce the need for physical barbarism in the practices that derive from the psy lexicon.

Most important, it was with witches that the gaze of science first began the transition from punishment to treatment: from the idea of heresy to the idea of mental illness.[2] But while the vocabulary began gradually changing, the goal did not: the control of deviance in service to the established order.

Like the *Malleus*, today's DSM codifies social ideology and legitimizes the technology that is the practice of intervention. What makes it far more sophisticated is not the clarity of its diagnoses, but its elegant adaptability. Capable of apparently infinite linguistic mutations, it is excellent at masking the desire for control in the guise of concern—thus serving the more repressive urges of the conservative while appealing to the benevolent impulses of those more liberal and humane.

Particularly illustrative is the case history of a diagnosis—now known as "Attention Deficit Hyperactivity Disorder" (ADHD)—along with its sibling, "Learning Disorders" (LD).

Gerald Coles, author of *The Learning Mystique*, writes, "Attention deficit has become the 'official' medical category for diagnosing LD. . . . Attention deficit disorder is different from other LD classifications in that it is both educational and medical. The medical use of the diagnosis, whether it is called attention deficit disorder or one of the earlier terms, has been the official basis for treating this 'disorder' with drugs, mostly Ritalin."[3] Coles classifies the description of a child with ADD (with or without hyperactivity) as being "vague and preposterous."[4] (The "essential features" of the disorder being: "often fails to finish things he or she starts; often doesn't seem to listen; has difficulty concentrating on school work; often acts before thinking; frequently calls out in class." As he says, "If the diagnosis is faulty, prescribing the drugs becomes questionable However, for those who prescribe drugs to children diagnosed as having an attention deficit disorder, poor definitions and a classification system with questionable grounds has not hampered their practice any more than it did when the 'disorder' was called something else."5

≈

The history of the ADD (or ADHD) diagnosis (which began life with the humble name of *hyperkinesis*) brings together most of the elements currently at play in the world of kiddie psy: entrepreneurial technology (pharmaceuticals); the demand for conformity suited to the prevailing social climate; the changing role of schools as agents of that conformity; the shifting of focus from institutional deficits to individual diseases; and the uncanny way in which psy techniques are able to gain support from both those who seek to control and those who seek to "help"—without discomfiture to either.

In terms of young people, two major social concerns served to invite the psychiatric gaze. One, *in theory* conservative-driven, has long been juvenile delinquency (or vagrant youth, wayward youth, rebellious youth). The second, *in theory* liberal-driven, was concern with helping children by improving their education. In fact, since learning disorders and hyperactivity were quickly identified as leading to poor school performance and then juvenile delinquency, and since poor school performance and juvenile delinquency were seen as stemming from individual learning disorders or hyperactivity, the differences quickly became far more theoretical than actual. Nonetheless, candor about the one has a history of proving impolitic, while espousal of the other—concern for children's education—plays well.

In 1969 Dr. Arnold A. Hutschnecker, then a practicing psychotherapist, proposed to President Richard M. Nixon that "the Government should have mass testing done on all 6–8 year old children . . . to detect [those] who have violent and homicidal tendencies."

The gist was that the "delinquent tendencies" could be identified and given "corrective treatment." When this leaked to the press, it generated an uproar. Apart from the clearly implied step toward preventive detention, it was almost impossible not to detect an underlying racism. Liberals were outraged.[6]

One week after the Hutschnecker proposal broke before the public (April 14, 1970), James E. Allen, Jr., the assistant secretary for education and U.S. commissioner of education, spoke at the annual convention of the National School Boards Association. His credentials were as a liberal, and he would later be forced to resign because of his anti–Vietnam War stance. He proposed a plan under which "there would be available in the school district a Central Diagnostic Center to which, at age 2½, a child would be brought by his parents or guardian. The purpose of the Center would be to find out everything possible about the child and his background that would be useful in planning an individualized learning program for him. This would be accomplished through an education diagnosis, a medical diagnosis, and home visits by a trained professional who would in effect become the child's and family's counselor. By the time the tests and home visits were completed, the Center would know just about everything there is to know about this child—his home and family background, his cultural and language deficiencies, his health and nutrition needs, and his general potential as an individual."[7]

While the one proposal frankly seeks to spotlight and target the potential delinquent for "medical" intervention,* beginning at ages six through eight, the other—apparently more benign because of its holistic intent—proposes to place all children, beginning at two and a half, under chronic "medical" surveillance, using educational "diagnoses," medical "diagnoses," and family harmony "diagnoses." In other words, the medical language facilitated liberal support of a

---

* " 'In medicine,' Hutschnecker had written, 'we seek preventive measures: we vaccinate, we quarantine, we immunize' " (Peter Schrag and Diane Divoky, *The Myth of the Hyperactive Child: And Other Means of Child Control* [New York: Pantheon Books, 1975], p. 9).

degree of invasiveness greater than that proposed by a conservative. How could this be?

As Peter Schrag and Diane Divoky reasoned in their seminal 1975 work, *The Myth of the Hyperactive Child*, Allen's proposal—and others in the same vein—caught liberals at a time of disenchantment about the possibility of changing social institutions and susceptible to the alternative passion: changing individuals. If it was fruitless to place the onus for social ills on social forces, here was a way to attend to the ills suffered by the individual, in language that appeared to avoid the imputation of blame.

One of those ills—a very visible one—was the restlessness of some kids, which led to school behaviors that, in turn, brought them censure instead of success. Since these same behaviors had been identified in the 1940s in postencephalitic children,[8] who had suffered some degree of brain injury as a result of their disease, it was now possible to posit the reverse: that if children exhibited these behaviors, they must have some degree of brain injury, encephalitis or no. It was the ability to conjure this kind of logic that made Lewis Carroll and later the Marx brothers such entertaining fellows.

Thus, hyperkinesis became "Minimal Brain Damage" (MBD) and—when the "damage" could not be physiologically verified—"Minimal Brain *Dysfunction*" (which allowed the acronym to stay the same). This was soon held accountable for "everything from learning disabilities to divorce and homicide."[9]

The conservatives unabashedly continued to play the same tune of "Borderline Eugenics" ("You will find that whereas slums make people, the basic truth is that people make slums; they cannot do otherwise," said one psychiatrist. "Their deficits and their lack of equipment make it inevitable that they will create a shambles. They ought not to be permitted to bring children into the world to perpetuate their own misery and inner and outer poverty,"[10] etc.) . . .

. . . While the liberals went enthusiastically on their own way—in much the same general direction. In fact, they offered psychiatry a much greater, and much richer population to mine: one that would bring under psy's sway not only poor children from socially anarchic circumstances, but middle-class children who simply were not achieving in school at the level the schools or their parents thought they should.

Johnny was not lazy, nor was the school failing to educate him decently: He had a learning disorder. Or he had an attention disorder. And the root of these disorders was a biological or neurological or genetic glitch. Poverty was let off the hook. Social injustices were let off the hook. Parents were let off the hook. Lousy schools and dysfunctional teachers were let off the hook. There was simply something biologically wrong with these children that accounted for all the things that teachers, parents, and Boy Scout leaders did not like about a whole panoply of childhood behaviors: not sitting still, not paying attention, not learning to read correctly (on time), butting in . . .

School personnel were elevated to the front lines: They were now the customs agents who were to identify the early symptoms of all these disorders. By the end of the sixties schools were spoken of as laboratories filled with "learning clinicians," offering "psychosocial treatment" for kids. [11]

The newly promoted "learning clinicians" took their mandate to heart. Educators lobbied for congressional passage of the Early and Periodic Screening, Diagnosis and Treatment Program (EPSDT) as part of the Medicaid package. (It passed in 1967.) This called for screening for physical, mental, psychological, and behavioral deviations of all children who were Medicaid eligible (that is, the poor) to search out "their physical or mental defects" and to provide measures to "correct or ameliorate defects and chronic conditions discovered thereby, as may be mandated by the Secretary." [12]

And so unacceptable behavior, problems in school, began to fall under the medical rubric, and—as good-news legislation led to more good-news legislation—schools themselves gained a measure of medical authority: gatekeepers, as it were, to the psy world, which—as we shall shortly see—began to court them for referrals. Learning disabilities became a subcategory under the general DSM heading of "Developmental Disorders," alongside some behavioral problems, all broadly conceptualized as due to biological or neurological deficits.

When Congress passed the Education for All Handicapped Children Act[13] mandating specialized educational services for children whose handicapping conditions included sensory or orthopedic impairment or mental retardation, it included children with serious emotional disturbance or specific learning disabilities—thus including as potentially "in need of" special ed all children identified as ADHD or who were claimed to have LD.

Since funding existed, research was generated: tons of it. But, as saner voices pointed out, the entire, ever-expanding grab bag of "indicators" was fundamentally flawed because it was circular: The behaviors or misbehaviors were signs of brain damage because brain damage could produce similar behaviors.

The same circularity was applied to the prescription of Ritalin: "if a drug 'improves' a problem thought to result from a brain dysfunction, that demonstrates that a brain dysfunction is the source of the problem."[14]* In 1972, 396,000 prescriptions for Ritalin were written by private physicians for children examined in their offices (thus not including prescriptions that might have been written in hospital or clinic settings). The number jumped to 480,760 by 1974, leapt to 608,660 in 1975. The manufacturer, CIBA, claimed that in 1985, Ritalin was prescribed to treat attentional deficit disorder in up to 500,000 children, but they expected that to increase as the number of children diagnosed increased.[15]

All along, saner voices *did* exist: In 1971, William M. Cruikshank of the University of Michigan, a national authority in special education, "had complained that the LD label was being applied to children who stuttered, teased the family cat, had night terrors, couldn't swim, masturbated, didn't like to go with girls, bit their nails, had poor eating habits, didn't keep their room neat, wouldn't take baths, or didn't brush their teeth."[16] Saner voices continue to speak. But saner voices have not prevailed.

---

* The alleged "improvement" was that some children placed on the drug became markedly more subdued, less obstreperous. If I am not mistaken, in the not so long ago, mothers figured out the same thing about moderate amounts of brandy. However, when the doctors prescribe a drug, it is evidently science. What the mothers did, we now consider an outrage.

Without leading us into the steamy jungle of studies that have been done attempting to validate the administering of Ritalin to five- and six-year-olds, nor through the thicket of meticulous documentation that refutes those studies, let me simply quote from the manufacturer's own fact sheet about the drug—a fact sheet available in any decent pharmacy.

Here, it is written that "Ritalin is a mild central nervous system stimulant. . . . The mode of action in man is not completely understood, but Ritalin presumably activates the brain stem arousal system and cortex to produce its stimulant effect.

"There is neither specific evidence which clearly establishes the mechanism whereby Ritalin produces its mental and behavioral effects in children, nor conclusive evidence regarding how these effects relate to the condition of the central nervous system. . . ." About attention deficit disorder the sheet tells us, "Specific etiology of this syndrome is unknown, and there is no single diagnostic test." Contraindications: "Marked anxiety, tension and agitation are contraindications to Ritalin, since the drug may aggravate these symptoms." Warnings: "Sufficient data on safety and efficacy of long-term use of Ritalin in children are not yet available. Although a causal relationship has not been established, suppression of growth (i.e., weight gain, and/or height) has been reported with the long-term use of stimulants in children. . . . [A]dministration of Ritalin may exacerbate symptoms of behavior disturbance and thought disorder." Also, "Careful supervision is required during drug withdrawal, since severe depression as well as the effects of chronic overactivity can be unmasked."[17]

Whatever "unmasked" may mean, according to Peter Breggin, the 1990 *Physicians' Desk Reference* "has a special box on 'Drug Dependence' for Ritalin, including warnings that drug withdrawal can be accompanied by 'severe depression' and hyperactivity."[18] As Breggin says, "It seems to have escaped Ritalin advocates that long-term use tends to create the very same problems that Ritalin is supposed to combat—'attentional disturbances' and 'memory problems' as well as 'irritability' and hyperactivity. When children are prescribed Ritalin for years because they continue to have problems focusing their attention, the disorder itself may be due to the

Ritalin. A vicious circle is generated, with drug-induced inattention causing the doctor to prescribe more medication, all the while blaming the problem on a defect within the child."[19]

One can only view with awe the fact that a diagnosis that is problematic and has been authoritatively and persuasively challenged can be matched snugly with a chemical response that is problematic (and has been authoritatively and persuasively challenged)—and continuing success nonetheless guaranteed. And view with awe the fact that this is called science, much less medicine (with its historical promise to "first do no harm"). Place this alongside the fact that on the street, Ritalin has a market value as "speed." And consider that without knowing what, precisely, it does to the young body (but with considerable evidence that it can not only cause physical damage,* but actually cause the symptoms it is meant to address), Ritalin is nonetheless routinely administered to children whose major "symptom" is that they are annoying someone in authority, or are not doing as well as it is thought they should in school. Now place all that against the fact that marijuana continues to be forbidden as a prescription for the relief of pain in terminally ill cancer patients. . . . Awe becomes amazement.

≈

Not only was the ADHD diagnosis being enthusiastically marketed by the schools, the pharmaceutical companies (particularly CIBA, the manufacturer of Ritalin), and the psy establishment, but it was being enthusiastically reported on in the press and enthusiastically embraced by the public.

The cause for the first group is not difficult to determine: dominion and bucks. As for the second, if nothing else, MBD, ADD/LD played to the apparently endless American passion for educational self-flagellation. As for why the public embraced it? To say that it let

---

* About Ritalin's effects, Peter Breggin reports, "Many cases of full-blown Tourette's syndrome are reported, characterized by both facial and vocal tics. Sometimes these neurological disorders do not subside after temination of treatment, and tragically, neuroleptics may be prescribed to control them, increasing the risk of further neurological disorders."

parents off the hook is inaccurate: It let mothers off the hook. But to say that is to neglect the damage that had been done to women in the forties and the fifties, the early sixties—when the Freudian worldview held sway—by that hook.

As feminist Florence Rush has written about her own experience of motherhood during that time, when her son "Bill" was failing in junior high school: "He had never been a good student and since third grade I ran regularly to school conferences, supervised his studies and forced him to do hated homework. Nothing helped. The counselor offered no solution . . . thought the difficulty might stem from the home, put it to me to figure something out, and of course I did. I found a very expensive private school fully staffed with hand-picked educators and psychiatric experts dedicated to help the underachiever. . . . The school, steeped in [then prevailing] psychiatric principles, maintained that students who could not function academically usually suffered from disturbed parental relationships. Since Bill's father had little to do with raising his son, it was naturally I who was the controlling and domineering parent unable to let her son grow up. With years of experience and authority in all matters pertaining to education, and in order to obtain each student's confidence, the school established the rule that parents were not permitted to communicate with any staff member. Since the mother was usually the greatest threat to the child, the school director emphasized for my benefit that I would not be given any information regarding my son's progress. I was not permitted a phone conversation with a teacher and I was warned against trying to wheedle information from my son. . . .

"One year later, I received a phone call from the school psychiatrist who did not bother to disguise his annoyance and impatience with me. He questioned my lack of interest in my son, wondered why I never contacted the school or asked for a progress report. Before I could protest, I was informed that my son was not only failing everything, but was also using hard drugs. When I broke down in tears and confusion, I was told I had good reason to cry because my son was seriously emotionally ill and needed to be hospitalized."[20] Bill, as it turned out, was not on drugs; was not emotionally ill, and was not hospitalized. He simply did not like school. Bill went on to become a successful entrepreneur.

Compared with the authorized vilification of mothers that had gained legitimacy during the reign of the Freudian view, it is no wonder that MBD-LD—the *idée fixe* of a mysterious no-fault neurological handicap—was greeted by women as a gift from the gods.

Most crucially, however, as one critic pointed out, "Another possible explanation for parents' misguided acceptance of the LD explanation was that they lacked the expertise for evaluating it."[21] Florence Rush, among others, went on, in the late 1970s, to explode Freud's Oedipal theory, which suggested that women who told him of sexual abuse as children were simply fantasizing.* As has since become common knowledge, Freud originally believed the women. He had originally formulated this belief as the seduction theory— that sexual abuse in childhood was what led to later "hysteria" in women. It was only in the face of the jeers, hoots, and catcalls of his colleagues that he said, in effect, "I take it back."

The critical point here is that Freud was writing in common parlance. He was speaking of events (or eventually, imaginings) and of feelings, of (if you will) human drama. He was speaking of experience and reaction—all of which are accessible to us; about all of which we are *competent* to have an opinion (whether professionals choose to take us seriously or not). Once the playing field is shifted to neurotransmitters and norepinephrines and suchlike it is as though we have been transposed to another planet, where we are at the mercy of Other Creatures who speak an Other Language, claiming Wondrous Knowledge. And hey—the teacher says my kid's not doing good. What's that, doc? Give him this Other Bottle? The one that says, "Drink me"?

While conservatives continued to hanker after the kind of Pavlov-

---

* Her original article, "The Freudian Coverup," appeared in *Chrysalis* (No. 1, 1977) and was included in her book *The Best Kept Secret: Sexual Abuse of Children* (McGraw-Hill: New York, 1980). Jeffrey Moussaieff Masson elaborated powerfully on this in his book *The Assault on Truth: Freud's Suppression of the Seduction Theory* (Farrar, Straus & Giroux, Inc.: New York, 1984).

ian methods used during the Soviet regime, the more moderate investors in the new ideology of reform bought stock in philosophies derived from B.F. Skinner and his psy-fi of behavior modification[22]—again begging to differ by advocating much the same thing. The reasoning mind might well ask why, if all these children suffered actual neurological or biological malfunctions—if it was not something they were doing willfully—it made sense to treat them with a system of punishments and rewards that implied what they needed was *reform*, a system of institutionalized *correction*. But reason did not rule in this kingdom. Passion did. And politics. And commerce. And turf.

No one appeared to suspect that, with the shift to the biological, neurological, genetic paradigm, what they had just welcomed in the door was a Trojan horse. Because it is possible to argue with a wrongheaded belief system. Despite psychiatric arrogance, "complexes"—as a concept, a formulation or interpretation of life experience—lend themselves to rational inquiry, to reference to one's own feelings and experience, to discourse. As long as psy was a belief system about human *being*, human beings had the *wherewithal* to challenge it, whether they chose to do so or not. But once the human dimension began to be removed, once the discourse took place on a linguistic plane of pure science, in the language of neurotransmitters and chemistry, none but a very tiny percentage of the species was in any position to engage in conversation or to challenge received wisdom.

Consider, for example, trying to think about, much less discuss, the content of a chapter titled "The Neurobiology of Developmental Disorders." We are only on page 4 (of 52) and only at the twenty-eighth day of gestation here: "By 28 days of gestation, the brain has expanded in size and forms three vesicular swellings: the forebrain (prosencephalon), the midbrain (mesencephalon), and the hindbrain (rhombencephalon). In the fifth week, the forebrain divides into the telencephalon and the diencephalon, and the hindbrain divides into the metencephalon and the myelencephalon. These five vesicles differentiate into the final structure of the brain. The telencephalon gives rise to the cerebral vesicles, the diencephalon forms the thalamus, the mesencephalon becomes the midbrain, the metencephalon becomes the pons and the cerebellum, and the myelencephalon differentiates into the medulla oblongata. . . ."[23]

It is enough to make one nostalgic for the good old days of penis envy.

Of that tiny percentage among us qualified to authoritatively read and comment, any who did pose challenges could effectively be pilloried as faulty scientists, without being able to appeal to the wider (uncredentialed) public for support.

As it would turn out, women had traded the helplessness of guilt for just plain helplessness: had unwittingly traded a reliance on experts for an abject dependency on them—void of all ability to rebut.

Given the exclusionary nature of the new bio-psy language, given the service the bio-psy system renders the status quo, and given the common-law marriage between alleged biological disturbance and biochemical interventions, it is impossible to overestimate the power of the psychopharmaceutical complex, particularly where juveniles are concerned. Once the *Parham* decision put the federal judiciary's stamp on psychiatry's medical nature, there was a chilling effect on further legal challenges. As in the case of California, to contemplate adversarial action against outfits like Teen Shuttle is seen as risking the loss of even those protections that exist.

The field is thus wide open for creative entrepreneurialism: the generation of new drugs, new diseases, which both pharmaceutical companies and hospitals then market to the schools, to the public. So long as they do not descend directly to the level of snake oil salesmen—as happened with the private, for-profit hospitals' advertising in the late eighties—they rest with ever-increasing security on their power as the authoritative emissaries of pure "science."

"Throughout the late sixties and early seventies," Schrag and Divoky write, "the CIBA literature was backed by a direct sales campaign in which company representatives were urged, in the words of one CIBA executive, to become 'more effective pushers.' The objectives were teacher training institutes, juvenile probation officers, PTA meetings and whatever other community groups might be hospitable. 'Your ingenuity in the promotion of Ritalin,' the executive said in his 1971 territorial sales report, 'is becoming more apparent.' "[24]

If the pharmaceutical industry was the original pioneer in addressing the psychiatric anomalies of kids with the traditional tools of corporate America—advertising and marketing—the private, for-profit psychiatric hospital chains followed close behind, bringing fresh ingenuity to the business task at hand. To the chains' great benefit, they had available for their employ a whole pool of people who were true believers; people able to provide them a front of genuine caring and credibility; people *willing* to do so. At least to begin with.

Max Schilling is currently a program specialist in the Teenage Parent Program in Fort Myers, Florida. For three years during the late 1980s he was a marketing representative for Charter Glade Hospital in Fort Myers.

Schilling had a B.A. in psychology and had graduated with a commitment to the mental health field; a commitment to help. He worked at a couple of halfway houses with aggressive retarded male adults before getting a job on a sort of subcounselor level at Charter Glade. To begin with, quite content to work with the kids and admiring of the competence of the staff, he saw no problems. Fairly quickly he was moved up to doing psychometrics, psychological testing.

When a job opened up in the marketing department he was placed there. His assignment: to develop employee assistance programs with large and small employers in the area, and to promote the chemical dependency unit. When, three months later, the marketing director left, Schilling was asked to become the adolescent unit representative: to represent the program and its staff in the community. "Initially," he says, "this was not uncomfortable for me. I was confident that I was essentially bringing teenagers to the treatment . . . that would significantly and positively impact their quality of life, self-understanding and functioning in society."

At the time, 1987, Schilling says that the hospital's annual marketing budget exceeded $650,000.[25] Schilling directed his efforts to the high schools and middle schools, to the juvenile justice system, and to other public and private residential treatment programs. As

well, of course, as to the media. His initial task was to make connections ("develop referral sources"). He says, "I tried to meet the
administrators from as many high schools and middle schools as
possible. These included principals, assistant principals, deans,
school psychologists, guidance counselors and social workers.

"At first, some school officials were wary of me—mental health
services for profit is a disquieting notion for some people. But I was
armed with statements and figures that presented the hospital in a
positive light." He would inform people, for example, that Charter
Medical Corporation was the largest health care contributor to the
United Way in 1988. He would announce the hospital's strong
support of the Mental Health Association and other related groups,
the corporation's generous contributions. He would also say, as he
then believed to be true, that "a considerable percentage" of patient
billing was written off every year—meaning the hospital was treating kids independent of their ability to pay. In general, he presented
this for-profit operation as one with a social conscience, committed
to helping kids, to "serving the community." Schilling's demeanor is
forthright and confidence inspiring. It helped immeasurably that, at
that point, he believed he was telling the truth.

Given Schilling's intelligence, his direct manner, his apparently
intimate knowledge of the hospital's workings, it is no wonder that,
as he says, "Most school officials came to regard me, and indirectly
the hospital, rather positively. If there were a question concerning a
child who was on our unit or needed to be, school officials knew they
could call me and I would respond immediately."

Schilling's attentions were directed evenly across the school
hierarchy—from principals down to school social workers. They,
after all, monitored school attendance and so would be the first to
notice school absence, which might be a warning sign of drug or
alcohol involvement, of family problems, of adjustment problems.
Worthwhile people to know.

Schilling says, "It was also worthwhile to invite them to a moder-
ately lavish luncheon in the hospital gym during Social Worker's
Month. Since the facility is a pleasant environment and tastefully
appointed, we frequently invited large groups for presentations and
luncheons, and small groups and individuals for tours. This made

a positive impression on those in a position to refer prospective patients."

He also staged events, calculated to further cement the hospital's role as benign and community invested—providing speakers who were authorities on a variety of mental health and substance abuse topics; informative speakers for seminars and in-service training of school personnel. He says, "Often, a captivating and authoritative adolescent psychiatrist or psychologist speaking to dozens or even hundreds of schoolteachers and administrators goes farther than hours of television commercials."

Talks on eating disorders, child abuse, crack-cocaine, teenage suicide, attention deficit disorder—these "events," often open to the public and to professionals (for credit), cemented alarm about today's "troubled youth" in the guise of concern and education.

Nor, of course, did Schilling omit that concern so prevalent among middle- and upper-middle-class parents (with plentiful insurance): goof-off kids. For this he provided an "Underachievers Seminar." For this one he would find smooth speakers from within the school system to talk about how parents could motivate their kids. "The response to these," he says, "was excellent and the group who attended was cleverly targeted." And—the suggestion was sure to be planted that the problem with kids who were underachievers might well be a "clinical one."

If you're having an event, people need to know about it. So promotional newspaper ads were placed to announce the event— linking the name of the hospital with the school name and thus implying cooperation and endorsement. That, Schilling says, "was seen as a major coup by my superiors."

Under his guidance the hospital contributed to the drug- and alcohol-free graduation parties at local high schools; gave graduating students key chains with the hospital logo on one side (and the school emblem or mascot on the other). They courted school athletic coaches, giving recognition to their importance as role models, offering them "the opportunity" to express their thoughts on how to help kids in trouble—and offering a tasty free lunch.

Starting adopt-a-school programs, sponsoring skating parties, forming "Just Say No" clubs, contributing to the schools' dropout prevention programs—Charter Glade came to seem just all heart. It was too good to last: disillusion awaited.

Schilling began teaching a weekly Junior Achievement class at one of the local schools—something he enjoyed and the school appreciated. The school, however, was zoned in an area including some of the poorest neighborhoods in the county. "Every time I secured funds for a project, such as sending well-behaved special education kids to Sea World, they wanted me to arrange for us to adopt a different school. They wanted these contributions to be influencing a school where the student demographics included more insured families." For Schilling, this was the first glimmer of dawn. In return for all the goodies the hospital so charitably provided the school community, Schilling states, "these bright educators and administrators understood that the hospital would like just one small thing: referrals." The message was unstated but hardly subtle. According to Schilling, the message was: "Though we are capitalists, part of a corporation with profit margins and stockholders, we can do this mental health and addiction thing much more effectively than the public providers. We can't help everyone but those who can take advantage of us get damn good treatment. And we want to work with you toward our mutual benefit. Let's work together and fulfill some of each other's needs."

Then came the Episode of the Scholarship Bed.

The idea was that one of the adolescent unit's beds would be set aside at all times for a teenager who "could greatly benefit from" six or eight weeks in the inpatient program—but was not covered by insurance. The hospital would pay the attending psychiatrist half of his or her regular daily fee and would simply take a loss on other expenses. Over the course of a year, this would "serve" six to eight kids who would otherwise not have gotten treatment. A goodwill gesture: a marketing ploy. ("In this for the insurance? Who, us?")

Schilling believed: He wanted to believe. He enthusiastically worked to implement the Scholarship Bed program. But he was growing canny. "It was an ongoing struggle for me to convince an indecisive administrator and three psychiatrists, having abundant clinical skills but varying degrees of greed, that the benefit in terms of increased referrals eventually would far outweigh their respective investments of time, energy, and gratis service." And indeed, the program gained tremendous appreciation from Fort Myers High School, the Abuse Counseling and Treatment Shelter, and the local Guardian Ad Litem Program.*

Then came the Kid Who Couldn't Leave, whose complex family circumstance defied efforts to discharge or place him. Loud grumblings were heard. The census of paying inmates was at capacity; a middle school assistant principal and a guidance counselor from the area's largest hospital were both pushing several other prospective Scholarship Bed occupants.

The hospital decided to cancel the whole deal. Schilling fought it, but since business was booming, he was shouted down. It was a substantial blow. Schilling says, "If those in decision-making positions were shortsighted enough to undo the positive public relations that had been generated, that was one thing. But to feel that my own integrity in the schools and community had been compromised was very hard to accept."

Then there were those "free evaluations" so generously offered by so many hospital chains. Theirs, Charter Glade called a "Teens at Risk" evaluation—which involved a height-weight-blood pressure screening; a look-see at the child's scholastic history and grades; an evaluation of "family issues or recent psychosocial stressors"; an interview with a recreation therapist about leisure activities; and a discussion about substance abuse issues—all information then given to a professional for recommendations. As Schilling describes it, "Let's say thirty teenagers go through this process over six or eight hours' time. The hospital pays the professional staff $1,000 or maybe $1,500 for their work during that time and spends maybe another $1,500 to promote the event.

"For this price, the hospital has (1) gained positive public relations for providing a free yet valuable screening for families in the community, (2) presented itself as having a pleasant, nonthreatening environment and demonstrably qualified professionals in its employ, (3) involved perhaps five teenagers, whose problems might [with any

---

* A program whereby citizens, not necessarily attorneys, are appointed by courts to represent a child's interests.

luck] worsen, in outpatient therapy, (4) identified, let's say, two adolescents who need intensive inpatient treatment, and, (5) admitted one patient who is covered by an insurance policy with psychiatric or chemical dependency coverage.

"One month's stay on the adolescent unit averaged about $13,800 in billing. The average length of stay on the unit was fifty-two days. . . ." Not a bad haul for one day's work.

It was the Demise of the Scholarship Bed, finally, that was the catalyst triggering Schilling's conscience. "It was like, 'You sons-of-bitches. Here I have gone out and pumped this in the community— people who know me and trust me are just calling me all the time, saying, "Listen, I have a kid who needs to come through. They're not covered." And now—you guys are telling me we've got this "temporary" suspension. Until you can't fill the beds with paying customers.

" 'That's it. I can no longer sleep at night, or live with myself, or whatever. I've been your whore long enough. I've gotta get out.' Toward the end, the last two or three months I was there, I was not just saying, 'We do good things for kids.' I had become an instrument of them. Of the administration and the corporation. To continue gaining admissions. It was not just a matter of helping kids, or helping some kids who were covered by insurance. It was a matter of filling beds. And doing their bidding."

Trolling for admissions, Schilling and the hospital also developed a relationship with the juvenile courts, offering the service of evaluation (and receiving in return, perhaps, juicy, insurance-covered court-ordered placements).

And so, the tentacles of psy power extend throughout the official worlds ordering children's affairs—the courts, child welfare. As Dr. Bernice Bauman, director of the Independent Consultation Center in New York, testified before the Committee on Family Court and Family Law, Association of the Bar of the City of New York,[26] for over thirty years, "I have seen a great number of parents and children referred by the courts for such things as psychotherapy, counseling, parenting skills. . . . It has become increasingly clear that these referrals which are involuntary and court-mandated are at best useless and at worst a cruel hoax. Most often these 'referees' are people confronted with the worst kinds of *real* problems such as lack of housing, money for food, escape from abusive husbands, lack of extended family support, etc. . . . Often, when they find themselves seeking assistance from the courts or government agencies, they find themselves labeled in one way or another and sent to have therapy, as though this was a relevant solution."

Bauman tells of one case where "a 14 year old boy . . . was summarily placed in a group home because his mother fled an abusive husband and asked for brief assistance in caring for her children. Instead she was charged with neglect . . . and her children were kept from her for over 2½ years. . . . Her 14 year old son was diagnosed as having 'parentification syndrome,' a serious-sounding way to say he looked after his younger brother. This had been used in an attempt to place him in residential treatment. . . ."

She concludes: "When a parent comes to a modern psychiatrist for advice on how to deal with a child there is little reason to assume that the psychiatrist's ideas on the subject are as sound as those of a kindly experienced neighbor or grandparent. Increasingly, psychiatrists are predominantly trained in the 'hard sciences,' such as medicine, biochemistry, neuroanatomy and psychopharmacology. Naturally, the psychiatrist will turn to solutions that he or she identifies with and knows best—diagnosis, drugs and hospitalization. Unfortunately, the direction of the fields of psychology and social work is also toward this same medical model."

But it is the school connection—because of its infinite reach, across all circumstantial lines—that stands out as most ominous. It is hideously, crazily democratic, capable of victimizing not only the poor nine-year-old ghetto child whose drug addict parents, and then his grandparents, had died, but all kids who pose challenges: the individuals, the different.

One young woman reports to me:

"At the end of my first-grade year, the school psychologist decided I had 'difficulty adjusting socially.' My teachers reported that I wasn't doing well in school because I refused to do long, tedious, repetitive assignments that I didn't see any meaning in. I cried and raged each morning when it was time to go to school. My parents were confused. In their loving, hopeful eyes I was just a wonderful little girl who had everything going for her; they couldn't imagine how there could be any difficulties in my life.

"At the same time, I was angry at the limitations on what I could be and do as a girl. I could run fast like a boy, and fight like a boy, and played hard with the boys across the street. I was angry that their father kept me from playing sports with them, and sometimes forbade them from playing with me at all for days at a time. I was angry at the way my father interrupted my mother, angry that she didn't stand up for herself. I was angry at dresses that we couldn't run and get dirty in, at the way we were supposed to walk and giggle and act silly and stupid.

"The school administration told my parents to go to Family Services. My second-grade year was filled with interviews, IQ tests, neurological evaluations. The professionals found 'no sign of psychosis,' no neurological damage. They announced that I was simply 'an unhappy little girl who hasn't learned to accept authority.' "

Nonetheless, she was sent to live and go to school at Children's Psychiatric Hospital (with weekend passes).

"I knew, anyway, what *psychiatric* meant. It was about being 'crazy.' It meant there was something wrong with you. It was what my playmates and I had jokingly threatened each other with. 'If you don't stop acting like that, the men in white coats are going to come and take you away.'

"My parents weren't wearing white coats when they delivered me to the hospital. . . .

"As a child, I was accustomed to being punished for 'bad' behavior, used to being scolded and devalued for not knowing how to do something 'right.' I had been taken away from home and school because I did not know how to get along with people. I took it to heart: There was something wrong with me, a natural ability lacking. I decided to try hard to 'get better.' I tried to figure out how to act like other people. I knew it was only an act: Inside I was as alone and scared and confused as ever. But apparently an act was all that was expected. Anxiously I asked the staff, over and over, if I was doing better yet. They reported this as a sign of progress."

What was school like?

"Once the teacher showed us the room behind the one-way mirror and explained that the staff would come in and watch us sometimes. They had to leave the lights off so we wouldn't be able to see through the mirror. I felt sorry for them, sitting there in the dark.

"There was another little room, the Quiet Room, plain concrete block walls without chairs or windows. Instead of making us stand in the corner as punishment, like my second-grade teacher did, the staff here put us in the Quiet Room. We were locked up here because our parents and our schoolteachers didn't know what to do with us, children who were afraid and hurting and angry. We were locked up here with professionals who were advertised as knowing what to do with our fear and grief and anger, how to heal our hurts. And when the professional training didn't tell them what to do with our pain, the staff locked us in the Quiet Room.

"I think they must have put Jana there first thing as soon as they brought her in. I remember watching when she was admitted. She was fighting for her life with her entire body, kicking and biting and cursing. It took four adults to carry her in. I went easier, conscious of my smallness and of the larger world's disrespect for my opinion. I never tried to run away, either. A couple of the boys did once, climbing over the high chain link fence around the playground. They didn't get far before they were caught and brought back.

"Once a week we went upstairs to see a psychiatrist. The man I saw had determined a specific prescription for me; each week he gave me a phone book to tear up 'to get my anger out.' Each week I remained unimpressed. I hid in his office closet, pulled the table in front of the [open] closet and the chairs around the table, made myself a fortress, and refused to come out until the time was up and I could go back downstairs. Week after week he sat out there at his desk, telling me to come out and tear up his phone books. It never occurred to him to get down on his hands and knees and peek through the chairs into my hiding place, to play hide-and-seek with me, to make a game out of begging me to come out and play. Finally they assigned me to a different psychiatrist. . . .

"My parents tell me that according to the elementary school psychologist I fought a lot, which doesn't fit my own memories of those years. But when I got out, I had something to fight about."

Again, I recall that wonderful word that peppers the psychiatric literature: *iatrogenic*—meaning that the treatment is what is causing the problem. It is interesting at least as speculation that it is precisely the *psychiatric treatment* of kids that is outright *causing* kids' problems in many cases. And in other cases, it serves simply to exacerbate and calcify problems the individual child, lent dignity, would perhaps (independently) grow to resolve. In fact, the whole system seems designed to create that which it purports, in its expertise, to "medically" treat.

Given the authority of the weighty Book of Judgment, the DSM, and the puffed-up power psy authority invests in an institution such as the schools, it is not surprising that those who dare challenge it find themselves in Psy-Fi City: entangled with a formless phantom, which then may instantaneously, and without warning, mutate into a giant wad of energetic Double Bubble: Burst one pink, sticky mass and another erupts, altered—if negligibly—in its shape and description, but not in its essential character.

9

The School
Connection II

IN OCTOBER 1990 the Education of the Handicapped Act was amended and renamed the Individuals with Disabilities Education Act (IDEA). I do not know whether this change was due to the cuter acronym gained, or to the fact that the word *Disabilities* was taken to be more user-friendly than *Handicapped*—(or perhaps to the fact that disabilities could be more inclusive than handicaps?).

The act is designed to aid states in meeting the educational needs of handicapped children by providing them with a "free appropriate public education." Children who fall under the act must be provided with an "individualized education program" (IEP) in order to trigger federal funds. Local school districts receiving IDEA funds through the state education agency must likewise comply with the act. Parents are meant to be participants in designing the IEP, and any complaints they have must be reviewed by an impartial due process hearing.

The point of the act was to allow for keeping handicapped kids in the *neighborhood* of the mainstream, even if not exactly *in* the mainstream, but in "special education," which could be a part of the school day spent in special classes in the regular school or could be a special school—or could even be placement in a public or private residential treatment center. (The law does, however, require the least restrictive environment.)

As practicing school psychologist Scott Sigmon writes, "Learning disabilities as a field really originated from psychology, medicine, and mental retardation as a result of work with brain damaged (retarded) children. Developing better methods of educating brain damaged children, both retarded and those who were intellectually normal—especially the cerebral palsied, even in their own separate classes—made a great deal of sense. However, as the intact children started being classified LD and were placed in special classes, both psychology and education subtly became perverted. . . . Virtually none of the research on LD students . . . is valid, as it mistakenly discusses many dissimilar LD children as if they were a homogeneous grouping, which they cannot possibly be because of the broad definition."[1]

Here again we witness the birth and empowerment of an entire field of new professionals (special ed experts, school psychologists) in the service of a new psy diagnosis—with an apparent goal of continually expanding the population in its domain. From 1976 to 1977, prior to passage of PL 94-142, to 1982–83, LD students more than doubled in number, while during these same six years the national mentally retarded group shrank by almost 20 percent.[2] An additional 600,000 children were classified LD, with a growth of roughly 25 percent being those labeled emotionally disturbed (ED). There are now over 4½ million kids who are formally classified as being educationally handicapped, almost half labeled LD. "Other uncomfortable statistics were found which strongly suggest that special education has become the means for containing the types of children which general American public education cannot effectively deal with in regular programs, i.e., those who are not white females from English speaking homes."[3]

So what begins as a good idea, a *liberal* idea, indeed what the public continues to believe is a good and liberal idea, again is brought to serve a conservative, even reactionary, agenda: containing, isolating, labeling kids who stand out as different. Sigmon writes, "Liberals show concern for the plight of the individual doing poorly within America; and they attempt to slowly modify, reform, and bring about the realization of democracy via the schools—but this has not worked. The destitute individual, from the conservative viewpoint, is merely of inferior biological stock and reproduces other, similar persons and therefore reform is useless. . . . Education, or more specifically schooling, is designed to prevent real change because it is charged with preserving dominant class interests within the culture."[4]

As Sigmon further says, "Special education, perhaps more than any other component of the educational system, is influenced by psychology; and mainstream, establishment psychology is, for the most part, ideologically linked to the dominant culture."[5] Public education is a state function, and as such it seeks to serve the demands of the prevailing powers. But some kids don't accede. Not only black and other minority kids, but even kids like Delia. "It is possible for a rather alienated pupil to do well in school academically without internalizing the dominant ideological line. However, it is quite likely that the alienated student will refuse to do much schoolwork. Such a student is not scholastically motivated, and will herein be described as a *school resister*. It is proposed that many student resisters have been formally classified with various special education labels such as emotionally disturbed, socially maladjusted, and especially learning disabled . . . by a general education system unable to deal with them."[6]

Ironically, most of these school resisters *do* have a handicap, a severe one: They cannot articulate what is going on, what is at the root of their resistance. This is not due to the fact that they have an "Expressive Language Disorder" (315.31 in the DSM-III-R). It is due to the fact that they are six years old.

Take Casey Jesson.[7]

When Casey was four, his parents, Valerie and Mike, put him in a local New Hampshire fundamentalist Christian school–a nursery school–kindergarten—largely so that he would have other kids to mix with. As Valerie says, "The room they were in had no desks. No particular seating. A lot of it was up and down and singing and dancing. A lot of touching, a lot of interaction. Casey did just wonderful." But: "After two years he went to the kindergarten. And that's when the trouble started.

"The teacher was coming to me and saying Casey was like a class clown. Being silly. Then that class clownness turned into being disobedient. Not stopping when she said, 'Enough.' The big difference is—now you've got a room that looks just like a first-grade classroom, even a third-grade class. All desks, very structured. Even probably more difficult than a public school first-grade class because they wanted the children's hands folded; they wanted their feet flat on the ground.

"So it just kept getting worse. And we'd never had any of these kinds of problems with Casey. I was bringing the news home to Mike, and we'd say, 'Gee, Casey, what's the problem here? You've gotta cut it out. Just do what you're told.' We'd never had this kind of problem. We didn't understand what was going on."

What was happening was that Casey was being sent down a long road, along which various dubious tags—"hyperactive," "learning disabled," "emotionally disturbed"—would, at one time or another, be randomly stuck on his forehead.

Casey's now twelve and Valerie says, "Interestingly, it was just this past year that Casey really started opening up a little bit more. And I said, 'Gee, Casey, what happened in kindergarten? Was it just hard for you to sit still?' You know what he said to me? The first time—you know how many years we're talking? He turns and looks at me and he says, 'Ma, it wasn't that at all. You know what it was?' I said, 'What?' He said, 'The teacher would write three sentences on the blackboard, and the children would have to copy them to a piece of paper with a pencil.' He couldn't do it. He couldn't write the letter *t*, for instance. He would have to look up—there's a straight line down, a straight line across. He said the other kids would get done writing these three sentences in maybe twenty minutes. He said he'd be there an hour doing it. And he'd end up losing recess. And in the teacher's eyes, he could do it. He was just being defiant.

"Finally, Casey said, he would just refuse to do it. Or he would start to do it and then get frustrated and throw his pencil down and rip his paper up. And then the kindergarten teacher started throwing him back into the nursery school. And I didn't understand the harm she was doing. But now that I know more—that kind of humiliation had to be pretty terrible."

Every day, Valerie says, the kindergarten teacher would call and ask her to come in. She'd be brought to the person they called the "reverent," invited to sit and to hold hands while the reverent intoned, "Let's pray for Casey. That he can obey."

The more the school leaned on Valerie and Mike, the more Valerie and Mike leaned on Casey. It's easy, looking at what happened, to say they shouldn't have. But—if they'd known then what was *going* to happen, if they'd even suspected such things could happen, they wouldn't have. Parents, however, are expected to be school *assisters*, school boosters: Val did what many parents under the circumstances would do: She assumed the school was correct, and therefore it must be Casey who was wrong.

"You mean," I say, "now *you* were trying to correct Casey?"

"Right. We're trying to correct him. We can't understand why Casey's having these problems. Just, 'Casey, do what the teacher says. We won't have to go through this. What is the problem?' And I've got them on my back, saying I don't discipline the child enough. That if I really loved my children, I'd spank them."

Now, predictably enough, with everyone on his case, Casey started to be more defiant—even at home.

"And after the Christmas holidays I was at the school—Mike and I had talked—and I said, 'Well, Casey, if you can be a good boy, we're gonna go to Disney World in April.' And the teacher said, 'Yeah. We'll make it like a contract. If he can do that, keep it all together, he can go to Disney World.' Well, what Casey did was he got worse. And then I got challenged by the school and everybody was involved. Mike and I got put into a position—what do we do? Technically, he shouldn't go. The school said, 'I hope you stick to your ground.' I was under a lot of pressure. It's something I have tremendous guilt about because no child does not want to go to Disney World. But we went. We took his sister. But we didn't take Casey.

"Then the teacher said, 'You've really gotta bring this child to a doctor.' So I brought him to my pediatrician. And he said, 'Well, I don't see anything wrong with him. But if I were you and if he were my child, I would bring him to this pediatric neurologist.'

"I brought him there and I told him about Disney World, what happened. The doctor said, 'I agree. You did the right thing by not bringing him.' He agreed Casey shouldn't have gone to Disney World—for behavior reasons, as well as—he gives me this line about this hemisphere of the brain or this wiring where one side is overactive and one side is underactive—some theory . . ."

"Meaning—what? Casey couldn't have tolerated Mickey Mouse?"

"Right! He couldn't have tolerated Mickey Mouse and taken in Pluto at the same time."

We both laugh.

Val says, "I told this doctor I don't feel him to be hyperactive. But he said he probably was and that 'if you want him to have a good start in first grade—if you really care about this child and what kind of start he gets in school—then I would definitely try this drug test called Ritalin.' And he did a ten-minute field test on Casey—measured the circumference of his head."

Gosh. Like phrenology.

"And he had him walk toe to heel, toe to heel in a straight line."

No. Like a DWI test.

"He said it was a medical problem. And he made the Ritalin sound as though the only side effect was maybe a little insomnia and maybe a little bit of weight loss. But otherwise it really helped the child focus and do a lot better in school. I came home with a scrip for Ritalin. That was the summer of 1985. A few weeks before school started."

Casey was on twenty milligrams, time release. It made him sick: severe stomachaches, headaches, vomiting. . . . The doctor switched him to ten milligrams, morning and afternoon. So when Casey started public school, first grade, the school nurse had to give him his second dose. Thus, from the first day, the public school knew Casey was on Ritalin. They pre-knew, pre-accepted, pre-sumed that Casey was hyperactive. They were looking for and expecting trouble.

"So about a month and a half into school, the teacher called me up and I go and I see her, and she's saying to me that Casey needs a lot of attention. He can't work independently. You're talking about a first grader, for crying out loud! She said he was always asking, 'Is this right? Am I doing this right?' But this was her first year of teaching. She did give Casey a lot of individual attention.

"Time goes on and she calls me up and says, 'Now Casey is outright refusing to do any kind of pencil work.' And how did I feel about her keeping him after school? And I said, 'If you think it will help.' I tried to be cooperative.

"And the drug, as far as the side effects—the biggest thing I started seeing was that Casey started having a really hard time winding down when he got home from school—and then into the night. Meanwhile, his behavior became even more exaggerated. More defiant. More—moody."

He began stealing. He began lying.

Gradually, on Ritalin, Casey was becoming a wild child, suffering some of the adverse reactions the manufacturer's warning sheet describes. Staying just with ones most of us understand: "Nervousness and insomnia are the most common adverse reactions. . . . Other reactions include . . . anorexia; nausea; dizziness; palpitations; headaches; dyskinesia; drowsiness; blood pressure changes, both up and down; abdominal pain; weight loss. . . . There have been rare reports of Tourette's syndrome. Toxic psychosis has been reported. . . .

"In children, loss of appetite, abdominal pain, weight loss during prolonged therapy, insomnia, and tachycardia may occur more frequently; however, any of the other adverse reactions may occur."

The psy practitioners, however, did not even suspect the drug. Rather, they availed themselves of the only other possible explanation:

Valerie says, "When I told the doctor what was going on with the lying and stealing, he said to me, 'Oh! He's got it bad! He's got it bad!"

In other words, that the behavior began only after the administering of Ritalin is not considered fact. What is considered fact is that the behavior is further evidence of the disorder.

Valerie took Casey to a child psychologist: " 'This child is classic hyperkinesis. Just keep him on Ritalin.' "

She took him back to the neurologist: " 'Oh, he has to stay on Ritalin. You can't even think of taking him off it.' "

"We proceeded to have a terrible, horrible summer. Casey couldn't sleep. It took him till maybe eleven-thirty, midnight. Sometimes he'd just sit there in his bed and cry because he couldn't wind down."

The next school year, Casey got an even less flexible teacher.

"And she started calling: 'He's disrupting the class.' And that Christmas holiday—'86–'87—my sister flew out from California. She looked at Casey and she said, 'Val, what the hell are you doing to this kid?' 'What are you talking about?' And she said, 'Look at your son. He's skinny. His face is sunk in. He looks like he doesn't sleep. He doesn't eat. He looks terrible.' I was—defensive. I said, 'Look, he has to be on this.' I remind myself of some of the parents I talk to now whose children are on Ritalin and they're so defensive. You can understand why, when you have doctors telling you, 'He's got it bad.' Right?

"It just hit me. Like—what am I doing? What is going *on*? Our lives are all screwed up. This kid—Casey was out of control, *in* control—you know what I'm saying? If we had a good day, it's only because Casey let us have a good day. If we had a bad day, that was Casey, too.

"January, February, the teacher is calling me up constantly. Now she's like, 'You're not addressing his behavior problems.' I said, 'What do you want me to do? What would you like me to do? I've got my child on a drug that I'm starting to believe is ruining our lives. And it's not even the same kid I had. He's just going down the tubes—physically, mentally. He can't look you in the eye anymore when you talk to him.' You want to know what Casey was, now I look back on it? You ever read the back of *TV Guide* or in a magazine what a person who's addicted to cocaine would be like? That's what Casey was. And we believe—now that we've started talking to other doctors—that Casey was starting to develop Tourette's syndrome. He'd end up kicking and screaming. He was so frustrated, Louise, it was just awful.

"You'd try to physically assist him to his room and he'd kick and fight all the way. Then he'd go in there and he would literally make animal noises. Repetitive noises. Have facial tics. I'm talking weird stuff."

Valerie and Mike were both reaching the limits of fear and frustration. To the point where Valerie would entertain the thought that Casey was possessed. To the point where Mike would say to Val, "I can't take it no more. I'm gonna take the kid and I'm gonna put him in the car, and I'm gonna go hit a stone wall. We can't go on like this."

Casey's third-term report card was a disaster.

"So," Valerie says, "I just said—that's it. Casey is coming off of the drug. Because by now I knew it was the drug that wasn't letting him sleep. I knew it was the drug that wasn't letting him eat. He was now underweight. He was not growing the way he should have been.

"The day I took him off it, I called the pediatric neurologist. 'I'm just letting you know I'm taking him off it.' He says, 'I just have one question: Is it helping or isn't it?' I said, 'I don't know what this drug is supposed to be doing. All I can tell you is I don't have the same kid I had. I've got a mess.' I says, 'I don't know how to put this into words—open your finger two inches? I started out with that many problems. Now I open my arms as wide as I can. And I've got this many problems. I don't even know where to begin.'

"So I take him off the drug. The doctor never told me to wean him off the drug—to watch out for depression, *anything*. And I'm so angry at that doctor because I shouldn't have done it like that. But see, my whole discovery about the drug doesn't come until later."

Since Valerie sent no more Ritalin to the school nurse, the school knew Casey was no longer on it. The school called an immediate conference team meeting: " 'Why did you take Casey off Ritalin?' "

Valerie says, "It's so upsetting—because I couldn't have been any more honest with these people. I didn't have to tell them about Disney World. I didn't have to tell them anything. I told them everything. I left myself wide open. And as far as I'm concerned they shoved it right up our ass. I said, 'We can't go on like this. We've got to do something. We've got to help Casey.' And they said, 'We can't even begin to do anything for Casey unless you medicate him.'

"They are not getting the message."

The school officials asked if their psychologist could evaluate Casey. Valerie agreed. The evaluation was done while Casey was undergoing Ritalin withdrawal, with the depressive symptoms the manufacturer's warning sheet allows can occur. The psychologist detected worries about death, a lot of sadness, a lot of loneliness. Naturally he did not suspect the drug connection. Nor did he consider the effect the school's treatment of the child might be having; rather, he suspected the Jessons of child abuse.

Valerie says, "He kind of tiptoed around—'I don't *think* there's been any abuse—but, you know, I wonder.' When we sat down with him, he was a little bit more direct. It was a lot of intimidation, is what it was. 'You put your child on the drug and we can just let this ride.' So Mike challenged him and said, 'Hey, if you feel there's been any kind of abuse whatsoever, then you turn us in.' Of course he never did."

What the school did do was to keep kicking Casey out: They kept calling Valerie: " 'Casey's out of control. Come get him.' " Finally some friends of theirs who had a severely handicapped child told Mike this was illegal: that they had some rights. The Jessons called a group of parent advocates and were told that indeed, under the law, Casey was entitled to a public education. That if this school couldn't do it, they had to find somewhere that could.

Valerie says, "So once again the principal called me up: 'Casey's out of control. Come get him.' Not 'would you,' 'can you.' So I says, 'I don't have any problem in disciplining the child if the child is learning something from it. Casey's not learning anything from you throwing him out of school every other day. I can't support this.' So you know what he said to me? 'Hey, lady, you want to play hardball?' I am stunned. It was like somebody slapped me across my face. I was taken aback. I go, 'Excuse me? I didn't know we played hardball with little children's lives. I don't know what you think you're doing here, but you're not gonna push me around. Because I know that it's his right to have an education. If you want to call that hardball, then I guess that's what we're doing here.' I says, 'But I'm not picking Casey up.' Because the advocates have told me not to. But I feel bad. Guess who's caught in the middle of this?"

By now the school year is nearly ended. The school recommends a summer program for Casey, a program for emotionally disturbed kids. (Is attention deficit hyperactivity disorder an emotional disturbance, then? I thought it was a biologically based brain disease. Sometimes it seems real hard to distinguish diagnoses from epithets.) Valerie went up for an interview and made it perfectly clear that she wanted the staff to work with Casey without medication. Initially they agreed. But then the camp director called up to say they would accept Casey only if she gave them written permission to provide medication if they decided they wanted to. She said no.

Meanwhile, the school kept calling more and more meetings: " 'We just don't see Casey going anywhere without drugs. There is gonna be no learning process until you get him back on drugs.' " Valerie says, "They kept saying he needed *more* drugs. That's what was wrong. We should have given him *more*. And the school psychologist who's not even a Ph.D. but he might as well have been a doctor the way he was talking, like he knew everything medical: 'What went wrong is we should have been giving him more drugs.' 'But he don't sleep.' 'Well, there's drugs for that.' 'But he don't eat.' 'Well, there's drugs for that.' I looked at these people, I looked at Mike: This is insane. I said, 'This is a developing child, with still-developing brain cells. His reproductive system is still not there. No.'

"So finally the parent advocate said, 'Look, the parents have made themselves clear. They don't want to use drugs. Why don't we try Casey at the Rye Learning Skills School?' It's a small little school for learning-disabled children. 'We'll use it as an evaluation process. Maybe that's all he needs. Obviously, you can't do the job here.' They shook their heads no: 'He's not learning disabled.' "

In case you have not yet suspected it, what is going on here is a war against Valerie. These school authorities are not going to tolerate this mother-lady defying their professional judgments about her child.

What got decided at that meeting was that Casey would go to Children's Hospital in Boston for evaluation. The hospital's opinion (evaluation) was that Casey was learning disabled because he was 'deficit' in all subjects. A year behind in everything. Well, of course he was—by now. The staff recommended special education, individual help. And they said that "if the parents agree," a course of psychostimulant medication could be helpful. Since they knew the

Jessons would not use Ritalin, they recommended Cylert—a drug that the doctors told Valerie can cause liver damage.

Valerie says, "They said Casey would first of all have to have his liver tested to make sure it's in great shape. Because Cylert leaves enzymes in the liver which can deteriorate the liver. And I said— forget it." Although Children's had not said Casey had attention deficit disorder, the school wrote to Valerie saying that it agreed with the diagnosis of attention deficit disorder—and when was Casey going to be medicated?

What is interesting here is the way in which Valerie is being driven to the belief that Casey is indeed something called learning disabled—as the least god-awful alternative, the one least likely to do the child bodily harm. After more kicking, and screaming, and meeting, and begging, the school finally agreed to put Casey into its special ed program, which had six or seven kids in it, a teacher, and an aide. "So," Val says, "we said, 'We gotta try it. My kid is entitled to an education. He's learning disabled. He obviously needs more help. He's behind.' So finally they agreed to a forty-five-day place-ment in one of their special ed classrooms—which was basically an ED program, an emotionally disturbed program."

"What," I ask Valerie, "does 'emotionally disturbed' mean to you?"

"I don't really know what it means. At that time, they told me they were mostly kids like Casey."

"Is all this interchangeable? I'm getting lost in the language here."

"Well, I was too, Louise. I was too. Because at this point—I had no choices. I know what you're saying, and by now my opinions have changed drastically. But I'm trying to keep myself in the past— trying to make people understand what I was up against at that point. When I said, 'What does that mean?' they told me it was kids who had behavior problems."

It's a phenomenon: The more they explain, the less can be under-stood.

"All I know," Valerie says, "is I'm trying to find a safe place for Casey. He wants to go to school. Here's a child who *wants* to go to school."

Casey was bused to the school that had the special program. Every day as he walked back to front to get off the bus, he would be kicked, hit, punched, slapped by the other kids. There was no monitor on the bus. Valerie started protesting *that*.

The Derry school district ended up providing a taxi for Casey.

Despite all the adversity, when the first report card came out, Casey had actually made some progress. Valerie says, "He told me that he was more comfortable; that when he needed to ask the teacher for help, the teacher would help him. Where in the regular classroom, there was no way the teacher would help him. He wanted to fit in, but it was like there was no way they were gonna let him succeed. I mean by that, the teacher and everybody involved. About six weeks into that program we had a meeting with the special ed teacher and one of the counselors. And the teacher said to me, 'I really feel that Casey doesn't have an attention deficit disorder, but I feel he is very emotionally disturbed.'"

"But what does that *mean*?" I ask, purely out of exasperation.

"I'm not sure. I don't know what it means. I don't *know*. But he certainly had his own opinion. He said to me, 'I'd like to see Casey on medication because I'm a special ed teacher and I know what to look for.'"

"I thought," I say, "that Ritalin was specifically for attention deficit disorder, not for feeling emotionally upset."

"Well, they use it for everything, evidently. I said, 'All I know is we're trying to do the best we can. Casey's at least more consistent at home. He's more predictable than he was on Ritalin. The lying, the cheating, the stealing—we don't have those behaviors to deal with anymore. He's sleeping. Physically he looks a hundred percent better.

"I think one of the things that broke my case wide open when this thing ended up in due process up at the state capital was the pictures of Casey. There's a picture of Casey in the second grade, on Ritalin. He literally looks retarded. And then there's another picture in third grade, off of Ritalin, and he looks like a different child. These are school pictures. They ended up in *USA Today*—'Two Faces of Ritalin,' they called it.

"Was he all better? No, he wasn't. Because there was no resolution. We were going at it with the school. And they were still, every once in a while, throwing Casey out of school—not as bad as they were in the mainstream.

"But finally, the forty-five days came and went. They drew up this IEP—individualized educational plan. They write it up without any of our input, and the law says we have every right to have input. It was a very self-serving IEP. It really did very little for Casey. Then—this was the kicker—on the back of it, it said, 'a contingency clause.' In other words, you want this? This is what you gotta do."

"And that was?" (As if, by now, I couldn't guess.)

"The parents *will* medicate their child. The parent will *not* suspend medication. The parent *will* provide the school district with medication. The parent *will* pick the child up when they throw him out. The parent *will* agree to suspension. Un-be-lievable."

So there was—another meeting. Val says, "We went round and round. I left there with such a headache. And my parent advocate says, 'We got a problem. We're in a power struggle here.' She says, 'I don't even know if I'm gonna be able to help you. And if I do help you, we've gotta go to due process. I need five hundred dollars up front. And really, I would recommend you get a lawyer.' So I started looking for a lawyer. And—the cheapest one wanted a twenty-five-hundred-dollar retainer."

Remember what we are talking about here? A child who, for the first six plus years of his life, showed no observable problems or deficits; who was identified as unconforming in kindergarten; who was then placed on Ritalin, thereby confirming for the first-grade public school that he had a disorder; whose behavior, as a result of the Ritalin, triggered further rejection; which further rejection more than likely triggered worse behavior; a child who was not, in all the chaos, being taught in any consistent or meaningful fashion, and thus was not learning in any consistent or meaningful fashion—which led to a lack of information and skills, which then was translated by school and psy practitioners as a learning disorder.

As horrifying as anything going on here was that Val and Mike were now themselves forced to identify Casey as having a disability. Educationally handicapped law formed the only ground on which they could hope to find recourse and seek remedy. They contacted the Disability Rights Center in Concord, hoping they would take the case for free. At that time they would not. There were worse cases. (Later on the center did get involved.)

Val continued to say to the school, "Look, this is unacceptable to me. We're not using drugs. And this is America, and you can't force us."

The school, says Val, continued to say, " 'Well then, we're not doing anything for Casey.' " In other words, no services unless they agreed to medicate.

Without counsel, Val was forced to cancel a due process hearing, asking it be postponed until she could get representation. The school wrote saying the Jessons had now violated the school's rights by not exercising their due process rights.

And where, I ask, is Casey in all of this?

"Poor Casey is still in that special ed class. And then they threw him out of there. Casey didn't understand, Louise. Casey didn't understand any of it. He just wanted to go to school. And nobody would let him. He just kept saying, 'All I need is a little more help.' So they threw him out and put him back in the mainstream. I called them up and said, 'I can't believe you would do this to a child. You're setting him up for failure.' Because he'd been improving. He was at least starting to learn."

The school continued to push the amphetamine-like drug, which the Drug Enforcement Administration (DEA) has classified as a Schedule II controlled substance, the most potent category of drugs that can be prescribed.[8] (And you thought it was a major crime to push drugs near a school?) The teacher called Val and Mike in, saying, "I think you're making a big mistake. If he was a diabetic, wouldn't you give him his insulin?' "

It is everywhere in the literature, this diabetes/insulin connection—a dubious simile, but a lurking menace because medication corroborates *medical*; thus, the parent who refuses to put the child on drugs can face an allegation of medical neglect, thereby placing the parent at risk of a charge by Child Protective Services.

Val remembers something: "I didn't even tell you that the doctor from Children's Hospital, she wrote me a letter and said, 'How can you do this to your child? If your child needed antibiotics, wouldn't you give him those antibiotics?' I was outraged that anyone would compare a ten-day course of antibiotics with a drug that totally affects your child's personality. But by now—it's just gone on so long. I kept thinking they were gonna come to their senses. They were gonna know they can't force us. We just kept hoping something was gonna happen.

"So anyway, Casey goes back to the mainstream and he's just falling on his face. Falling, falling, and falling. He's not doing the work—*he can't do the work*. He don't know what he's doing. He needs more assistance, he needs more help, because by now he's actually been deprived of education. He's spent more time out of school than in.

"So mid-March I get a call from the superintendent: 'Just so you're not totally shocked, you're gonna get a letter in the mail tomorrow. I'm suspending Casey for twenty days. I'm petitioning the local school board to have him thrown out of school for the rest of the year.'

"*What!* What is *that!* Basically, the letter said his being at school is an absurdity; that there's no learning taking place whatsoever. That Casey rocks, he hums, he gazes out the window. And cannot follow simple rules. Doesn't finish work assignments. Those are actual quotes. I'm crushed. I'm devastated. Oh! And. He's giving me one week to make up my mind."

"About what?"

"Med-i-ca-tion. I was totally distraught because along with that letter—guess what! I got another letter from the school attorney, saying, 'We are taking you to due process to see if the IEP that the school district has made is appropriate for Casey.' Anyway, I call up the Department of Education: 'Look, they've thrown my kid out for twenty days. They're petitioning the local school board to expel him for the remainder of the year. Can they do this?' So the lady goes, 'Calm down. What did the kid do? Did your kid bring in a loaded weapon?' "

The absurdity of the contrast is so abrupt, we both laugh.

Val continues, " 'Did he try to kill a teacher? Did he set the school on fire? What did he do?' I told her—'He rocks, he hums, he gazes out the window. Doesn't finish school assignments. And doesn't follow simple rules.' She goes, 'I never heard of this. How old is this kid?' I say, 'He's just in the third grade.' 'I—never—heard—of this. Never heard of such a thing happening to such a young child. Maybe a kid sixteen years old, coming in with an attitude.'

"Meanwhile, Casey was totally distraught that they were throwing him out of school. He couldn't believe it. And they said they were going to provide him with a tutor. Meanwhile, I requested a meeting with the superintendent. Louise, I begged them. I begged them. 'You can't believe, you're gonna hurt this kid so bad. His ego—he's so fragile already. Try to think of this kid. Can't we fight this out and just leave my kid alone? Let him be safe. We can take it. He can't. Put him back in the special ed class. He was more comfortable there. He was making some gains. It's not right. You can't do this. You can't force us to drug the kid.' It ended up getting pretty nasty. That's when it hit us—even if it meant hurting my kid, that's what they were gonna do. Mike said, 'So. We're playin' hardball, huh? Well, get ready—because we're gonna throw the first pitch.' Mike said, 'I think we'll go to the town newspaper and let's see what the townspeople think about what you're doin' to this kid.' "

Val went to the newspaper. Eventually, the case made *People* magazine, *USA Today*. The Jessons were on *Nightline*.

While they lost in the administrative hearing, they won on appeal. But not until 1991. Not until Casey was twelve years old. Casey is now in a residential school for children with emotional problems and/or learning disabilities. I ask Val—does Casey believe he is emotionally disturbed? Learning disabled?

"Oh, Louise, everything. It's terrible. He doesn't know what to feel, how to feel, how to act, what to be, who to be. But he feels better about where he is now. Because he told me that he doesn't feel stupid where he is. That most of the kids have the same problem he does."

"Which is?"

"That they need more time to finish work. They need help. When they ask a teacher for help, they get help. They don't get what he got here: 'No. You have to do that paper yourself.' He's doing very, very well now in school."

Yes. But at what price?

≈

It is instructive to listen to a psy practitioner explaining to a young patient, alleged to have ADHD, what is wrong with him. If you remember Thurber (and Mr. A, Mr. B, and Mr. C and their variant adventures with traffic), you will, I think, be impressed.

Barbara Ingersoll, Ph.D., writes, "I have found that even young children can understand the analogy of a car that is out of gas. The brain, I explain, is a complicated and wonderful machine but, just like a car, it needs fuel to operate properly.

" 'What happens when a car runs out of gas?' I ask.

" 'It won't go,' is the inevitable response.

" 'Right, it won't go. Does that mean that there is something wrong with the car—that it's a bad car?'

" 'No.'

" 'No, there's nothing wrong with the car. It can be a great car, a super car. But it won't work without the right kind of fuel, will it?' "9

Ingersoll goes on to explain (to the child) that the child's brain is just like that car: It may be a super brain, but it isn't getting the kind of fuel it needs to make it work as well as it should. Ritalin (street description: speed) is, presumably, the fuel the child's brain "needs."

So now the car, once a sex symbol, has been adopted as a brain symbol. Can't *anybody* in the psy universe let the car be what it is? Simply a gas-guzzling, ozone-depleting means of transportation?

Along with many others, Ingersoll also tells children "about eminent people who have had ADHD. Thomas Edison, for example, was constantly in trouble as a child and was removed from school after attending for only three months. Former governor and U.S. Senator Huey Long was also a hyperactive child, as was Winston Churchill." Now this piece of information is worth the price of admission all by itself, since it is self-serving retrospective diagnosis based only on the biographical reports of apparent orneriness. However, now we read, "While this information is not comforting to every child (one of my young patients objected, 'Yeah, but they're famous and I'm not!'), some hyperactive youngsters do enjoy reading biographies of famous people who had problems similar to their own."

It is hard to be calm in the face of the points raised by this.

1. These days, any young child who knows who Winston Churchill was—much less Senator Huey Long—deserves to be skipped at least two grades, in fact maybe to high school.

2. None of the folks mentioned were put on a regimen of amphetamine-like substances. They were left alone, to develop as they would and ultimately to prove that the assholes in authority during their youth were wrong.

The case that is actually made by invoking famous folks as comforting company for kids with this "affliction" (apparently these folks also include Einstein, Rodin, Patton, Yeats, and Hans Christian Andersen)[10] is precisely the opposite of the case the psy practitioners seem to think they are making. It is a case for *leaving the kids alone*.

10

The School

Connection III

As I WRITE THIS, reports of scandal are erupting everywhere: the shellfire of multiple skirmishes is ubiquitous in the distance. On one business front, private, for-profit psychiatric hospitals continue to take heat. Scandal continues over kids dragooned into hospitals, over families (like Katie's) who seek help and are conned. Over financial fraud, bounty fees, patient intimidation, fees for referrals, guerrilla marketing. Zillions of stories, tons of ink, from Maine and Massachusetts to Florida, California . . . and, most vigorously at the moment, in Texas.

In Houston alone, discharge data show an increase from just over 20,000 in 1984 to 48,798 in 1987. [1]

In Texas, the scandals appear, literally, without end, and not all of them are directly about inmates. A jury in McAllen, Texas, orders Charter Palms Hospital and its parent company, Charter Medical Corporation of Macon, Georgia, to pay nearly $4 million in damages to a former nursing supervisor who was fired for refusing to dummy patient records in order to maximize insurance benefits. [2] In Fort Worth, a psychiatrist and medical director of a Psychiatric Institutes of America hospital who tried to blow the whistle on corrupt practices is fired—and a psychiatric salvo is, additionally, fired off. The hospital alleges that the psychiatrist suffers from bipolar personality disorder—characterized by loud and rapid speech and a condescending attitude toward the staff (on three occasions in six years). The psychiatrist countersues for wrongful removal.

The sheer magnitude of what is going on is enough to ensure static in transmission—extending, as it does, from the psychiatric and hospital business interests, to the insurance business interests, to the interests of corporate America in general; and then to the psy world itself and the dissonance over its theoretical base; to the world of pharmaceutical companies and the physiological damage done by psychotropic or neuroleptic drugs; and to the world of affluent families, the world of poor families; and extending (as I will get to shortly) to some rather sinister interests of conservative government.

Take something simple—like the fact that the number of health industry lobby groups in Washington has grown from 117 in 1979 to 502 in 1986 to 741 in 1992,[3] many of them trying to influence legislation by contributing to lawmakers' reelection campaigns. You've got everything from the American Medical Association, the American Psychiatric Association, the American Hospital Association, to the National Association of Private Psychiatric Hospitals, the National Association of Residential Treatment Centers, the health insurance associations, the pharmaceutical associations—all representing major corporate interests.

In terms of kids and psychiatry, the unstable climate is being produced by something that simply will not stay discretely defined—thus creating turbulence as language fluctuates to accommodate expedience.

It would seem sensible to respond to such an egregious hoorah by crying out for oversight. (It *would* be if one did not understand that, given the ambiguities of what we are talking about, chaos is more than likely simply endemic.) But the fact is there is already so much oversight as to preoccupy hospital administrations for the greater number of days of the year. "The [mental health] bureaucracy consists of all those monitoring and regulatory and oversight agencies, from the Joint Commission on the Accreditation of Health Care Organizations (JCAHO) on down, through state departments of mental health and county or city offices of mental health, to local associations of mental health who sponsor citizens' committees to comment on the doings of mental health programs. . . . The trouble with the mental health bureaucracy, as seen from the field, is that it doesn't listen to practitioners, much less patient/consumers, so its spokesmen don't know what they're talking about."[4]

Ann Braden Johnson is in charge of mental health services for women in the jail at New York's Rikers Island. She writes, "Among the various bits of practice-based wisdom I have heard about auditors is that they will never address a serious problem for fear they will get in trouble for not having spotted it before . . . , [that] if something untoward were to show up, the overseers would then have to do something about it and run the risk of being blamed for having let it happen in the first place. There are two results of this reluctance to find anything seriously wrong in the agencies one is reviewing: (1) program directors and their auditors can and do collude to keep potentially damaging problems covered up as long as possible; and (2) auditors give so much advance warning of their visits that an agency's administration would have to be truly incompetent to fail to clean up its act in time."[5]

In fact, there are already enough overseers and regulators, external and internal, running around in facilities to generate an aspect of farce: Apart from the outside folks there is UR—for "utilization review"—"a required system of internal checks to determine if a program's services are both necessary and provided in a cost-efficient manner."[6] Then there is QA, which stands for "quality assurance": "a required system of internal checks on the adequacy of a program's work."

Not only is all of this mainly concerned with matters of plant safety, but it focuses entirely on paper procedures, the existence of credential and protocol standards, the keeping of records. It is not even remotely interested in how the inmate feels, or feels about what is being done to her—much less in the aptness of the ostensible reason for confinement.

It is not surprising, then, that this leads many facilities to indulge in creative writing. In FAKING HOSPITAL RECORDS: A CASE OF DOUBLE JEOPARDY, the *New York Times*[7] tells of the rewriting of minutes, the altering of case information in New York hospital records. For-profit psychiatric hospitals for children and adolescents have been accused not only of altering records to pass JCAHO inspection, but of altering diagnoses for insurance purposes.

The more psychiatry becomes perceived by practitioners as a market item, a mental health Hula-Hoop or Barbie doll, the sillier the idea that it is a helping profession becomes (except in the sense of helping itself). "The reality," Sheldon Galin, M.D., writes, "is that psychiatry now must be understood as comprising a group of marketable products. Indeed, one author concludes that 'the position of psychiatry in the health marketplace may be the most advantageous for growth of all medical specialties.'" . . . Further, "a product need not necessarily be tangible. It is a good or service exchanged for either money, time, or other personal valuables." Thus "considering psychiatric health 'products,' you would do well not to fall into myopic marketing."[8] I like "myopic marketing." It calls to mind Mr. Magoo hawking empty eyeglass frames. "The marketing approach pressures psychiatry to define clearly what it does for whom, to assess and evaluate systematically its efforts, and to communicate responsibly but assertively its value to health and society."[9]

In fact, to review the composite news clippings is to go from horror for the kids to hilarity at some of the behavior of the adults.

A March 31, 1991, *New York Times* story reports that Community Psychiatric Centers wants to spend $1.1 billion to buy Charter Medical Corporation.[10]

The story starts, "Call him dedicated. Call him a tightwad. But when James W. Conte visits one of the 50 psychiatric hospitals owned by his company, he refuses to pay for a hotel room, preferring instead to stay at the hospital—behind locked ward doors. That way he can try out the mattress, the air conditioning and cafeteria food."

As though under the impression that he is a Leona Helmsley do-alike, running a hotel chain, Conte says, "Our competitors say we do it because we are cheap, and that's part of it. . . . But I want all of the hospitals to be places where we're not ashamed to go. The last one we stayed in we found out the purchasing department decided to buy plasticized mattresses because it saves staining. Well, it's great until you try to sleep on them. It's like sleeping on a slab of ice. You're sliding all over and have to hang on at night."

Also, we are told, "Mr. Conte frequently makes jokes about lunatics running the asylum—perhaps to attempt to rise above the suffering he sees in his hospitals." Perhaps. Or perhaps he doesn't see any such thing.

This would not be unusual. As we have learned, the oversight bodies do not see it either, but instead do the same kind of tire kicking. (And it is instructive that nothing is said about his sampling the psychotropic medications like Thorazine and Elavil along with the food.)

And so, in one panel of what starts to seem like a frieze you have the (sometimes clownish) entrepreneurs.

In another panel you have the guys in rowboats dreaming up new diagnostic categories—(any number of which are said to reflect underlying depression, and thus require not only treatment programs, but medication). In the *New York Times* report of March 27, 1991, STUDY DEFINES "BINGE EATING DISORDER,"[11] we meet our old friend, Dr. Robert L. Spitzer, as he presents the findings of his study to the annual *scientific* meeting of the Society of Behavioral Medicine in New York. As with masochism (or DSM's "Self-Defeating Personality Disorder"), this one is not actually *new* either. It had been flown before. As with the earlier battles, here one sees being waged the battle between the psy folks and the bio-neuro-psy folks. Spitzer said that "the binge eating disorder had been recognized as early as 1959 by Dr. Albert Stunkard, a psychiatrist at the University of Pennsylvania who is a leading expert on the causes and treatment of weight problems. But it fell into the shadow of a unified theory of obesity that holds that obesity results from genetic or metabolic problems. The disorder was further eclipsed by recent attention to the eating disorders of anorexia and bulimia." (All of which has the character of "my specialty disorder is more disordered than your specialty disorder.")

Not surprisingly, "The figure suggests that for as many as five million Americans this complex disorder may account for their seeming inability to shed unwanted pounds once and for all." And—certainly not surprisingly—"The problem is considerably more common among women than men."

(In what is surely unconscious irony, the *New York Times* printed the results of this study next to a report by William J. Broad that begins, "A surprising one in four scientists suspect their peers of engaging in intellectual fakery, according to a new survey.")

The antic behavior of the adults makes that of the "conduct-disordered" or "adjustment-disordered" kids seem not only normal response, but positively responsible.

It is discoveries—or rediscoveries (or reinventions?)—of life problems that make the psy world appear to be helping and that make it appeal to the liberal interest in human concerns, in relieving individual distress. Because individualized problem management does not *appear* to be political, does not *appear* to be connected to large-scale social management, the more sinister potential for social abuse offered by the psy sector, when reported, seems anomalous and perplexing.

It is when, regularly as a cuckoo clock, overtly political interests pop out and announce their hour that there is occasion for a proper clutch of alarm—as with Dr. Hutschnecker's proposed plan, in 1970, under which the government would have mass testing done on all six- to eight-year-old children to root out those who might have violent or homicidal tendencies. (By comparison, entrepreneurial capers tend to seem merely fantastical.)

It suits the conservative wish list to identify violence, particularly that of male youth, as a public health problem and to invite the use of psy technology as a cure for the disorders of those identified (in kindergarten) as being "at risk." So, at this writing, we see the cuckoo pop out again.

It was pretty carefully set up: First, a report of a seemingly scientific study. STUDIES FIND A FAMILY LINK TO CRIMINALITY.[12] "More than half of all juvenile delinquents imprisoned in state institutions and more than a third of adult criminals in local jails and state prisons have immediate family members who have also been incarcerated, according to figures compiled by the Justice Department. . . . 'These are stunning statistics,' said Richard J. Hernstein, a professor of psychology at Harvard University and an expert on the causes of crime. He said they were fresh proof 'that the more chronic the criminal, the more likely it is to find criminality in his or her relatives.' " Meaning—it's biological, genetic, generationally transmitted.

There followed letters of protest, including one that says, "There is a long and sad history to this type of genetic determinism: trait after trait, including anorexia nervosa, schizophrenia and alcoholism, has been claimed to be genetic solely on the ground of familial transmission. There are clear dangers to such unfounded assertions. Before 1935, for example, 20,000 Americans were sterilized for 'hereditary feeblemindedness.' Although eugenics may no longer be a problem, more subtle dangers remain, such as the willingness of society to change the environment to cure what is seen as a genetic problem."[13]

Following release of this study, on February 11, 1992, Frederick K. Goodwin, then administrator of the Alcohol, Drug Abuse and Mental Health Administration, speaking before a department advisory council on mental health, compared violence by inner-city youths with the behavior of "male monkeys" in the jungle. Goodwin said, "If you look, for example, at male monkeys, especially in the wild, roughly half of them survive to adulthood. The other half die by violence. That is the natural way of it for males, to knock each other off and, in fact, there are some interesting evolutionary implications of that. . . . The same hyperaggressive monkeys who kill each other are also hypersexual, so they copulate more and therefore they reproduce more to offset the fact that half of them are dying." He then likened the aggressive behavior of these monkeys to violence in high-impact inner-city areas, which lack "some of the civilizing evolutionary things that we have built up."[14]

Since Goodwin at that time oversaw the funding of most federal research dealing with drug and alcohol abuse and mental illness, this had far-reaching implications. A fracas ensued. Goodwin moved to the post of director of the National Institute of Mental Health, a move that was publicly proclaimed a demotion (although it was evidently a job Goodwin wanted and was going to get anyway).

On Goodwin's side were the American Psychiatric Association, the Society of Neuroscience, and the National Alliance for the Mentally Ill. Also Leonard Garment, a Washington lawyer who was White House counsel under President Nixon (and whose personal physician Dr. Hutschnecker had been just before his famous memo).

Opposing Goodwin's appointment as director of NIMH were the American Psychological Association, the National Association of Social Workers, and the American Orthopsychiatric Association.

What Goodwin was proposing in his monkey speech was a "Violence Initiative" as a priority. ("What I am referring to is our number one initiative is the violence initiative.")[15] On February 11, Goodwin said (with considerable convolution), "What we have as an agency that isn't represented anywhere else in the Public Health Service is we have the expertise in individual vulnerability and I think if one is looking at sort of a triage look at how you actually get at this extremely complicated problem which ranks always number one and number two in everybody's public concern list, drugs is the number one public concern in society's eyes, and of course related drugs—and we will have a drug component of our plan."

More coherently, he said, "But the point is that if you are going to leverage that at all, in my view, you are going to leverage it through individuals, not through large social engineering of society, not through things as politically hot as gun control because by the time you get that passed you could rack up quite a few more violent deaths."

His scheme, of course, was early detection. "On the early detection front, the literature has, I think, been enriched by the advances in diagnostic precision, particularly around conduct disorder. . . . There are also some interesting new studies which relate to potential biological markers, at least in terms of some of the brain imaging studies that are being done with regard to prefrontal changes that may well be predictive of later violence."

As Edward M. Opton, Jr., Ph.D., counsel with the University of California, wrote to the Committee on Government Operations, "The plans developed by Dr. Goodwin's predecessors in the early 1970's were first revealed quite offhandedly, and probably unintentionally, just as has occurred for the new Violence Initiative. When a number of people, including myself, asked for the documents underlying the initiative of the 1970's, those who had developed the documents used all of the usual stratagems to avoid releasing them, including, especially, denials that any such documents existed. In spite of the denials, the documents eventually were pried out, and, in the daylight of exposure to the public and to the political process, the biomedical violence-control program of the 1970's was dropped."[16]

Yet even after Goodwin had publicly apologized for his monkey business, it seemed clear that his contrition did not extend to retracting the Violence Initiative proposal. On the contrary. As Eli Newberger, M.D., then president of the American Orthopsychiatric Association, wrote to Louis W. Sullivan, M.D., secretary, Department of Health and Human Services, on March 11, "Subsequent to those remarks and prior to his resignation as head of ADAMHA, Dr. Goodwin attended a February 25, 1992 meeting of the Mental Health Leadership Forum for the purpose of apologizing to the heads of some 37 national organizations. After characterizing his earlier remarks as inadvertent and misunderstood, Dr. Goodwin responded to a question about his approach to the problems of urban violence by reiterating his views in essentially the same terms, shorn only of references to jungles and monkeys. At this moment of heightened sensitivity, in the immediate aftermath of his personal apology, Dr. Goodwin elaborated on his position by outlining his proposed federal programs for dealing with violence among inner-city adolescents. The plan calls for establishing biological markers for the early identification of conduct-disordered youngsters. It aims to predict by the age of five—and at that point to intervene with—those children most likely to become disruptive and violent in adolescence."[17]

Newberger continues. "This proposal for a program that would label and stigmatize poor five-year-olds in the name of prevention is of particular concern to the American Orthopsychiatric Association, which has championed a preventive approach to mental and emotional disorders since its founding in 1924. Dr. Goodwin confounds punitive and preventive, while advocating a rehash of 'preventive' intervention that has been soundly discredited in its prior incarnations. (Notable among these have been the proposal by President Nixon's personal physician that all five-year-olds be tested to identify potential presidential assassins; the highly publicized and ultimately futile efforts to link XYY chromosomes to hypermasculinity and violence; and the hypothesis proffered by several psychiatrists during the civil disorders of the '60s that participants in the inner-city uprisings were suffering from 'temporal lobe epilepsy.' It is more than just ironic that the definitive refutation of the last of these endeavors came from careful studies conducted at NIMH in conjunction with the Kerner Commission, which concluded that the disorders were deeply rooted in social and economic conditions and which found no evidence that riot participants were more 'pathological' than nonparticipants.)"[18]

As Peter Breggin, director of the Center for the Study of Psychiatry, writes, "The violence initiative is essentially a biomedical approach to social problems. It is one example of a remarkably consistent viewpoint that has recycled in modern history at critical periods of social conflict in the United States and Europe. It rationalizes social ills and instead blames the victim—in this instance the young inner city black man—by declaring him genetically and biologically unfit.

"The transformation of criminal justice issues into psychiatric issues is always a hazard to individual rights. When the focus is upon the *potential* for violence, the threat escalates. And finally, when *early detection* is the theme, the civil libertarian implications are horrific."[19]

Here, as elsewhere, it is the legitimacy vested in psy technology that makes it so attractive to the powers that be. Bathed in the glow of science and medicine, it sustains the public appearance of neutrality. Because of this patina *it can be used*—in the same way that psychiatric hospitals for kids can be used, where public flogging would be frowned on. It is this quintessential pragmatism that for many obviates debate.

Given this—and regardless of whether the present Violence Initiative can be short-circuited or not—it seems more plausible than paranoid to suspect the psy sector of being a virtually irresistible control technology; one that can readily service the irrepressible longing of conservatives and reactionaries as a way to mark, intervene, and control (by segregation or by psychopharmaceuticals) uppity youth (most especially inner-city youth). Psy-fi.

As for the school connection here? That is where five- and six-year-olds are already required by law to go; schools are already empowered to evaluate, to judge, and to cause psy intervention.

A taped speech by Goodwin, in fact, makes the school connection explicit. He says: "The important thing is to recognize the continuity between disruptive childhood behavior, delinquent behavior, and violent behavior. . . . Early identification which has been tried with the so-called sequential gating procedure, the teachers identify perhaps 12, 15 percent of the classroom of the kids who are showing disruptive behavior. From that, one goes to a telephone interview with the parents. This costs about seven cents per child to administer and the telephone interview with the parents is about seven dollars per potential client. And then, finally, a structured parent-child interview. In other words this is sort of a triage operation where you gradually increase the level of clinical scrutiny and then of course the interventions would target the risk factors. . . ."

Goodwin adds that "there are indeed clinical treatments that can be brought to bear in a routine way."[20]

So. Although this is clearly scenario and not (yet) fact, such connections would permit the psy sector to set up a sort of psy-military presence in ghetto schools. Psy-fi.

11

Whose Drug
Problem
Is It?

I AM (ONCE AGAIN) sitting in the meeting room of a private psychiatric hospital. The chief psychiatrist is there briefly (he has a meeting in fifteen minutes), and the director, vice-president of administration.

The psychiatrist has told me that 25 to 30 percent of their inmates are preteen, and so I have asked about some of the young children who have been admitted. The psychiatrist tells me about one young boy who had been battered, sexually abused by his father: detailing the whole panoply of ugly events that had been visited on this kid, which have resulted in the "emotional disorder" with which he has been charged.

And do you, I ask, feel that this child's problems are "biologically based"?

He does.

You mean that, had this kid been treated lovingly by caring parents, if none of this stuff had happened to him, he would still have a biologically based brain disease?

247

He does mean just that.

What a remarkable piece of knowledge.

Trying another tack, I say, "What if a kid says, 'This is not what I need'?"

They look at each other and grin: "Most of them say that!"

"But—suppose—what if—they were right?"

This provokes, from the psychiatrist, the curious response that "the system is flexible enough to allow each kid to be treated individually."

"But if it's the family that has the problem or is the problem, what is the child doing in the hospital?"

"That is how you can most effectively and most rapidly engage that family in treatment."

Right about here the psychiatrist rushes off to his meeting, and the director expounds on the hospital and insurance business. But toward the end (I can't help it) I raise the issue again: "Take the kid's position for a minute." And thinking of Delia, I say, "Suppose Mom and Dad just tricked you into a hospital, and you're somewhat annoyed about that. Mom is saying you're depressed, you're anorexic." (I am trying to be politic here.) "Maybe Mom was convincing enough, or the kid is angry enough in the circumstance of the interview with the psychiatrist, and the kid was admitted. But supposing the kid was really right, that she'd been gaslighted. Is there any way that kid could convince the hospital of that?"

At this point, what he says, in effect, is that the insurance companies decide such matters. "Insurance companies are not gonna pay if there's not medical necessity. You have to be able to show medical necessity."

But the *evidence* of medical necessity, of course, is the psychiatrist's say-so: the diagnosis: the prescription for meds.

I am getting as frustrated as the kid I am conjuring here. "But the doctor can believe there's medical necessity. The kid can disagree."

He looks at me, truly perplexed. "Why would you believe the kid more than you'd believe the physician?"

Given what I have looked at and listened to, a thousand reasons come to mind. What I say, wearily, is, "I'm just thinking to level the playing field. Right at the moment, not only do the kids not have rights—but their testimony is totally disbelieved."

≈

Mixed into the hodgepodge of kids said to suffer from "atheoretical" psy disorders is a substantial portion of kids who have been sexually abused by fathers and stepfathers: Mind, the diagnosis is not "sexually abused"; more likely it is adjustment reaction, conduct disorder, oppositional defiance disorder. . . . In fact, a child's disclosure that she is being sexually violated in the home, and the subsequent intervention by the Department of Social Services this triggers, puts her at extreme risk of psy surveillance and a whole panoply of irrelevant and punitive "treatment" interventions, including psychiatric hospitalization.

Because? Because virtually from the moment of its birth as a publicly spoken-of social problem, incest was gobbled up by the psy sector as falling under the medical/psychiatric domain. Indeed, treatment for adult survivors—and for the concomitant ills from which they are said to suffer: codependency, multiple personalities, posttraumatic stress disorder, sexual addiction, substance abuse, eating disorders—has, in the past ten years, become one of the most lucrative specialties in the overall psy industry. Psychiatric hospitals have specialized survivor treatment programs. Individual therapists have specialty practices. Psychologists advertise survivor retreats. The language of healing, empowerment, of hugging the toddler within, is now ubiquitous.

The assumption is that the child who discloses sexual abuse is destined to suffer—not appropriate sadness or rage, but lasting emotional disorders, a deformity of being.

That the medicalization of social problems, deflection of attention onto the individual's illness, is a powerful technique for defusing concerted action for change is abundantly clear in the issue of child sexual abuse. Here, briefly, is how it happened.

In the latter part of the 1970s, a time when women were speaking out about rape, about battering—when those were emerging as strong feminist political issues—some women also began thinking and speaking about child sexual abuse by male parents and authority figures. At that time Freudianism still prevailed, and Freudian theory was holy writ.

As I noted earlier, Freud originally believed the women, suffering from what was then diagnosed as hysteria, who told him of childhood rape by male parents. Since most of his female patients were the daughters or female relatives of affluent citizens, he was not *happy* about it, but he did, to begin with, accept it. When, however, he presented this "seduction theory" to his colleagues, he was mocked, attacked, and generally threatened with professional rejection. And so he decided that the women had simply wanted the "seduction" to occur; dreamed it; imagined it. And he declared what was simply an about-face decision to be, in fact, a *discovery*. The discovery not of a social reality but of an individual female disease: the Oedipus complex.

This "Freudian cover-up" Florence Rush first exposed in 1977.[1] Meanwhile, as I discovered when I began researching *Kiss Daddy Goodnight*,[2] one had but to ask and women poured forward to speak of what had been done to them as children. What we discovered was that what had happened to each of us had several things in common: The primary discovery was that the fathers had all said it was natural; they had all done it not in spite of the fact that they knew it was wrong, but because they believed it was their right; at the very least, they believed it to be *justifiable*.

This discovery was so congruent with the politics of rape, the politics of wife battering, that it seemed, at the time, irrefutable: What we were talking about was a tacitly licensed abuse of power.

But what women saw as an opportunity for social change, the psy practitioners (once their heads cleared) saw as an opportunity for expanding dominion, and doing so in the service of the status quo. Once it was clear that it would no longer be possible to turn back the testimony of thousands of women, it became necessary for someone to formulate a theory that would support problem management: the appearance of response without the upset of change. The very thing at which the psy sector excels.

Once again both conservatives and liberals disagreed by running off in the same direction. No one, after all, can be *for* child abuse. And the idea of "treatment"—particularly the treatment of what was quickly declared a symptom of "family dysfunction"—removed the onus from any offender so unlucky as to be caught; it actually obliterated the idea of an offense. From a conservative viewpoint, the family would be preserved (that was the goal of treatment: keeping the family intact). From a liberal viewpoint, treatment was help; it was understanding; it was compassion for the victimized child.

The machinery was already in place to ensure that child sexual abuse could be "decriminalized." The 1974 Child Abuse Prevention and Treatment Act authorized social service intervention. All that was needed was to "educate" the public about the psychological trauma of incest; the emotional damage; the warning signs; whom to call (social workers). It took only three or four years to go from zero to cruising speed, gathering ever more child victims in the glare of the headlights and gaining ever-expanding dominion over the adult survivors, ensuring that they, too, thought of themselves not as victims of a political license, but as individually emotionally damaged.

≈

I first met Tracy and heard parts of her story five years ago. Not only is her experience of what happens to victimized kids far from atypical, but it is illustrative as well of one issue that has been threading not only through this work, but through much work on the increasing use of the psy sector to subvert and manage what might otherwise be social and political issues. In this case, the issue is incest.

Let me recount Tracy's background as concisely as I can, then ask her, today, at twenty-two, what her multiple hospitalizations were like: see if any relevance can be found between what was done to her by her father and the response: the way in which she was "treated."

Tracy's father began sexually abusing her when she was nine. Routinely. Weekly. A feisty kid, she decided at thirteen that she didn't have to take this anymore. It was 1983: The bombardment of (dis)information about incest had not reached its peak: The news had not yet reached her. She didn't even know what to call what was happening, didn't know what to do.

She tried calling several psychiatrists; none responded. Finally she called a rape crisis center. The counselor asked whether she wanted the abuse to stop, whether she wanted to do something. She said she did. That was the last decision Tracy would be empowered to make for the next five years.

Tracy was yanked from the home. Since her mother was not supportive, Tracy was put in foster care. She was coerced into going for counseling, group therapy; made to tell her story over and over. Angry that she had been, effectively and summarily, orphaned; appalled at abruptly finding herself in a severely religious household, Tracy was told her foster placement was not working out. She was placed in a second foster home. From there she was sent to a hospital for psychiatric evaluation. From there to a state hospital for nine months. From there to an aunt (briefly). Then, for another nine months, back to the state hospital. And on and on it went, until she was seventeen.

At seventeen, when I first met her, Tracy was plenty enraged at the "treatment" she had received. Even then, though, she was one of the most articulate kids I had ever met. That is one reason I have come back to talk to her. Another is that her experience was with public, not private, for-profit, institutions. These few years later, she says, "I think I can explain a little more about how they run the places and stuff; explain the rules better because I was—a little angry at the time. Feeling a little hostile, put it that way." She is also, she tells me, now able to talk about some of the things that went on, things she saw, that were too painful to remember at the time. "I didn't really explain when we talked before what happened to *other* kids.

"The first place I was in was the psychiatric unit of a general medical hospital. That was for my evaluation. Technically speaking, the longest people are supposed to be there is like two weeks. That's the one I was in for a month and a half.

"They didn't really have a lot of juveniles in there. One guy who was seventeen. And another girl who was about fourteen. But almost everybody was on drugs of some kind. The minute you walked in they would put you on something or other. They had me on Elavil. And Haldol. For if you got upset or anything—if you 'went off' [transl.: got angry] like I did.

"There was an older lady there that was, I would say, pretty much insane. Maybe Alzheimer's, I don't know. But she didn't have any memory and she'd babble a lot about nothing and it was very weird.

And if she did—like, anything? I don't think she was really at fault for it? I mean she didn't know what the hell she was doing most of the time. So every once in a while she'd refuse to eat, and then they'd calm her down with drugs. She couldn't walk, she was in a wheelchair. What is she gonna do if she sits there and screams? She really couldn't do anything to anybody.

"Everybody was on meds: kids, adults. I think the guy, Stan, was on more Elavil than I was. Then they put me on thirty-five milligrams. Three times a day."

Elavil is a tricyclic antidepressant, about which Dr. Peter Breggin writes, "The tricyclic antidepressants originally were tested as neuroleptics because chemically they are very similar to Thorazine. . . . They are, in many ways, neuroleptics in disguise. Their side effects stem mainly from suppression of the cholinergic nerves of the autonomic nervous system and the brain. . . . Nearly all of the antidepressants commonly produce the following side effects: various autonomic nervous system signs, such as blurred vision, dry mouth, and suppressed function of gut, bladder, and sexual organs, as well as low blood pressure on standing, weight gain, sleep disturbance, seizures, and impaired cardiac function. . . . They frequently produce sedation, lethargy, and a blunting of emotional responsiveness."[3]

About Elavil, Tracy says, "It's really interesting because I remember when they first put me on it and I was basically like completely asleep. In a chair. Out in the lounge. For about six hours. Gone. Out. Whhhuh. I was tired all the time. And that was supposed to be an *anti*depressant. I don't understand how that could be an *anti*depressant if you're sleeping all the time. Whenever you start taking a drug like that, it's going to have some drastic effect, especially if they just start you on it. They're not supposed to do that. They're supposed to gradually ease you into and ease you out of it— and ease you onto something else. They cannot just go boom, here's some drugs, take them."

"But they did."

"But they did. The first three days I was there—they make you take the MMPI; the blob test. Fifty thousand other stupid tests. They did a complete physical on me. I saw a shrink every week. . . ."

"What did the shrink do with you?"

"Not a hell of a lot. He—asked me why I was angry—a lot. 'Why are you angry?' For me, I was just basically angry because I was there. I was angry that people were telling me what to do, when to do it, and how to do it. I was angry that I wasn't allowed to listen to music." (Remember Anne, the thorn in Dr. Masterson's paw?) Tracy says, "There were a lot of things that ticked me off. He would tell me all the time that I'm gonna be getting my own clothes back. And of course I never got them until three weeks before I left.

"We had a group every week; another group we had every day. Another group that was—every week we'd sit and watch movies and shit."

"Just regular movies?"

"Yeah."

"That's called a 'group'?"

"Everything's a group. Every morning we'd have this group where we'd sit and confess our sins."

"What did the kids confess to?"

"It seemed to me that the majority of the problems people were talking about were just being unsatisfied. Really nameless stuff. Nobody would 'confess' to anything heavy. Things like, 'This person was pissing me off.' Those groups seemed kind of weird to me because—it was all bluff. Most of the time, nobody talked about anything heavy."

"But there were restraints and isolation?"

"Oh, yeah. Yeah. There were restraints and isolation in almost every single place I've ever been in.

"Other places, like the state hospital: There's two buildings; one had the guys in it, one had the girls. There were four levels that you could be on. You had Step 1, Step 2, Step 3, and Step 4. You also had orientation when you first came in, in which you were basically on Step 2, but you didn't quite get to do everything. You were kind of just there—allowed to do stuff but not as much as a real Step 2 person. You basically just learn the rules and stuff. And then if you do anything wrong, you're demoted and you're not allowed to go to the bathroom unless you ask a staff person. You're not allowed to talk in the hall. You're not allowed to go out on the porch. Just sit in the dayroom."

"Didn't you tell me before that you had to do your own wash?"

"That wasn't rules, per se; that was *goals.*"

Silly me. (It is worth noting that even after wandering in this world for a year, I have not really picked up on an order of things that any kid is—on contact—supposed to master.)

"The *rules* were like you couldn't go upstairs to your bedroom after the morning was over with. What you'd do was, you woke up in the morning, you took your shower, did all that stuff. Went downstairs for breakfast. After that point, you could not go upstairs again until—I believe it was nine-thirty at night. Lunch and dinner were always at the same time. Rules were you had to do your things when you were told to do them.

"You went to your groups, you made sure you were at all these places. After breakfast you'd go to school; then you'd come back and go to your groups. You always had two or three. They had so many groups it wasn't even funny. Orientation group, occupational therapy group, recreational therapy group. Occupational therapy has nothing to do with the name itself, because the name sounds like you should be learning an occupation. You sat around and made ceramics and stuff; did crafts. Recreational therapy was—you did sports shit. And there was a group for certain people who had problems like—if their coordination were bad?

"There was another group for sexually abused kids, which I refused to go to. Another group for guys who were abused. There was volleyball group, softball group, all of it's group."

≈

So far, it is difficult to see what conceivable relevance any of this has to Tracy's disturbance over having been sexually abused and subsequently deparented. What it has to do with is dominance and submission.

Tracy continues, "There were several things that happened that—really freaked the shit out of me." She pauses and sighs. "Um. I'm trying to put it so it's easy for other people to understand. I think that's why it's so hard to describe it—is because it's such a different world that *nobody* can understand. Like—what I understand does not make sense to anybody else."

Try me. "You mean it's like a trip to a different universe."

"Yeah. Basically it is." Tracy tries to be particular, to offer the details that will allow us to imagine the universe she is describing. "The whole state hospital—we had our own little cottages, but we went to what they called the canteen. A little store. With soda and all that. And cigarettes. So basically you never went outside—except to go to a movie or something if you were good.

"We saw all the nutso people, too. The MIDs—'mentally ill and dangerous.' The CDs—'chemically dependent.' Adults. There were usually about twenty-nine to thirty guys on the guys' cottage. Usually no more than twenty girls. And about seven kids in PC (Protective Care)."

"What got a kid into Protective Care?"

"I don't know. Because if they came in there, they came straight from the outside quote/unquote. There were two stories in our cottage. The downstairs had the living room and the offices and the bathrooms. Upstairs had two halves. It had one side, which was the bedrooms—four girls in a room. And on the other side was the Protective Care Unit. There, they had three Time Out Rooms. Our side had only one.

"Time Out Rooms had nothing in them except one of those—mats, like you do gymnastics on? And a light overhead with a little metal shit around it, so that you couldn't break the bulb and kill yourself."

So far, this reminds me of nothing so much as a psychiatric hostage camp; or a Gulag. Again, what has all this to do with any real will to repair the hurt Tracy suffered? Why would anyone expect this kind of (mal)treatment to result in a restoration of balance and confidence in a badly hurt kid?

Having looked long and hard at several such (and been impressed), I ask Tracy about the Time Out Room doors. She says, "Very, very, very thick. The front of the door, when you close the door and look at it from the outside? Was wood. The inside—was metal. A little window in it about five inches long, three inches high. We went up to the PC Unit twice to watch a movie. Just like ours, the Time Out doors had the windows with the metal stuff in it. And the TV had plastic over it. They weren't allowed to turn on the TV or touch the VCR. And the Time Out Rooms were right next to the door."

I can tell from her softened voice, her demeanor, that remembering back this concretely—reinvoking the images—is tapping feelings Tracy did not give room to five years before, not the least of which is awe that she was actually in that universe, that galaxy; that, at the time, it was a daily reality.

"Basically," she says, "what they tended to do with us was, you sat on a chair at the end of the hall. And if you didn't do that, or if you smart-assed too much, you'd just sit on that chair for the rest of your life. They had them in the basement where we had school, too.

"When they Timed Out somebody, generally speaking—getting them into a room or making them sit on a chair, whatever—they would basically force them on the floor and hold their arms behind their back—so that their hands were up, kind of? One time, Jane— this is a girl that later had electroshock therapy—before she was sent down for that, this is what occurred. What happened was she was kind of pissed off one day, because—every once in a while, we all got mad. Because we were there. She was just in an argumentative mood. Basically, Jane was an artist—very good; very sensitive; a very nice person.

"She was angry about something and it escalated into a huge argument with one of the staff people. He made a derogatory remark—and she basically swung at him. And she ended up very quickly on the floor. They dragged her down to the Time Out Room. They had to call a couple of staff from the guys' side because there was nobody watching us; they were all busy dealing with Jane."

In contrast with her normally buoyant and rapid pattern, Tracy's speech is now subdued. "They dragged her into the Time Out Room. She was not calming down. They had to continue to hold her down. So finally they called a nurse. And she came down. And they shot her up. With Haldol."

Haldol is a neuroleptic—a category of drug also known as *major tranquilizers*.[4] According to Breggin, "[W]ell over a million people a year are treated with neuroleptics on the wards and in the clinics of state mental health systems." Also, "In recent years, haloperidol, sold by McNeil Pharmaceutical under the trade name Haldol, has become the most prescribed neuroleptic. In a letter to attorney Roy A. Cohen dated August 13, 1987, McNeil's director of medical services, Anthony C. Santopolo, provided a glimpse of Haldol's escalating use. The figures for patients first treated with Haldol grew from 600,000 in 1976 to 1,200,000 in 1981."[5]

Tracy says, "They shot her up. She slept in the Time Out Room that night. I remember she did not come upstairs until the morning. And in the morning, she was so drugged out—she was drugged out all day. It happened a couple of more times that week, and then finally—they just took her to the university hospital and—gave her shock treatments. She—came back a zombie. Yeah. She was really different. And—um—I couldn't stand to be around her.

"After that she was very, very suicidal. That's how it got with me. It got to the point where—it didn't matter anymore because you feel it's all out of control, and they're just gonna do what they want with you anyway."

"How old was Jane?" I ask.

"Seventeen."

"How long had she been in treatment institutions?"

"From what I could tell, since she was nine. The kids coming in got younger and younger every year. When I first went in there, the youngest kids were about fifteen. Not even a year later, they were down to thirteen, twelve. I constantly heard staff remark on that— how much younger the social workers were referring kids." Tracy is quiet a moment, then says, "Jane didn't tell me about the shock until much later, but I just knew. I just knew—from the way she was—it wasn't drugs. Later on, she told me. Because it took her a while to get out of the haze." She stops again, then, "Ah, man. This shit is really hard to talk about."

"Hey, Tracy, we don't have to do this all in one day."

"No, I'd rather do it and get it over with. It gets—easier. That sounds callous, but it gets easier. See—I never talked about any of these people before. Because I—I couldn't. It's—very hard to see people your age be treated like this all the time."

Gamely, Tracy goes on: "The other major thing that happened in that place was—Caroline. She, basically, was just a runaway. She ran like three or four times. And they finally put her on all these drugs. I know what some of it was. I don't know what all of it was. I know she was on like eight hundred milligrams of Haldol twice a day.

"They finally took her off it. But from what I can tell—I don't think they really eased her off it. Because she went through DTs while I was there, for like three weeks. Drooling. Couldn't feed herself. And we had to look at her every day. She still went to school with us. She still ate with us. And somebody would have to feed her, and somebody would have to get her ready in the morning. And a lot of times we ended up doing it. Walking with her to classes and stuff. . . .

"It was terrible. All of her clothes eventually had this big drool stain. It was just—gross. Terrible. And it wasn't *her* that was gross. You know what I mean? They had drugged her and—uhhh—it was nasty."

The astute reader may have noticed that I appear to be paying only passing attention to the issue of the widespread dosing of kids with neuroleptic and antipsychotic medication. This very hesitancy on my part makes a point: If credentialism reigns even where the DSM is concerned (a work that is written in some sort of English); if, even there, hangs a warning that all who presume to enter a dialogue must have received the proper indoctrination/education— then what awaits the investigator who is not a neuroscientist and has the audacity to challenge chemicals (medications)? Indeed, as I have suggested, that is the strategic brilliance of shifting the psy sector onto a biological base; and one of the major, major dangers.

However, it seems inarguable here to quote from the publication *Science News*. Its November 2, 1991, issue reported on a study, the results of which were first published in the October *American Journal of Psychiatry*, that showed that one-third of all children and adolescents treated with antipsychotic drugs in a New York psychiatric hospital developed symptoms of parkinsonism. "Richardson's team studied 104 youngsters, averaging 15 years old, living in or admitted to a state-operated child psychiatric center in New York during a six month period. The patients' diagnoses ran the gamut, including conduct disorders, schizophrenia, severe depression, drug use and hyperactivity.

"Of 61 youngsters who received neuroleptics upon entering the study 21 displayed clear and often 'striking' parkinsonian symptoms, Richardson says. Those with longer histories of anti-psychotic treatment developed the most severe rigidity and slowed movement. Of all neuroleptic-treated children who took specific drugs to quell those symptoms, three nevertheless exhibited parkinsonism."

One of the major things troubling the researchers was that those diagnosed with *severe* disorders "accounted for only slightly more than one-quarter of the diagnoses among youngsters receiving the drugs."[6]

One has to wonder: So much is made by psychiatry of kids and the drug problem, but *whose drug problem is it*?

Tracy is talking about another psy setup she was placed in: "It looked like a group home," she says, "but was considered a treatment facility. They could house nine, all girls. The way it was set up, there wasn't a Step 1 or Step 2. But it was set up so they had a problem sheet that had a list of different problems: authority problems, drug and alcohol problems. . . . And people would check your behavior. Constantly. About every little dorky thing." Ah yes. Like the place we found Mike in. "Like if you didn't plug in the van in the winter, it was considered an authority problem, because you knew you were supposed to do it. Having to ask the staff to use the bathroom.

"We had groups every day right after school. In the basement. And you'd have to somehow remember all the problems you had that day. I was never able to do that. And—that was automatically a problem. We'd sit there and go through a list of problems and say what happened with each circumstance: who checked your behavior, why that person checked your behavior; analyze every little dumb thing—including forgetting the ketchup on the table. But they'd never really talk about why anybody was there. Nobody had any idea what my real problems were.

"By the time people got out, basically they were robots. One time, one of the girls got Timed Out. And they expected *us* to do it. To hold her down. Or else you had an 'authority problem.' "

"*You* had to do it? The *kids*?" For some reason, this strikes me as more invidious than even the abuse of massive drugging. (Maybe because it is so reminiscent of the use of inmates to control inmates in Nazi concentration camps?)

Tracy says, "Mm-*hmmm*. Exactly. I refused to do it at first. Like, 'I'm not gonna Time Out somebody.' But they expected us all—with the staff—to hold somebody down."

"So you were forced to turn on each other?"

"We were forced to turn on each other. I will never understand exactly what the basis of this was. I don't understand how it's helpful to anybody."

That's easy. It's extremely helpful to the staff. And of course it helps to break both potential solidarity and kids' wills—and to maintain control. "So," I say, "you didn't dare rebel?" (What am I saying? Rebel how? Rebelling is what got many of them in there in the first place.)

Tracy says, "You couldn't get anybody to do it, simple as that. Technically speaking, you'd think—five or six kids against one staff person meant that we could go, 'Screw this!' But it didn't happen."

"Because?"

"I feel—maybe this is going to sound weird, but I feel it was almost like a brainwashing kind of thing. Consider—you take all these kids in, okay? And when you set a bunch of kids up in a system like that, treat them that way, it makes people question what their real values are." Exactly what Alida Jatich said about Bettelheim's regime at the Sonia Shankman Orthogenic School. "Like, for me, the idea of holding somebody down is the most abhorrent idea—it makes me sick. But somehow—I did it anyway.

"And—just the fact that it was powerful enough to make me do something that I find absolutely disgusting . . .

"I guess what continues to bother me about the whole thing, taking everything that happened in 'treatment,' is—I can't believe that I saw the things that I saw. That—these things exist. That—I did what I did. All of the ways I reacted—or didn't react. Like the fact that we all put up with the fact that on withdrawal Caroline was shaking her arms off, and we just dealt with that every day. The fact that it happened.

"That shouldn't have happened. Jane shouldn't have had shock treatment. Kids shouldn't be forced to hold down other kids. That's against everything I believe in.

"I'm not going to say all my values are 'normal,' because I do have ideas that people find—different. But being in the situations I was in—anybody would have been disgusted by that. Would have been—horrified."

"To what extent do you feel the treatment fucked you up more than the abuse and the events that led up to the treatment?"

"I think it's obvious that it has. I came into the whole thing with fairly low self-esteem. But I think there's no way in hell anybody could get out of treatment—no matter how they were when they went in—without their self-esteem ripped to shreds.

"And I think it made me a psychological hypochondriac. At this point in my life—and probably for a long time to come—I sit here and go, 'Okay, what problems do I have, and blah blah blah?' Maybe I'm not nuts, but I always think I am. And I think most people who go through treatment come out with this problem: thinking you're worse than anybody else; that it must be your problem if somebody's pissed at you. It's always there—that you're completely different than anybody else. And that you are the one who is causing any problem.

"I'm always telling myself, 'No, this is not my problem.' But there's always this little tweak back there—because of the way the treatment treated me, and the way they put everything as being *your* fault—somehow you have done something—you're always wondering, 'Is it me?' "

What is ironic here is that Tracy, when she was first ordered to go to sexual abuse counseling, to groups, kept being told, over and over, that the *sexual abuse was not her fault*. As she said to me five years back, "Over and over, 'It's not your fault, it's not your fault.' And I'm like, 'I *know* that. If I know it and you know it, why do you have to keep saying it?' "

"Tracy, at what point did this start to get to you? You go in and you're angry and—'Let me out of here. I don't belong here.' At what point does it convert into—you somehow believe them?"

"For me? I think I fought back the most when I was first in the state hospital. But once I realized I had to play the game . . ."

"You mean—they win?"

"Pretty much. When you realize that you're not in control. When you realize you can't really fight back. That's when they win. When you realize that you no longer have your own life.

"And that probably happened for me after being two or three months in the state hospital. You get so separated from everything else that you can't discern the difference between what reality in your mind is—what you think is right, your beliefs—and what *their* beliefs are. You can't believe in what you believe in anymore— because it isn't your life you're living. You're living your life how *they* want it.

"Nothing is yours. Your thoughts aren't yours. Your beliefs aren't yours. Your things aren't yours. Nothing is in your control anymore. So nothing is yours."

"And the goal of all this is conformity?"

"Yeah," Tracy says. "Definitely. Kid control."

"One last question, Tracy," I say. "What did all this 'treatment' have to do with what started the whole thing: the fact that you'd been sexually abused and did, then, what we now encourage kids to do? Blow the whistle. Speak up. Do you see any conceivable relevance of the response to the problem?"

"I—do—not—understand. I do understand that it was important a dozen years ago for you to tell people this stuff happened. Back when nobody knew. To break the silence and all that. But we *did* that.

"Now we're just going over and over the same shit over and over again. It's kind of like, 'Okay, guys, well guess what! We've dealt with this.' At least I have. And I think it's now time to deal with how we're *dealing* with it. Fine, we know that incest is there. We know that these things exist. We know that it's happened to a lot of people. And I think—who spoke up recently? Suzanne Somers, Roseanne Barr, Oprah?—I think we all feel that we're not alone anymore. I mean, give me a break: I do not feel alone.

"There's groups everywhere, 'counseling' everywhere. There's so much 'treatment' out there it's not funny. But they don't discuss what *kind* of treatment it is. They don't talk about how this stuff is helping *nobody*."

"Well, but there's more money in just medicalizing the problem. It sure creates a lot less social chaos than trying to seriously sanction the offenders."

"Well, yeah. The difference between saying, 'Yo, this happened to me, too,' and going out after the offenders is that all this speaking about it just makes you a patient or an inmate. It doesn't challenge power. Because if you say, 'My daddy's a big, rich man over there, and he did this. Go do something about him,' then you're challenging a higher power. I feel there's a war going on with all this who's gonna get which kids in treatment.

"And I feel in my mind that there should be a war on the treaters. Some days, I just want to go in and let all the kids in 'treatment' go free—let them out, like the animal rights groups let minks out. Set them free. But—what are the kids gonna do then?"

Afterword:
Emerging

ON APRIL 28, 1992, the U.S. House of Representatives Select Committee on Children, Youth, and Families held a hearing entitled *The Profits of Misery: How Inpatient Psychiatric Treatment Bilks the System and Betrays Our Trust*, the committee chair, Representative Pat Schroeder, reported that the committee's investigation found: that thousands of adolescents, children, and adults have been hospitalized for psychiatric treatment they didn't need; that hospitals hire bounty hunters to kidnap patients with mental health insurance; that patients are kept against their will until their insurance benefits run out; that psychiatrists are being pressured by the hospitals to alter their diagnoses to increase profit; that hospitals "infiltrate" schools by paying kickbacks to school counselors who deliver students; that bonuses are paid to hospital employees, including psychiatrists, for keeping the hospital beds filled; and that military dependents are being targeted for their generous mental health benefits. According to Schroeder, a briefing she received from the Department of Justice revealed "current intelligence shows that psychiatric hospitals and clinics are defrauding Government programs and private insurers of hundreds of millions of dollars annually. Patients have been forcibly admitted into psychiatric treatment programs in situations where they posed no threat to the community or themselves. Often patients are subject to batteries of blood tests, x-rays, shock treatment, and other services. Investigations by the FBI to date have disclosed billings to the Government in the hundreds of millions of dollars."[1]

Testimony at the hearing revealed that the Civilian Health and Medical Program of the Uniformed Services (CHAMPUS) showed increased costs of 126 percent between 1986 and 1989—to $613 million dollars in 1989. And that this increase could be attributed almost entirely to the inpatient treatment of children and adolescents. CHAMPUS has offered private, for-profit facilities—both acute care and residential treatment—a bonanza: Its coverage includes 30 days annually of inpatient care for adults, 45 days annually for children, and 150 days of care annually for children and adolescents in residential treatment centers. (Most private insurers do not cover residential treatment centers.) Thus, the only cap is annual, not lifetime.[2] (All of which gives new meaning to "military spending.")

It was the testimony of state Senator Mike Moncrief of Texas that "In Texas, we have uncovered some of the most elaborate, aggressive, creative, deceptive, immoral, and illegal schemes being used to fill empty hospital beds with insured and paying patients. Probably the most widely known case, and the one that really started the investigation, involves an adolescent boy who was apprehended at his grandparents' home in San Antonio by employees of a private security firm who were not even certified peace officers—although they flashed large police badges. The firm was being paid between $150 to $450 for each patient delivered to certain private psychiatric hospitals in the area. This young man was admitted to the hospital for a substance abuse problem without ever being examined by a physician. His records show that he wasn't even given a drug test until four days after admission, and the results of the test were negative."[3]

Moncrief's investigation turned up one young woman who was billed for eight, ten, and twelve hours of group therapy each day. And the same patient was billed on one day for thirty-six prescription drugs. Her itemized statement shows 8,400 milligrams of Lithobid (lithium). "The PDR (*Physicians' Desk Reference*) lists the maximum dose at 1,800 milligrams. This amount of lithium alone or in combination with the other drugs would have been lethal if it had actually been given to the patient."[4]

Moncrief raises the point that it is not just the health care providers who are at fault, but the insurance industry, which "has not offered any acceptable explanations for their failure to monitor and investigate these claims for potential fraud."

What *might* the explanation be? (You may be wondering. I am.)

Moncrief says, "One possible explanation, as reported last October in the *Houston Chronicle*, is that several major health insurance companies own large quantities of stock in the corporations that, in turn, own private psychiatric and other health care facilities. In my opinion, this is a blatant conflict of interest. What possible incentive is there for an insurer to help hold down costs if, by paying these exorbitant claims, the company will improve the return on its investment and just raise the policyholder's premium to adjust for the escalating health care costs?"[5]

Cozy? But after all, insurance is an *industry*: We speak of the insurance *business*. Business seeks its own benefit in the form of profit. We may be outraged. But we have no reason to be surprised (other than a wistful wish to believe that the insurance we pay for is there primarily to help us in time of need).

And Moncrief adds, ". . . let me share just one more case that was reported to our Committee by the Chief of Police of Shenandoah, Texas, a small city outside of Houston with a large, 150-bed, private psychiatric hospital. The Chief said his department had responded to numerous complaints about this facility. One particularly memorable incident involved a four-year-old girl who was admitted to the hospital for evaluation after a physician concluded she may have been sexually molested by a family member." And—(remember the sexual abuse–psych hospital connection? Remember Tracy?)—"the child's mother was persuaded to check into the hospital with her young daughter for a few days to help the child get adjusted. Both were covered by CHAMPUS. Promptly after checking in, mother and daughter were separated and were only allowed to see each other at meal times. When the mother demanded to be released, she said that several hospital employees overpowered her and gave her an injection. Mother and daughter were finally released but only after she contacted the Shenandoah Police Department."

And—(remember the Little Rock initiative to fund 100 percent of kids referred by schools for inpatient substance abuse treatment?)—"It might interest you to know that the facility has since been converted into a rehabilitation hospital."[6]

Curtis L. Decker, executive director of the National Association of Protection and Advocacy Systems, Inc., recounted further abuses, including an Alabama case where Larry and Patricia Barker, foster parents of an eight-year-old boy, Daniel, were having a little difficulty in toilet training Daniel. They thought maybe a little counseling might help. "After an initial session Daniel was removed from the custody of his foster parents and placed in a seven-month in-treatment program. The Barkers have alleged that within the treatment center their foster son was overmedicated, put in isolation, and came out a withdrawn and disturbed little boy. The Barkers were restricted from seeing Daniel, permitted to only specific and limited visiting hours. Only after the Barkers sought legal and political help nation-wide was the boy returned to the family."[7]

The testimony of Russel D. Durrett—from November 1988 through July 1989 the controller of Twin Lakes Hospital in Denton, Texas, a Psychiatric Institutes of America facility—was even more detailed and more chilling about gross fraud and corruption than the testimony we listened to from Max Schilling. He recounted violations of Medicare regulations, state regulations, Internal Revenue Service regulations, and of acceptable business practices, including:

- Psychiatrists were recruited by paying for the establishment of their practices and in addition were paid salaries of anywhere from eight thousand to fifteen thousand dollars a month (for roughly ten hours a week);
- The chief medical officer, who might spend two hours a day in the hospital, earning a 50 percent bonus, while office rent, renovation, furniture, and equipment were paid for by the hospital;
- The medical director for the Twin Lakes drug and alcohol abuse program being an ob-gyn physician, not a psychiatrist. He was given a loan of thirty-five thousand dollars with the understanding that as long as the number of patients on the

program was above a certain level, the loan would largely be written off.

- One consultant, active on the speaker circuit, was paid four thousand dollars a month for mentioning Twin Lakes while on speaking tours.
- Art therapy, recreational therapy, music therapy, and biofeedback sessions, which would not be covered by insurance, were shown on bills as group or individual therapy.[8]

Psychiatrist Duard Bok, a former hospital employee, testified to abuses he had witnessed in private psychiatric hospitals in North Texas, including:

- unlicensed staff members doing work with patients that "involved a certain percentage of them going into hypnotic trance and many of these counselors not knowing nor understanding what was happening to these patients";[9]
- some of these hypnotized patients being given "false memory implantation"—false memories that would stay with them forever. ("The reality of their personal history can be irrevocably changed," Bok testified);[10] and
- some concoction called "rage reduction therapy"—later amended to pose as "trust development therapy."

About this last item Bok testified, "Not only is there no professionally recognized validation of 'rage reduction therapy,' but it involves holding the young person down by one or more adults while another person usually verbally taunts them and beats him/her in the rib and chest areas often causing severe pain and bruising.

"In some of the female preadolescent and adolescent patients there was tissue injury in the form of severe bruising incurred in the nipple and breast areas. The nursing staff were concerned about fractured ribs as a result of this procedure."

Further, and arguably most appalling, "Many of these children were probably the victims and survivors of physical, sexual and psychological abuse by their various major caregivers.

"In these youths the verbal taunting and the beating while being forcibly held down would often have been reminiscent of the type of terrifying abuse many of them had experienced before admission.

"To label that experience 'trust development therapy' was completely ironic. It probably compounded these youths' confusion and mistrust." *Probably*? (What would *your* reaction be?)

Bok also detailed "double-bind" scenarios: Kids who complied were told they were faking it. Kids who did not comply were told they were "sick" or disturbed; their levels were dropped, their passes withheld.

Why didn't nurses or technicians complain? Because these jobs were their livelihood, and because, as whistle-blowers, they would have had difficulty securing other employment. As Bok says, "Hardly anybody addresses the elephant in the metaphorical living room. Woe betide the person who does."[11]

Also, Bok claims, medicated/sedated kids were deprived of sleep—allowed to sleep only between 10:00 or 11:00 P.M. and 5:30 A.M. "If they fell asleep or misbehaved in school or a therapeutic activity, they were often penalized or it was noted on the record, or reported at the weekly team meeting, that they were unmotivated and/or 'not working their program.' "

Psychiatrists, psychologists, and therapists who referred to the hospitals got hospital referrals for postrelease treatment. Psychiatrists, psychologists, and therapists who did not, did not.

Psychologists and therapists who referred got lucrative contracts to do hospital-based group therapy.

Bok says, "I have knowledge of lies told to patients by their 'team coordinators,' usually chemical dependency counselors who ironically profess to promote spiritually based twelve-step programs, the essence of which is integrity.

"I've had 'team coordinators' come to me and literally beg me not to discharge patients until the administration blessed it."[12]

Clearly Bok was a renegade troublemaker and, as the hospital figured that out, they did what these sorts of places do: "[T]heir executive committee then wrote a letter to the Impaired Physicians Committee of the Texas Medical Association in Austin, claiming

that I had become 'incommunicado,' and suggesting that I had
become this way as a function of being mentally ill."[13]

There is more—some of it the usual (sexual assault of kids by
physicians), and some of it indicative of what we might call Mafioso
Delusional Disorder (forging physicians' signatures; paying off recovery hot lines for referrals; bugging phones).

"I have heard," Bok says, "of a case in Nevada where one young
person was confined to a psychiatric hospital for four and a half
years.

"I have heard of cases in Dallas where young people have been
confined in four-point restraints in hospital beds or wheelchairs for
weeks at a time.

"I have heard of cases where, recently, children were placed in
'body bags' in Virginia. . . .[14]

"I have heard of cases in Nevada where young people on orders
from psychiatrists, and with the compliance of other staff and administration, deliberately and systematically have kept youths
awake for several nights at a time 'to break them down.'"

Some of these abuses were reported to child protective agencies,
yet none were acted on. Why? Because, Bok suggests, workers in
those agencies saw the hospitals as potential employers should
social service agency budgets be cut.

What we are clearly talking about here is financial interest. No
matter how many neurotransmitters are tossed into the conversation—it is *not* science.

≈

On the whole, the testimony at the select committee hearings offers
powerful evidence that Delia's experience—Mike's, even Joey's,
Tracy's—are actually on the benign (rather than the sensational)
side of what is being done in the name of treatment; in the name of
assisting kids' mental health; it is what the grown-ups are up to in
the world kids enter once they become psy fodder.

While the scandals at the moment are focused on acute care
psychiatric facilities, there is, if anything, reason for even greater
concern about residential treatment facilities. They are far more
hidden, more loosely regulated, and—faced with criticism—they

tend to claim that they deal with the kids no one else will deal with; that their population is the most troubled, the most difficult, and, it is implied, the most violent. Thus, it is further implied, extreme circumstances demand extreme measures.

David Baine, director of federal health care delivery issues for the United States General Accounting Office, testifying at the select committee hearing, said, "As of March 31, 1992, HMS had conducted an on-site survey of every CHAMPUS-approved residential treatment center at least once and [of] 44 facilities that had applied for CHAMPUS certification. In all, 137 surveys had been conducted. Currently, there are 75 CHAMPUS-approved residential facilities."[15] *Nearly half* of the facilities surveyed did *not* qualify.

Among the abuses:

- unqualified staff providing individual, group, and family therapy;
- patient treatment not being directed by a qualified psychiatrist;
- registered nursing services not being available twenty-four hours a day, resulting in child care workers assessing the need for and administering medications;
- excessive use or misuse of restraints and seclusion as methods of behavior management;
- therapeutic services not being provided;
- restrictions being placed on mail, telephone calls, and visits with family for all patients regardless of individual circumstances;
- strip searches being conducted without justification; and
- admission, continued stay, and discharge criteria not being stated or followed.[16]

It's important to note that the fact that some facilities are no longer CHAMPUS-approved does not mean they are out of business. States, for example, continue to be free to use them as placement for kids in their custody.

It's tempting to look for solutions in terms of pragmatics: more review, more checks, more regulation. But so long as what we are talking about remains ill-defined, that strikes me as futile.

There clearly is a discrete population of children who are born brain damaged; a population that will require some degree of chronic care; a population that is woefully underattended by psychiatry and woefully underserved by society.

And then there is everybody else who is delivered to the psy purview. These kids represent not one problem called mental illness (or mental health, or psychiatric impairment or whatever) with a whole host of subsets. They represent the result of every conceivable personal and social problem—from child abuse to other real-life trauma to deliberate or nondeliberate nonconformity. They are the victims of increasingly unyielding and impersonal and inflexible education establishments; often they are victims of larger social oppressions played out on a first-person-singular plane. Sometimes they are just visited by bad luck.

Sometimes they are ornery. Often enough they are a pain in the neck. Some of them seem to be running for baddest kid on the block.

Because all these kids are lumped together as disease-ridden or brain damaged or genetically deprived, and because the "treatment" visited on them is rote (the steps, the levels, the consequencing, the medication), the state of affairs itself seems mad. Because the ideology of psy-think is so entrenched—the use of the medical model, of illness—it seems overwhelmingly out of control, certainly more so than do the kids. Assuming one were to buy the viewpoint that all of these kids, with all their different experiences, are similarly neurologically flawed (and that that is fundamental causation), the treatment response of rules and sin confessing (therapy) is awesomely irrelevant. It is clearly based on a contrary assumption: that the kids are merely spiteful and willful. The treatment the kids describe is the kind of treatment one might rationally design for kids one believed to be not fundamentally ill, but deliberately bad. It is a policing/punishing response, not one of respect, concern, and care.

On the evidence, however, the kids, individually, are not the point. Who they are, what has happened to them, the narrative of their lives and their circumstance, is an Axis IV afterthought. Many of the psy practitioners I met on this journey struck me as vaguely android: Not only did they seem never to have met a child, they seemed never to have *been* one. By definition, those practitioners who do truly listen to and care about kids cannot wield power in a system that identifies that as unscientific, defiance. The good guys blow the whistle—and are themselves labeled sick.

Psychiatrists, psychologists, and therapists are, to differing degrees, trained to a mind-set. While there is variation in kind as well as degree (and mavericks, rebels, and true befrienders notwithstanding), part of the training is that they know what they are about. That they are experts in wellness and know what it is: that judgment in such matters is their right (their birthright?). And that they deserve to be in control; to make determinations and binding evaluations about those who come or are brought before them. As Carl Jung wrote, "The cure works best when the doctor himself believes in his own formulae, otherwise he may be overcome by scientific doubt and so lose the proper convincing tone."[17] To parse what is implied here: Numerous doctors might *not* believe in the value of what they are doing (but keep doing it anyway); there may well be reason for overwhelming scientific doubt; the suppression of that doubt is essential in order to con(vince). What can this be called except excruciating intellectual dishonesty?

When applied to massive numbers of children of all manner of personality, circumstance, intelligence, alleged transgression; and where part of the deal is the prescription of powerful and potentially toxic chemicals—drugs whose benefits are in doubt but whose potential for harm is recognized*—it is grotesque to allege that this

---

* For instance, "One-third of all children and adolescents treated with antipsychotic drugs in a New York psychiatric hospital developed symptoms of parkinsonism—mainly muscular rigidity and slowed movement—that interfered with daily activities and often persisted for weeks or months after antipsychotic use stopped, researchers report in the October *American Journal of Psychiatry*" (B. Bower, "Antipsychotics Evoke Youthful Concern," *Science News* 140 [November 2, 1991], p. 276).

"treatment" is benign; and it is ingenuous of us to imagine that psy intervention can do children no harm.

That the DSM is a political document and that the psy continuum is rife with politics, and that the psy sector acts politically to extend its turf, does not mean that there inheres any passion for a particular social order (other than one that fosters its own eminence). For all their passion for professional and personal dominance, there is no reason to believe psy practitioners in the aggregate give a fig about any larger social issues, much less ones of social control. And yet, paradoxically, they are readily agents of others' agendas. As Robert Castel, Françoise Castel, and Anne Lovell write in their excellent book, *The Psychiatric Society*, "[E]ven those who don't care in the slightest about the social control function contribute to carrying it out. We can thus begin to identify several groups of actors, motivated by different interests and proceeding according to strategies that conflict on certain points and coincide on others.

"Financial motives, for example, are largely independent of the political aims of supervision and conformity. The mental health system, whatever else it may be, is also—and for many people, primarily—a market governed by the law of supply and demand under conditions of free competition. Capitalism dominates: Large sums of money, public and private, can be mobilized, especially when it becomes necessary to attack problems viewed at a particular moment in history as especially urgent or worrisome; drugs, violence, a high scholastic failure rate, etc. Subsidies make possible research, experimentation, and marketing of new products and techniques. New careers emerge, jobs open up, and judicious investments yield huge profits. Though not disinterested, these motives generally have nothing politically cynical about them. Still, to give only one example, the result is that hundreds of thousands of children are declared hyperactive, bombarded with drugs, and surrounded by well-meaning counselors. One may wish to say that they are being made more 'normal,' but by whom?"[18]

In fact, the most overwhelmingly potent part of the psy sector's usefulness as an agent of control is precisely that it *does not seem* political—even to its practitioners. They are thus free to act genuinely wronged and outraged when their actions or their judgments are alleged to reveal deep politics. And those whose agendas they are serving can similarly posture rectitude because what is at issue is said to be concern for children's health. All can then attempt to suppress public challenge by claiming that such challenge will prevent or inhibit kids (or their parents) from seeking the "help they need."

Indeed, it is the contrast between the grave potential for damage inherent in psy ideology and practice, and the behavior and beliefs of those vested in the arrangement (the mattress-testing executive, the wrangling DSM concocters), that resulted for me, at moments on this journey, in a sense of breathtaking banality.

Nobody is *trying* to hurt kids; that's a byproduct; the whole system, as Joey might say, is a little side-effecting. Under the patina of science, kids' troubles (or their troublesomeness) have been reconfigured to constitute market demand. The supply side is an ever-expanding psy-fi universe, largely exempt from the province of justice, in which obfuscation and circumlocution are the recognized coin of the realm.

It is a peculiar idea—that something is medical, and thus curative, because the persons who do it are called "doctor." It is certainly not borne out by psychiatry's history; most *especially* not by medical psychiatry's history.

Examples abound: Clitoridectomy as the cure for masturbation. Head-compressing machines with a clamp to the child's hair, another to his underwear, so that if he turned in the night there would be pain.[19] The physician whose solution to bed-wetting was, in boys, to apply to the penis "a tolerably strong current for one to two minutes; at the close, a wire electrode is introduced about two centimeters into the urethra—in girls I apply 'small' sponge electrodes between the labia close to the meatus urethrae—and the faradic current [is] passed for one to two minutes with such a strength that a distinct, somewhat painful sensation is produced."[20]

By comparison, heavy-duty tranquilizers and psychotropic drugs differ mainly in that they are less strenuous for the administrator, more efficient—and more potentially, even permanently, damaging (they have been widely likened to chemical lobotomy). Of course they alter behavior. So does electroshock. So does being dropped on your head.

While an inpatient, one young woman, Vicki, was variously dosed up with Thorazine, Mellaril, Cogentin, Stelazine . . . Her description?

"Mellaril is an antipsychotic drug. It's very sedative. The side effects of some of these drugs are just horrible. To me, it's like being tortured. Extremely dry mouth. So that—my tongue would crack. It would hurt to drink anything like orange juice. You'd be extremely sensitive to the sun—you burn, but it's not like a sunburn. It's—you burn and you itch and you certainly don't tan from it either. I had to stay out of the sun for years.

"You gained weight. Because it slows down your metabolism. It's like your mind turns to cotton candy. It's very hard to think. It's very hard to function. I had no energy. And I was on heavy doses because they wanted to use it for control. And it works. It really works. It slows you right down. Thorazine injections are extremely painful. It hurts for a couple of days. The shots would be if I would be put in the seclusion room. But I was also on regular doses. Three or four times a day.

"And I believed that I was sick, that there was something wrong with me. I was having a really hard time, and then you're telling me that I'm sick and I need help. Okay. So then you first have to accept that before you can get help. You have to cooperate. And at first I did. I was thirteen and I certainly wanted to get better. I wanted to go home. Home was not a good place. But I had built up home as this really neat place to be—because I was locked up in this room and anything was better."

≈

In the past decades, the American public has been trained away from a social response to problems and conditioned to a kind of psy reflex. Since the psy definition of health is not-female, women have been most targeted and been found most susceptible. As Peter Breggin writes, "The woman who seeks help from psychiatry or who is forced into the psychiatric system often is suffering from exactly those issues that feminism attempts to address—the feminine mystique of helplessness and dependency. On the one hand, she has failed in some important aspect of life, often with easily identifiable women's issues underlying her failure. She may be depressed in part because of conflicts related to being a woman. Or she may be anorexic, bulimic, or agoraphobic . . . obvious women's issues. . . . On the other hand, by going to a psychiatrist she is doing what women are trained to do best: she is placing herself in a dependent role, more or less at the mercy of an authority."[21]

But it does not stop at the edges of medical psychiatry. A barrage of challenges is constantly issued to women—as women and as mothers—by the media: the women's magazines, the talk shows. The solution is everywhere proposed: Seek help for this, seek counseling for that. Warning signs. In you. In your kids. Implicit is this: that psy intervention *can't hurt.* That you are acting responsibly by "owning" your problems (which, in the peculiar fashion of psy-speak, actually means turning them over to some psy authority's judgment).

Institutions that intersect with the lives of kids similarly believe that psy intervention *can't hurt.* The same schools that are happy to see Johnny placed on Ritalin by a psy authority would be incensed if Johnny were solicited to buy Ritalin (a relative of speed) on his own, in the schoolyard. The same drug—yet in one instance it would be thought "bad" for the kid. (Or bad *of* the kid, should he actually make the purchase.)

The root cause of the epidemic of kids dumped in psych hospitals, of kids placed under psychiatric surveillance, is an ideological virus, one symptom of which is mental mush: the willingness to have our realities and the feelings and actions they engender translated into a language that is able to express only one thing clearly: that those realities and those feelings are due to our deficits. Or to our children's deficits.

As my own journey into the psy world of kids concludes, it is clear only that the private, for-profit psych hospitals remain under blazing attack. Perhaps their prosperity will diminish. More likely they will attempt to mutate, retool the language, reorient themselves to the market as drug rehab centers or residential treatment centers or reeducation farms or learning enhancement centers or growth facilitation facilities.

It is conceivable that pressure will be brought on insurance companies—despite their own investments—to crack down. But since we really don't know what we are talking about in the first place, it is hard to know—crack down on what? (How can one effectively do this when, if you say you do not cover conduct disorders, it is proclaimed that these are merely symptoms of something else you will cover?) Most likely, insurance restrictions will (in that contrary way of such things) wind up having their major detrimental impact on the acutely or chronically damaged kids—as do current time limits and lifetime caps.

I emerge from this journey convinced that what most needs challenge is that which is least likely to receive it: the entire ideology that empowers the entire psy machine, that places it outside the arena of rationality and blocks rational discourse. An ideology that allows what is called treatment to enter where justice and punishment and concepts of personal dignity and privacy cannot. An ideology that, in its purest imaginable form, is pastoral—one of befriending, of acting to help; but one that has turned mutant beyond recognition, with tentacles everywhere. And with alarming ties to the state.

Notes

Out of Control: An Introduction

1. Richard Weizel, "State Widens Program to Improve Foster Care," *New York Times*, December 22, 1991, Connecticut section, p. 4.
2. Jamie Talan, "The Hospitalization of America's Troubled Teenagers," *New York Newsday*, January 5, 1988, pp. 3–6.
3. Katherine Barrett and Richard Greene, "Mom, Please Get Me Out," *Ladies Home Journal*, May 1990, pp. 98–106.
4. Calvin Pierce, "More Young Patients Being Hospitalized," *Clinical Psychiatry News*, April 1989, p. 12.
5. Ibid.
6. Ibid.
7. National Mental Health Association, Invisible Children Project, *Final Report and Recommendation of the Invisible Children Project*, 1989.
8. Ibid., p. 3.
9. Ibid., p. 3.
10. National Mental Health Association, *Invisible Children Project*, p. 4.
11. Ibid., p. 4.
12. Ira M. Schwarz and Jeffrey Butts, "Preliminary Findings from a New Research Program on the Psychiatric Hospitalization of Adolescents" (research brief, Center for the Study of Youth Policy, University of Michigan, November 7, 1989).
13. American Academy of Child and Adolescent Psychiatry, "Inpatient Hospital Treatment of Children and Adolescents," (Policy statement June 1989).
14. Sandy Rovner, "When Mentally Ill Children Are Overlooked," *Washington Post*, June 13, 1989, Health section, p. 11.
15. Ibid.

16. National Advisory Mental Health Council, *National Plan for Research on Child and Adolescent Mental Disorders: A Report Requested by the U.S. Congress*, DHHS Pub. (ADM) 90-1683, p. 2.

17. George Rosen, M.D., Ph.D., *Madness in Society: Chapters in the Historical Sociology of Mental Illness* (New York: Harper Torch Books, 1968), p. 289.

18. Ibid., p. 294.

19. D. Patrick Zimmerman, "Notes on the History of Adolescent Inpatient and Residential Treatment," *Adolescence* 23, no. 97 (Spring 1990), pp. 9–38.

20. Robert Castel, Françoise Castel, and Anne Lovell, *The Psychiatric Society* (New York: Columbia University Press, 1982), p. xi.

21. Paula J. Caplan, Ph.D., and Ian Hall-McCorquodale, B.S., "Mother-Blaming in Major Clinical Journals," *American Journal of Orthopsychiatry* 55 (1985), pp. 345–53.

22. George W. Albee, "The Futility of Psychotherapy," in David Cohen, ed., *Journal of Mind and Behavior: Challenging the Therapeutic State: Critical Perspectives on Psychiatry and the Mental Health System*, vol. 11, nos. 3 and 4 (Summer/Autumn 1990), p. 372.

23. Lois Weithorn, "Mental Hospitalization of Troublesome Youth: An Analysis of Skyrocketing Admission Rates," *Stanford Law Review* 40, no. 3 (February 1988), p. 822.

1. The Fake Police

1. All material relevant to *Parham* can be found more extensively in Louise Armstrong, *The Home Front: Notes from the Family War Zone* (New York: McGraw-Hill, 1983) in the chapter "Taps for Jackie," pp. 149–95.

The main sources used for this chapter are as follows:

Parham v. *J.R.* 442 U.S. 584, 61 L. Ed. 2d 101, 99 S. Ct. 2493, *U.S. Supreme Court Reports* 61 L. Ed. 2d, pp. 101–41.

J.L. v. *Parham* 412 Fed. Supp. 112 (1976), pp. 112–46, and materials supplementary to the trial.

Post Discovery Memorandum of Plaintiffs.

Defense Supplementary Brief.

Parham v. *J.R. and J.L.*, Minors, Jurisdictional Statement on Appeal to Supreme Court, 442 U.S. 584, May 1976.

Brief for Appellees in the Supreme Court of the United States (September 1977).

Brief for Appellants (August 1977).

Appellants' Reply Brief (November 1977).

Oral argument before the United States Supreme Court (no. 75-1690).

Personal interviews with attorney David Goren and Debby Goren.

Background news stories include:

Atlanta Journal, May 5, 1977, p. 2-A.
Gainesville (Ga.) *Times*, December 1, 1977, p. 1-A.
Gainesville Times, December 8, 1977, p. 12-A.
Gainesville Times, March 12, 1978, p. 10-A.
Macon Telegraph, August 6, 1976, pp. 1-A, 6-A.
Macon Telegraph, February 10, 1977, pp. 1-A–8-A.
Macon Telegraph, February 11, 1977, pp. 1-A, 9-A.

2. Gary Melton, "Family and Mental Hospital as Myths: Civil Commitment of Minors," in *Children, Mental Health, and the Law*, ed. N. Dickon Reppucci et al., (Newbury Park, CA: Sage Publications, 1984), pp. 151–67.
3. Ibid., p. 154.
4. Ibid., p. 159.
5. For a more detailed history of California's rulings on mental health and minors see (for example) Malissa D. McKeith, "Children Inpatient Mental Health Treatment: Extending Due Process to all Commitment Procedures," *University of San Francisco Law Review* 17 (Summer 1983), pp. 797–817.

3. *Bart Simpson Meets Bruno Bettelheim*

1. Charles Pekow, "The Other Dr. Bettelheim," *Washington Post*, August 26, 1990, p. C-1.
2. Ibid.
3. Ibid.
4. Michael Miner, "Hot Type," *Chicago Reader*, March 23, 1990, p. 4.
5. *Chicago Reader*, April 6, 1990, pp. 2, 32.
6. *Chicago Reader*, May 4, 1990, p. 27.
7. *Chicago Reader*, June 8, 1990, p. 36.
8. Charles Pekow, "The Other Dr. Bettelheim," pp. C-1, C-4.
9. " 'Beno Brutalheim'?," *Newsweek*, September 10, 1990, p. 59.
10. Ronald Angres, "Who, Really, Was Bruno Bettelheim?," *Commentary*, October 1990, pp. 26–30.
11. "Accusations of Abuse Haunt the Legacy of Bruno Bettelheim," *New York Times*, November 4, 1990, News of the Week, p. 6.
12. David James Fisher, "Last Thoughts on Therapy: Bruno Bettelheim," *Society* (Rutgers State University), March/April 1991, pp. 61–68.
13. *Newsweek*, October 8, 1990; excerpt reprinted in *Psychohistory Review* 19, no. 2 (Winter 1991), pp. 259–60.
14. Penelope Mesic, "The Abuses of Enchantment," *Chicago*, August 1991, pp. 82–87, 97–101.
15. David James Fisher, "Last Thoughts on Therapy," pp. 61–68.
16. Penelope Mesic, "The Abuses of Enchantment," p. 87.
17. Richard Bernstein, "Accusations of Abuse Haunt the Legacy of Dr. Bruno Bettelheim," *New York Times*, News of the Week, November 4, 1990, p. 6.
18. *Publishers Weekly*, February 22, 1991.
19. *Chicago Reader*, June 15, 1990.
20. Penelope Mesic, "The Abuses of Enchantment," p. 98.
21. *Encyclopedia of Social Work*, vol. 2 (Washington, D.C.: National Association of Social Workers, 1977), p. 919.
22. Ibid., p. 926.
23. Charles Pekow, "The Other Dr. Bettelheim," p. C-4.

4. A Brief Business Trip

1. "Little Rock Schools Insure Drug Treatment," *New York Times*, September 8, 1991, p. 19.

5. Sad (But Interestin')

1. George W. Albee, "The Futility of Psychotherapy," p. 372.

6. The Disciples of Dr. Bisch

1. Phil Brown, "A Sociology of Diagnosis," *Journal of Mind and Behavior* 11 (Summer/Autumn 1990), p. 388.
2. *Diagnostic and Statistical Manual of Mental Disorders*, 3d ed., rev. (Washington, D.C. American Psychiatric Association, 1987). See pp. xviii–xix for a brief historical background.
3. George W. Albee, "The Futility of Psychotherapy," *The Journal of Mind and Behavior* (Summer/Autumn 1990), p. 372.
4. Phil Brown, "A Sociology of Diagnosis," *The Journal of Mind and Behavior* (Summer/Autumn 1990), p. 403.
5. Theodore Millon, "The DSM-III, An Insider's Perspective," *American Psychologist*, July 1983, pp. 806–07.
6. Ibid., p. 807.
7. Ibid., p. 806.
8. George W. Albee, "The Futility of Psychotherapy," *The Journal of Mind and Behavior* (Summer/Autumn 1990), p. 369.
9. National Institute of Mental Health, U.S. Department of Health and Human Services, *Research on Children and Adolescents with Mental, Behavioral and Developmental Disorders*, DHHS Pub. (ADM) 90-1659, 1990, p. 19.
10. John Mirowsky, "Subjective Boundaries and Combinations in Psychiatric Diagnoses," *The Journal of Mind and Behavior*, Summer/Autumn 1990, p. 411.
11. Ibid.
12. James Thurber, "Sex ex Machina," *Let Your Mind Alone!* (New York: Grosset and Dunlap, 1937), pp. 57–65.
13. Ibid., pp. 57–58.
14. Ibid., p. 58.

15. Ibid.
16. Ibid.
17. Ibid., p. 59.
18. Ronald Levy, M.D., *The New Language of Psychiatry: Learning and Using DSM-III* (New York: Little, Brown, 1982).
19. Ibid., p. 37.
20. Ibid.
21. Ibid., p. 43.
22. Ibid.
23. Ibid., p. 7.
24. Ibid.
25. Ibid.
26. William H. Reid, M.D., M.P.H., and Michael G. Wise, M.D., *DSM-III-R Training Guide*, (New York: Brunner/Mazel, 1989).
27. Robert L. Spitzer, M.D., et al., *DSM-III-R Casebook*, (Washington, D.C.: American Psychiatric Press, 1989).
28. *DSM-III-R Training Guide*, p. 12.
29. Ibid.
30. Ibid., pp. 20–21.
31. Ibid., p. 22.
32. Ibid., pp. 22–23.
33. *DSM-III-R*, p. 330.
34. Joel Kovel, "A Critique of DSM-III," *Research in Law, Deviance and Social Control* 9, 1988, p. 135.
35. Ibid., p. 281.
36. *DSM-III-R*, p. 87.
37. *DSM-III-R Casebook*, p. 291.
38. Ibid., p. 308.
39. Ibid., p. 332.
40. Susan Faludi, *Backlash: The Undeclared War against Women* (New York: Crown, 1991), p. 356.
41. Ibid., p. 358.
42. Ibid.
43. Ibid., p. 359.
44. Ibid.
45. Ibid.
46. Ibid.
47. Ibid., p. 360.
48. Ibid.

49. Ibid., p. 361.
50. Ibid.
51. Phil Brown, *The Journal of Mind and Behavior* (Summer/Autumn 1990), p. 386.
52. Ibid., p. 387.
53. Ibid., p. 388.
54. Kaye-Lee Pantony and Paula J. Caplan, "Delusional Dominating Personality Disorder: A Modest Proposal for Identifying Some Consequences of Rigid Masculine Socialization," *Canadian Psychology*, 1991; 32:2, pp. 120–33.
55. Ibid., p. 121.
56. Ibid., p. 123.
57. Lenore Walker, "Discussion: DDPD: Consequences for the Profession of Psychology," *Canadian Psychology*, 1991; 32:2, p. 137.
58. Ibid.
59. Ibid.
60. Robert Castel, Françoise Castel, and Anne Lovell, *The Psychiatric Society*, p. 205.
61. James F. Masterson, M.D., *Treatment of the Borderline Adolescent: A Developmental Approach* (New York: Brunner/Mazel, 1985).
62. Ibid., p. 17.
63. Ibid., p. ix.
64. Paula J. Caplan, Ph.D., and Ian Hall-McCorquodale, B.S., "Mother-Blaming in Major Clinical Journals," p. 346.
65. Masterson, p. 116.
66. Ibid., p. 117.
67. Ibid.
68. Ibid., p. 121.
69. Peter Conrad and Joseph W. Schneider, *Deviance and Medicalization: From Badness to Sickness* (St. Louis: C. V. Mosby Co., 1986), p. 32.
70. "Borderline Personalities," *Sally Jessy Raphael*, Transcript 776, air date: August 27, 1991.

7. Believing in Bio-Psy

1. *Psychopharmacology: The Third Generation of Progress*, Edited by H.Y. Meltzer, M.D. in association with the American College of Neuropsychopharmacology (New York: Raven Press, 1987).

2. Letter from Enid Peschel, Ph.D., dated September 17, 1991.
3. *NAMI-CAN News*, Summer 1991, p. 2.
4. Enid Peschel et al., eds., *Neurobiological Disorders in Children and Adolescents: New Directions for Mental Health Services*, no. 54, Summer 1992 (San Francisco: Jossey-Bass).
5. Ibid., p. 1.
6. Lisa Amaya Jackson et al., "Attention Deficit Hyperactivity Disorder." *Neurobiological Disorders in Children and Adolescents*, p. 45.
7. Anne Marie O'Keefe, "Reforming Insurance Law to Provide Equitable Coverage for Persons with Neurobiological Disorders," *Neurobiological Disorders in Children and Adolescents*, p. 102.
8. Ibid., p. 103.
9. Roland D. Diaranello, "Brain Development: Pervasive Developmental Disorders and Infantile Autism," *Neurological Disorders in Children and Adolescents*, p. 13.
10. Thomas Detre, in the introduction to *Neurological Disorders in Children and Adolescents*, p. 5.
11. Ibid.
12. "Special Report: SB 595—San Diego County," University of San Diego Law Institute Patient Advocacy Program.

8. The School Connection I

1. Joel Kovel, "A Critique of DSM-III," pp. 139, 140.
2. Peter Conrad and Joseph W. Schneider, *Deviance and Medicalization: From Badness to Sickness* (St. Louis: C. V. Mosby Co., 1986), p. 43.
3. Gerald Coles, *The Learning Mystique: A Critical Look at "Learning Disabilities"* (New York: Fawcett Columbine, 1987), p. 43.
4. Ibid., p. 44.
5. Ibid.
6. Peter Schrag and Diane Divoky, *The Myth of the Hyperactive Child: And Other Means of Child Control* (New York: Pantheon Books, 1975). See chapter 1, "The Hutschnecker Memo."
7. Ibid., p. 6.
8. Peter Conrad and Joseph W. Schneider, *Deviance and Medicalization*, p. 156.
9. Peter Schrag and Diane Divoky, *The Myth of the Hyperactive Child*, p. 14.

10. Ibid., p. 15.
11. Ibid., 19.
12. Peter Conrad and Joseph W. Schneider, *Deviance and Medicalization*, pp. 154, 155.
13. Public Law 94-142, 20 U.S.C.
14. Gerald Coles, *The Learning Mystique*, p. 92.
15. Ibid., p. 93.
16. Peter Schrag and Diane Divoky, *The Myth of the Hyperactive Child*, p. 47.
17. Ritalin® hydrochloride methylphenidate hydrochloride C91-28 (rev. 7/91) 665617, CIBA Pharmaceutical Company.
18. Peter R. Breggin, M.D., *Toxic Psychiatry* (New York: St. Martin's Press, 1991), p. 307.
19. Ibid.
20. Florence Rush, "Woman in the Middle," in Anne Koerdt, Ellen Levine, and Anita Rapone, eds., *Radical Feminism* (New York: Quadrangle Press, 1973), pp. 46, 47.
21. Gerald Coles, *The Learning Mystique*, p. 197.
22. Peter Schrag and Diane Divoky, *The Myth of the Hyperactive Child*, p. 19.
23. John L. R. Rubenstein, Linda Lotspeich, and Ronald D. Ciaranello, "The Neurobiology of Developmental Disorders," in Benjamin B. Lahey and Alan E. Kazdin, eds., *Advances in Clinical Child Psychology*, vol. 13 (New York: Plenum Publishing, 1990), p. 4.
24. Schrag and Divoky, p. 91.
25. Max Schilling, written testimony dated January 30, 1989, directed to Jack Levine, Florida Center for Children and Youth, Tallahassee.
26. Dr. Bernice Bauman, written testimony dated January 25, 1990, directed to the Committee on Family Court and Family Law, Association of the Bar of the City of New York.

9. *The School Connection II*

1. Scott Sigmon, *Radical Analysis of Special Education: Focus on Historical Development and Learning Disabilities* (London: Falmer Press, 1987), p. 80.
2. Ibid., p. 72.
3. Ibid., pp. 73, 74.

4. Ibid., p. 76.
5. Ibid., p. 75.
6. Ibid., p. 77.
7. All materials on file as Civil Action #C-88-412-L, *Valerie J.* et al. v. *Derry Cooperative School District* et al., Derry, New Hampshire.
8. Diane Divoky, "Ritalin: Education's Fix-It Drug?" *Phi Delta Kappan* 70, no. 8 (April 1989), pp. 599–605.
9. Barbara Ingersoll, Ph.D., *Your Hyperactive Child: A Parent's Guide to Coping with Attention Deficit Disorder* (New York: Doubleday, 1988), pp. 47, 48.
10. Gerald Coles, *The Learning Mystique*, p. 129.

10. The School Connection III

1. Diana Hunt, "The Big Business of Troubled Teens," *Houston Chronicle*, May 14, 1989, p. 4.
2. Olive Talley, Jacquielynn Floyd, "Texas Targets Psychiatric Hospitals," *Dallas Morning News*, October 25, 1991, pp. 1-A, 14-A.
3. "Conflicting Aims in Booming Health Care Lobby Help Stall Congress," *New York Times*, March 18, 1992, p. A-17.
4. Braden Johnson, *Out of Bedlam: The Truth about Deinstitutionalization* (New York: Basic Books, 1990), p. 210.
5. Ibid., p. 241.
6. Ibid., p. 291.
7. Martin Gottlieb, "Faking Hospital Records: A Case of Double Jeopardy," *New York Times*, April 12, 1992, News of the Week, p. 6.
8. Sheldon Gaylin, M.D., "The Coming of the Corporation and the Marketing of Psychiatry," *Hospital and Community Psychiatry* 36, no. 2 (February 1985), p. 159.
9. Ibid.
10. Michael Lev, "Community Psychiatric Centers Is Ready to Take on Debt," *New York Times*, March 31, 1991, Business section, p. 8.
11. Jane E. Brody, "Study Defines 'Binge Eating Disorder,'" *New York Times*, March 27, 1991, p. A-16.
12. Fox Butterfield, "Studies Find a Family Link to Criminality," *New York Times*, January 31, 1992, p. A-1.
13. Letter from Jerry Coyne, professor of ecology and evolution, University of Chicago, *New York Times*, February 14, 1992, editorial page.

14. Michael Isikoff, "HHS Official Apologizes for 'Male Monkey' Remarks," *Washington Post*, February 22, 1992, p. A-5.
15. Partial transcript of February 11, 1992, meeting of the National Mental Health Advisory Council, p. 116.
16. Letter from Edward M. Opton, Jr., Ph.D., university counsel, University of California, dated March 19, 1992, to Carol A. Bergman, associate counsel, Committee on Government Operations.
17. Letter from Eli Newberger, M.D., dated March 11, 1992, to Louis Sullivan, M.D.
18. Ibid.
19. Peter R. Breggin, M.D., "A Dangerous New Biomedical Program for Social Control: The Federal 'Violence Initiative,'" background paper, available from Breggin, 4628 Chestnut Street, Bethesda, MD 20814.
20. Frederick K. Goodwin, "Conduct Disorder as a Precursor to Adult Violence and Substance Abuse: Can the Progression Be Halted?" Address to American Psychiatric Annual Convention, Washington, D.C., May 1992.

11. *Whose Drug Problem Is It?*

1. Florence Rush, "The Freudian Cover-up," *Chrysalis* 1, 1977, adapted for *The Best-Kept Secret: Sexual Abuse of Children* (New York: McGraw-Hill, 1980), pp. 134–42.
2. Louise Armstrong, *Kiss Daddy Goodnight* (New York: Hawthorn, 1978; Pocket Books, 1979, 1987).
3. Peter R. Breggin, M.D., *Toxic Psychiatry*, pp. 153–54.
4. Peter R. Breggin, M.D., *Psychiatric Drugs: Hazzard to the Brain* (New York: Springer Publishing, 1983), p. 13, n. 1.
5. Peter R. Breggin, M.D., *Toxic Psychiatry*, p. 52.
6. B. Bower, "Antipsychotics Evoke Youthful Concern," *Science News* 140 (November 2, 1991), p. 276.

Afterword: Emerging

1. U.S. House of Representatives, Select Committee on Children, Youth, and Families, *The Profits of Misery: How Inpatient Psychiatric*

Treatment Bilks the System and Betrays Our Trust (Washington, D.C.: U.S. Government Printing Office, 1992) Pat Schroeder, opening statement, p. 2.

2. Select Committee on Children, Youth, and Families, statement of David P. Baine, director of federal health care delivery issues, Human Resources Division, U.S. General Accounting Office, pp. 176–193.

3. Select Committee on Children, Youth, and Families, written testimony of Senator Mike Moncrief, p. 7.

4. Ibid., p. 17.

5. Ibid., p. 19.

6. Ibid., p. 20.

7. Select Committee on Children, Youth, and Families, written testimony of Curtis L. Decker, executive director of the National Association of Protection and Advocacy Systems, Inc., pp. 64–77.

8. Select Committee on Children, Youth, and Families, written testimony of Russel D. Durrett, former controller, Twin Lakes Hospital, Denton, Texas, pp. 100–107.

9. Select Committee on Children, Youth, and Families, written testimony of Duard Bok, M.D., psychiatrist, former employee of a psychiatric hospital, p. 110.

10. Ibid.

11. Ibid., p. 111.

12. Ibid., p. 112.

13. Ibid., p. 113.

14. Ibid., p. 115.

15. Select Committee on Children, Youth, and Families, written testimony of David P. Baine, p. 182.

16. Ibid., p. 183.

17. Carl Jung, letter to Dr. R. Loy, dated January 12, 1913, in the chapter "Some Critical Points in Psychoanalysis," *Freud and Psychoanalysis* (1961).

18. Robert Castel, Françoise Castel, and Anne Lovell, *The Psychiatric Society*, p. 315.

19. Louise Armstrong, *The Home Front*, p. 23.

20. Wilhelm Erb, *Handbook of Electrotherapy* (published 1881), cited in Leonard Frank, "Five Centuries of Perspectives on Psychiatric 'Treatment,'" *Dendron News* 27–29 (May 1, 1992), p. 12.

21. Peter R. Breggin, M.D., *Toxic Psychiatry*, p. 325.

Index